The Art and Craft of Screenwriting

The Urbana Free Library

To renew materials call
217-367-4057

ALSO BY SHELLY FROME
AND FROM MCFARLAND

_____

The Actors Studio: A History (2001; paperback 2005)

*Playwriting: A Complete Guide
to Creating Theater* (1990)

PO-8

The Art and Craft of Screenwriting

*Fundamentals, Methods and
Advice from Insiders*

SHELLY FROME

McFarland & Company, Inc., Publishers
Jefferson, North Carolina, and London

8-09

40-

LIBRARY OF CONGRESS CATALOGUING-IN-PUBLICATION DATA

Frome, Shelly, 1935–
    The art and craft of screenwriting : fundamentals, methods
and advice from insiders / Shelly Frome.
        p.   cm.
    Includes bibliographical references and index.

    ISBN 978-0-7864-3426-8
    softcover : 50# alkaline paper ∞

    1. Motion picture authorship.   2. Screenwriters—United
States—Interviews.   I. Title.
PN1996.F765   2009
808.2'3—dc22   2008050985

British Library cataloguing data are available

Manufactured in the United States of America

McFarland & Company, Inc., Publishers
   Box 611, Jefferson, North Carolina 28640
      www.mcfarlandpub.com

For Susan
and the magic of the silver screen

Table of Contents

Preface

It seems that each time I touch base with the movie industry, more books and products appear outside the gates promising the latest keys to success. And nowhere is this more prevalent than in the world of screenwriting.

In response, I've moved these shortcuts and tactics to the background in favor of the actual process, its rich heritage, and a variety of approaches from many sources including examples from distant shores. Moreover, the recipes take a backseat in favor of a match between material that's fresh and original and an appropriate venue. As a result, I've found that given a good background and wide range of options—mainstream and artistic, large-scale and less ambitious—a writer doesn't have to settle for the trendy and commercial.

In this way, you the reader may very well find your niche in a genre or sub-genre, the indie scene, adaptations and remakes, collaboration or even opting for a stint on the Web. But no matter what style or way of working touches a chord, the nuts and bolts of composition and scripting are fully covered, including a prime example of the slow but steady dynamics of development leading to production and full realization.

In addition, I talked with a top flight Hollywood agent and instructor of script development at the University of Southern California School of Cinematic Arts, a script reader from a commercial production company, a noted Hollywood producer and an independent producer, a film festival director, a seasoned screen actor, film and Emmy Award-winners, a team of Hollywood writers and a director. Going a step further, I drove to the Vermont-Canada border to visit an old student. There we traced the arc of his journey: how he found his own niche and what enables him to draw from a seemingly bottomless well and continue to thrive. This journey culminates the series of revealing interviews.

All told, you will be in a better position to decide whether to enter the fray, avoid Hollywood or mainstream cinema altogether, come at it obliquely or in increments, or stick to smaller ventures. You will hopefully also gain greater insight into what it takes for a compelling vision to reach the screen.

Introduction

Dateline Hollywood: First impressions.

Among the magazines and newspapers that line Al's open-air newsstand on fashionable Beverly Drive, arguably the most prominent are preoccupied with the entertainment industry along with screenwriting ploys to breach the barriers.

A featured article in one issue of *Los Angeles* declares that L.A. is the mecca of movies and television, "the two most powerful cultural forces of the last hundred years." It also underscores the city's preference for pop culture over high culture. For those who are adept at networking and trying to get an edge, there are the trades like *Variety* and *The Hollywood Reporter*. Here you will find the daily changing currents: which company is buying what kind of scripts and who brokered the deal, the movements of various development execs and story editors, a list of films that are going into production. For the seasoned veteran, these are clues to current trendy material.

For the hopefuls that are not in this league, *Fade In* magazine is available, touting yet another annual Hollywood Pitch Festival where, for the price of $400, starry-eyed screenwriters from all over the country are given a chance to be one of the first in line outside the ballroom of the Hyatt Regency Century Plaza Hotel (not far from Al's newsstand) to give a seven minute pitch of a sure-fire high concept. Those on the receiving end of each face-to-face encounter are Hollywood buyers and brokers, scouts from top talent agencies like Endeavor or management firms, studios and production companies. Aspirants who arrive later than 6:30 A.M. may find themselves pitching to lesser lights: younger agents and junior executives from second-tier outfits who, as a rule, don't accept unsolicited ideas or scripts. Though only a small percentage of those who have spent hours rehearsing their notions are deemed worthy of follow-up, everyone in line appears optimistic.

For those looking for strategies beyond a one-shot pitchfest, *Script* offers industry news, articles by and about screenwriters who have found commercial success, all manner of ads and services to enhance a novice's chances, and so forth. First and foremost, the reader can find out who sold what to whom. For instance, two first-time writers (one the son of a well-known TV actor) who met at a screenwriting class at USC may have sold a spec script (spec for speculation) to a production company about a bookstore clerk who discovers a museum devoted to his life. Warner Bros. may have acquired a comedy pitch to be written by an actor-writer attached to a current Warner Bros. movie. Columbia Pictures may have obtained a pitch from a woman about a bounty hunter hired to track and bring back his ex-wife, to be developed by a seasoned writer. A leading first article may advise the reader to take advantage of the summer months in L.A. when top executives have left town and the chances of a meeting with an assistant development executive or story editor are better. Said assistant might welcome a peek at a spec script during this time when the tracking board indicates the stream of available material has slowed to a crawl. The article may also reveal that pitching a writer-proof book adaptation is a safer bet than an idea or a spec script. In case the reader isn't ready for any of this, ads offer coverage (a grading system of potential must-see movies) and a draft-by-draft evaluation to perfect the marketability.

There are also ads for primers; classes (especially at University of California Los Angeles film school); consultations, weekend seminars and books by gurus who have jump-started the careers of screenwriters whose names are legend. One such text offers the credo that all notable screen stories are power struggles. The source is a theatergoer who wrote a book in the 1940s insisting that plays should be a contest between a protagonist and antagonist who won't quit until the struggle is played out. The authors of the text add that the struggle nowadays has greater rooting interest if the protagonist starts out to be a bit weaker.

Interestingly enough, at the time this primer was published, reviews of an action franchise attributed its success to the fact that it dealt with a struggle over identity (Who am I?), morality (What did I do?), and remorse and redemption (How can I make up for the terrible things I've done?). Moreover, in the *L.A. Times* the appeal of yet another slacker film was attributed to the fact that the leading character would have been happy to remain shiftless were it not for some unforeseen dilemma.

What to make of all this? So far screenwriting seems to consist of hawking a product using some kind of inconsistent recipe.

Back to another book ad. "The most sought-after screenwriting teacher in the world" apparently has no patience for any story headed in a single direction and opts instead for twists and turns at every interval.

Another variance. Arguably the most well-known author of screenwriting bibles and short seminars, Robert McKee (another guru with his roots in the theater) takes up an entire page with his ad in *Script*. In his popular book he claims that through the efforts of a driven hero or heroine, the resolution of a story proves the writer's message. He numbers among his students writers like Eric Roth and cites Roth's Academy Award-winning script *Forrest Gump* (1994) and Oscar nominations for *The Insider* (1999) and *Munich* (2005). However, you'd be hard pressed to find a self-generating protagonist in any of Roth's storylines as a way of proving a point. Forrest Gump, for example, is a guileless young man who is sidetracked in search of his sweetheart by cartoon-like happenstance and key events in history over which he has no control. In a later work, Roth's *The Good Shepherd* (2006) flits back and forth in time over a span of three decades revolving around a character who is painfully introverted and manipulated until he reaches a high position in counterintelligence. And all along he's simply a company man.

Speaking of company men, in Tony Gilroy's acclaimed script for *Michael Clayton* (2006), the title character has to be dragged into the action and shaken before he finally takes over almost three-quarters into the narrative.

By this point, any film buff can step in and offer countless other examples of why McKee's popular formula often just doesn't work. In the best-loved *Casablanca* (1942), our disenchanted hero spends much of the time brooding, reminiscing and being acted upon. Not until the trio of screenwriters came up with a last-minute solution did the storyline resolve. In *Psycho* (1960), the heroine is eliminated early on. In writer-director Michelangelo Antonioni's *L'Avventura* (1960), the heroine disappears and jaded members of her party begin to search for her, but the camera soon looks for other points of interest like the stark setting of the Mediterranean island and the playful rhythms of light and dark. Giving the characters a second chance and then another, the camera seems to find the overpowering flow of time and space much more interesting. The same sort of thing happens in Antonioni's *The Passenger* (1975). The lead character (Hollywood's own Jack Nicholson) attempts to find excitement as an investigative journalist, gives that up to be a passenger in someone else's life (taking over a dead man's identity as a gun runner) and still can't hold the camera's attention as it moves out the window, into a North African landscape and the greater drama of the world outside.

True, with Antonioni, we're dealing with the sensibilities of a European. But when you keep in mind that film is a collaborative venture, the great influence of Antonioni on the work of Oscar-winner Martin Scorsese, not to mention some of writer-director Woody Allen's movies, and the fact that Michael Curtiz, the director of *Casablanca*, was from Budapest, Britain's

Alfred Hitchcock certainly had an effect on the narrative of *Psycho*. In short, when you consider the background and sensibilities of many a Hollywood writer and writer-director and all the projects past, present and future, large and small, across the pond and all points of the compass, it's impossible to confine the process to products and recipes.

On the surface, of course, it's easy to imagine putting all this aside for the lure of the quick fix in pursuit of insider status, a great deal of money and a brush with celebrity. Consider all those exposés, especially from Hollywood itself.

For a start, there is Michael Tolkin's book, which he transformed into a shooting script of the same name, *The Player* (1992). At the outset, as a gaggle of writers jockey for position at a Hollywood studio, pitching notions like "*Out of Africa* meets *Pretty Woman*," the more wily of the bunch works after hours in tandem with a tracker. At a posh Bel Air hotel by the pool, the tracker catches a studio exec alone and distracted. Seizing the moment, he moves in, claiming that he and his partner have exclusive meetings at Paramount and Universal "first thing. Meaning, if you pass this up, you'll lose it." The writer-player goes into gear and acts out a movie trailer, framing key shots with his fingers. Pressing the issue, the tracker cuts in with, "No one yet has heard this; we should make a deal now." For a clincher, the writer adds, "No stars, no happy ending. That's the reality. And, I tell you, there's not a dry eye in the house." In this take on the industry, the writer's notion about a heroine who dies in the gas chamber is green-lit and a lucrative deal is struck. Under commercial pressure, however, box-office stars are featured along with a new ending: the heroine is saved at the last second. In terms of actually getting a picture made, the writer and tracker still win. As a counterpoint, a maverick writer (a poor man's Antonioni perhaps) who refuses to play the game, loses his life at the hands of the studio exec who gets off scot-free. In Tolkin's black comedy, this is simply how things work.

And there is the prototype of the screenwriter-as-opportunist in Billy Wilder's 1950s classic *Sunset Boulevard*. Here Joe Gillis's last-ditch pitch has been flatly turned down by a studio exec. Distraught and penniless, willing to do anything to keep from slinking back to his small-town Ohio newspaper, he agrees to turn a hopeless silent screenplay into a talkie. But little writing takes place. Gillis is only buying a little time, playing both ends against the middle. The hook: unknown to Gillis, his employer is not only a forgotten, deluded film queen, she's also deranged. In this earlier model, a former insider overplays his hand and loses both the game and his life.

There have been countless other examples in films and on TV of scripts tucked into slim envelopes passed on to stars, agents and moguls. These surreptitious hand-offs, usually during lunch at a Beverly Hills watering hole, only add to the belief that trying to out-guess the market, hawking material and scrambling for an edge come with the territory. Even companies distributing software for screenwriters have entered the fray, promising the latest insider tips if you hurry and buy the product now.

But for those still caught up in the hype that screenwriting is solely a crafty trade, Charlie Kaufman and his late brother Donald devised *Adaptation* (2002): a movie in a movie dovetailing into a character's mind. And, ironically, the cover of the DVD of the film is featured in McKee's full-page magazine spread advertising his course. In this screenwriting tale, the introverted Charlie Kaufman struggles to be true to a rambling non-fiction book about orchids. But his cynical agent wants the adaptation "fast and sweet." Buying into "the system," extroverted twin brother Donald and a complete amateur, bypasses Charlie's concerns about integrity, buys McKee's book and attends his workshop in New York. After learning that Donald has landed a major deal in no time flat, Charlie also enrolls in a second McKee weekend seminar. When McKee denigrates Charlie's belief in allowing the story to unfold organically, a crestfallen Charlie gives in. The movie in his mind transforms into *the* movie, replete with sex, drugs, a wild chase after a rare and priceless ghost orchard in the alligator-infested swamps of the Everglades and the death of an obsessed orchard poacher and brother Donald. As a bonus, Charlie loses his brother but, by following McKee's classic and timeless formula, he gets the girl and makes good in Hollywood.

Satires aside, digging beneath the surface and beyond the ads, primers and conventional wisdom, the options begin to open up.

There is the case of Nora Ephron. Though her parents were Hollywood screenwriters, she had no wish to follow in their footsteps. Her training came from stints in New York as a journalist. By a circuitous route she adapted her own bitterly humorous novel detailing the breakup of her marriage to the *Washington Post* columnist Carl Bernstein (of the famed Watergate team of Woodward and Bernstein). The script, entitled *Heartburn* (1986), led to *When Harry Met Sally* (1989) and *Sleepless in Seattle* (1993)— deals that helped pay the rent. But it was never a matter of following a formula or compromising her integrity. As she stated in Marsha McCreadie's *The Women Who Write the Movies*:

"As a woman screenwriter, my job is to write women who are real, whatever they are like. Who are loveable or not loveable, but who are comprehensible and complicated."

Ephron feels a writer should ask, "What's the truth here? And don't even consider screenwriting until you've spent enough time not just going to screenwriting boot camps but seeing and doing things."

Callie Khouri, after majoring in drama at Purdue University and working at odd jobs in Nashville, including waitressing at restaurants and bars, began working as a producer of rock videos. One night she got off the L.A. freeway, pulled up in front of her house and suddenly had an image of two working-class Southern women going on a crime spree. One thing led to another, a screenplay written on spec and an eventual Academy Award for *Thelma and Louise* (1991). No games or gurus. Just the makings of the first female road movie with an angry, feminist, anti-male tone.

If you take into account indie films, the prospects continue to spill over. Small, independently made films like *In the Bedroom* (2001), *Smoke Signals* (1998) and *Boys Don't Cry* (1999) and charming little comedies like Susan Sandler's *Crossing Delancey* (1988). Quietly observed movies produced far from mainstream Hollywood, centering on a disrupted life in a Maine village, an estranged father and son from an Indian reservation, homophobia in a small town in the Heartland, courtship rituals in a neighborhood in the Lower East Side, and so on. If you take a close look at *Little Miss Sunshine* (2006) you'll have a hard time dismissing it as just another road-trip comedy. If you examine the flow of incidents in a low-budget film like Edward Burns' *The Brothers McMullen* (1995) you'll find a loose, formless structure. And you also might come across Ali Selim's *Sweet Land* (2005), a 15-year odyssey bringing a short story he loved from his native Minnesota gently to life on the screen.

And we haven't even touched on the methods of writer-directors or actor-writers like Britain's Emma Thompson, Oscar winner for her literary adaptation of *Sense and Sensibility* (1995). Or Elaine May, the screenwriter of *Primary Colors* (1998), who honed her craft and developed her incomparable wit as a member of Chicago's improvisational Compass Players, a troupe that numbered among its performers Alan Arkin, Alan Alda and the noted actor-director Mike Nichols, whom May teamed up with in Greenwich Village. The further you delve, the more endless the list of possible approaches to the craft. In fact you can make the case that screenwriting and film go far beyond what we've touched on so far.

Put another way, it's a given that the best road maps give you a view of the whole terrain. A sense of trails that have been blazed, prominent vantage points and wilder, more obscure areas off the beaten track. You're also provided with a legend differentiating major throughways and secondary routes, along with a scale that enables you to gauge how far you'll have to go to reach any point. After taking all this into account, you can chart your own course while keeping abreast of conditions along the way.

Notes on Content

- Though there is no way to gauge how much talent, first-hand experience or knowledge of filmmaking a screenwriter needs before setting out, the opening chapters are based on the premise that every screenwriter should be at home with the medium.

- All of these chapters can serve as a stimulus or possible checklist, but in no way are they designed as a step-by-step guide; rather, they are only a means of drawing the reader deeper into the process.

- Because the primary focus is on creative screenwriting, tent pole franchises (those movies that hold up a studio financially) aren't given a great deal of emphasis. Like theme park rides, these features, for the most part, rely on special effects and continual amusement for its own sake, and are geared for a certain demographic, a 40 percent profit at concession stands, and repeat viewing. In their usual guise as pre-sold fantasy spectacles, they're driven by the pressures of profit margins and marketing goals—a calculated bet with a view toward spin-offs that will filter into other revenue streams.

- It should be kept in mind that scripts go through many revisions before becoming final drafts, then developed further into shooting scripts which are also subject to revision. Therefore, most films discussed are based on highly polished material. There are Internet sites like www.script-o-rama that contain an index of movie scripts that can be downloaded free of charge (more about this in Chapter 13). In many cases, you can examine first drafts, early drafts and final drafts of a given movie to see how it all evolved into its final version.

- Even though a number of these films can be rented from Netflix or obtained from other sources and studied in greater depth, it should also be kept in mind that no matter how effective a flat-panel video screen may be, every film was designed to be seen in a theater. In home viewing there is always the awareness of the outer edge of the frame and other distractions.

Seated in the dark, engulfed by oversized imagery, you can become lost in the experience, in a crowd and alone and transported at the same time. However, unless there is a retrospective or revival nearby, the home screen or computer may be the only option.

• It should also be mentioned that to keep things moving along, a lot of the most detailed information has been placed in the appendices. If, say, you want to know more about aspects of the shot (camera angles, long, medium and close-ups, mobile framing, duration of the image), official sites of the Writers Guild of America, West and East, and membership requirements, standard three-act formats, etc., you can find it there.

• By the same token, in keeping with this book's compact size, all script excerpts have been greatly compressed. As indicated at the outset of Chapter 13 on scripting and illustrated in Appendix B on the standard format (pages 239-241), these examples were taken from drafts that were on 8½ × 11 sheets of paper utilizing 12-point type floating on lots of blank space. In effect, these drafts were devised to give producers, actors, directors and others a provocative blueprint. Or, if you like, an open-ended guide. Ideally, the reader should imaginatively enlarge these excerpts in the same way that moving images on a standard sized TV monitor should be imaginatively enlarged.

• Last of all (also to keep things flowing), the pronouns "he," "him" and "his" should always be taken to mean "he or she," "him or her," and "his or hers."

I—THE ESSENTIALS

1. An Eye for the Camera

A SERIES OF STREET SCENES
Over them, the credits. These scenes should capture the tempo of Madison Avenue and Fifth Avenue in the fifties. Streets swarming with smartly dressed people. Revolving doors of sleek glass-and-steel office buildings spewing out streams of super-charged New Yorkers, hurrying for cabs and buses and subways and cocktail bars. Two bundle-laden women fighting over a cab. A packed bus closing its doors in the face of an irate would-be passenger. A shot of a newsboy in front of the Independent Subway entrance shouting, "Trouble in the Middle East! Get your trouble in the Middle East!"
INTERIOR. LOBBY OF OFFICE BUILDING—MADISON AVENUE
Four elevators in action. A starter keeping things humming. Doors close on an elevator. It starts up. Another elevator arrives at street level. The last credit fades. The elevator doors open. Crowds pour out and we hear a voice at the rear of the car even before the man is revealed to us by the off-going passengers. The man is tall, lean, faultlessly dressed and far too original to be wearing the gray-flannel uniform of his kind. His secretary, pad and pencil in hand, will have to scurry to keep up with his impatient stride when they leave the elevator and cross the lobby to the entrance.

These are the opening lines of Ernest Lehman's classic screenplay for *North by Northwest* (1959), directed by Hitchcock. As the words on paper became more and more graphic, Lehman succeeded in peaking everyone's curiosity including his director, cinematographer and, eventually, moviegoers everywhere. All wanted to know, "What is going on here? Where is this taking us?"

And, sure enough, the framed images begin to proliferate and the questions keep mounting. We quickly discover that, inside the Oak Bar of the Plaza Hotel, the lean, faultlessly dressed man (Cary Grant as Roger Thornhill) has harmlessly raised his hand at the same time an approaching bellboy is paging a Mr. George Kaplan. A cryptic line of dialogue tells us that Thornhill is about to intercept the bellboy in order to harmlessly send a telegram to his mother. In relatively no time, this man who seems totally at ease in this upscale environment is accosted and suddenly "emerges from the hotel to the sidewalk. Two 'unobtrusive' men take his arms and ease him inconspicuously past unnoticing passersby to a limousine parked at the curb. They open the rear door, push Thornhill into the back seat and follow him in. A third man sitting behind the wheel immediately starts the car and pulls away."

A moment later, Thornhill lunges for the door and struggles to open it but to no avail. The door has special locks. Almost immediately there is a dissolve to the exterior of a Glen Cove estate on Long Island. The car approaches. On the open gate there is a nameplate: "TOWNSEND." The car turns into the driveway. Thornhill looks out ahead: "A curving, tree-lined driveway. Through the trees, a red-brick mansion. The car swings around the circular driveway, pulls up before the entrance."

In quick succession, the screenplay tells us that a stocky, gray-haired woman wearing the uniform of a housekeeper opens the front door and Thornhill is ushered inside. Without a pause, Thornhill is past an oval foyer, taking in a curving marble staircase leading to a balcony, off which are many rooms: "Above the balcony, a stained-glass window. Everywhere, a kind of seedy grandeur."

Up to this point, the camera shots are not specified but clearly indicated. And these indications are much more than just prompts. At the outset, Lehman has established a sense of place, a tone and a seemingly self-generating storyline—a volatile world governed by sheer chance. Primarily through a set of moving pictures we find a Madison Avenue executive perfectly at home, completely unaware that at any moment and for no apparent reason he can be thrust out into a parallel universe where nothing he can say or do will keep him from being shuttled "north by northwest" into harm's way. All his assumptions are not only threatened but of absolutely no use.

So vivid is Lehman's screen story that we can almost follow the progression through the visual clues alone. Presently, our hero has a quart of bourbon poured down his throat and is shoved behind the wheel of a car with its motor running. Someone puts the car in gear and steps out of the way. The car begins to career down a twisting stretch of road while Thornhill desperately tries to keep his eyes open. Narrowly escaping with his life, he is taken into custody by the police for drunken driving and is unable to verify his story. Soon after, he goes to the United Nations in search of "Townsend" (a diplomat and his assumed kidnapper). In another twist of fate, he no sooner encounters the real Mr. Townsend when someone stabs Townsend in the back. Trying to come to his aid, then dropping the knife as the authorities close in on him, Thornhill is now on the run.

The next set of frames takes him on a train where an attractive young woman (again for apparently no reason) hides him in her compartment from searching plain-clothesmen. Once off the train in Chicago, we see Eve (the young woman) through the glass doors of a phone booth in the main lobby of the station, listening to someone, writing on a memo pad. The camera now begins to travel along the row of booths. The camera comes to a stop outside another booth. Through the glass doors we see the man who poured bourbon down our hero's throat and sent him careening down the treacherous drive. This same henchman is now apparently issuing instructions to Eve:

> SEMI-LONG SHOT: POINT OF VIEW
> EVE starts to move across the lobby after THORNHILL.
> CLOSE SHOT: THORNHILL POINT OF VIEW
> He comes to a stop at a secluded spot behind a column. After a few moments, EVE comes into the shot.

At this point, we are not only aware that Eve is manipulating Thornhill, but we can see that Lehman is also providing information that Thornhill is unaware of. Thornhill's point of view is limited; the viewer knows much more but can't come to his aid, adding to the moviegoer's involvement. And now Lehman is not only being visually suggestive, he is actually calling the shots.

Without going into too much more detail, let's glance for a moment at how this writer set up the famous crop-dusting sequence and Thornhill's near fatal brush with a buzzing, murderous biplane.

> EXTERIOR HIGHWAY 41—HELICOPTER SHOT—AFTERNOON
> The bus stops. A man gets out. It is THORNHILL. But to us he is only a tiny figure. The bus starts away, moves on out of sight. And now THORNHILL stands alone beside the road—a tiny figure in the middle of nowhere.
> EXTERIOR ON THE GROUND
> The terrain is flat and treeless. Here and there patches of low-growing farm crop. A hot sun beats down. Utter silence hangs heavily in the air.

After a brief encounter with a man who appears, waits and then boards a bus, Thornhill is alone once more. His only company, the drone of a crop-dusting plane in the near distance, dusting where there are no crops. "Almost immediately, he hears the plane engine being gunned to a higher speed. He glances off sharply, sees the plane veering off its parallel course and heading towards him. He stands there wide-eyed, rooted to the spot. The plane roars on, a few feet off the ground. He yells out but his voice is lost in the noise of the plane. In a moment it will be upon him. Desperately he drops to the ground and presses himself flat."

We could go on and underscore all the elements at work here, including the dramatic irony of a man being dangerously out of his element once he leaves the teeming throngs, rampaging taxis and hurtling subway cars of Manhattan for the wide open spaces of the Heartland. But for our initial purpose, it's more than evident that a person who writes stories for the screen is also writing for the camera. That he must somehow take in the scope of the project—whether it is a major, sweeping epic or a quiet, intimate comedy or slice of life—and, right off the bat, determine what kind of camera work will be needed, along with sound and lighting equipment. He must know, for instance, that a few lightweight digital cameras with a handful of interchangeable lenses can capture the interior family scenes and tightly-knit neighborhood activities he has in mind. In that case, helicopter, crane and tracking shots would be superfluous. So much so, that the writer need only jot down phrases like, "We peer into a spotless kitchen and see a lone figure in an apron sprinkling olive oil on a frying pan, her head bowed slightly, tears streaming down her eyes. Outside, in the back yard there are sounds of children at play." Once again, if it's working, the framed image piques the potential viewers' curiosity. They will want to know, "What is going on here? Where is this leading?"

Or, in the case of the opening moments of *The Player*, a long tracking shot follows two men in tropical sports clothes across a sunlit studio lot as they discuss a favorite opening long tracking shot in *Touch of Evil* (1958). The movie they're discussing begins with a close-up of a hand setting the timer of a bomb as the camera tracks right following the figure of an unknown assassin and then cranes up to a high angle as the assassin flees and the victims arrive and set out in a car, the camera rounding the corner, losing the car and tracking diagonally backward until it catches up with the car again, continuing on and finally zooming into a medium shot as a couple embrace, the embrace interrupted by the off-screen sound of an explosion, culminating in the end of the camera's anxious surveillance as it pans and zooms in on the victim's car in flames. In *The Player*, this tracking-shot-about-a-tracking- shot ends, not with a close-up of a catastrophe but with a close-up of a pitch session about a far-fetched "thriller that is cynical but with a heart." And now, having followed the crane shot to its ultimate destination, Tolkin (the screenwriter who indicated this kind of camera movement) assumed that viewers surely would want to know, "What is going on here? How are we supposed to take this? Where is this tongue-in-cheek stuff heading?"

And so it seems the wily writer in this film, the one touching his thumbs with forefingers outstretched framing shot after shot as he gives his pitch, was not just a parody but an indication of how a screenwriter sees his story unfolding. Though few, if any, may actually gesture like this, there's no doubt that peering through an imaginary lens comes with the territory. When this movie character slowly drew his fingers toward his eyes and said, "We pull back and see a crowd gathering in front of gray prison walls and a rain-soaked street," he was envisioning what would be projected onto a silver screen. And when he eased his fingers forward and said, "We notice the flickering flames of a candlelight vigil," he was cutting to the next shot.

It's as though a camera that could go anywhere in a writer's mind's eye is brought to life by irresistible sights. Ideally, this mental camera continues to track through the whole story until it plays itself out. Or, the moment the sights become commonplace, the camera shuts off and waits for the next promising opportunity. To illustrate, and to make this way of seeing less whimsical and more down to earth, a professor from UCLA's Film and Television Writing Program was fond of having students play the movie game. The rules were that you could only call out what you imaginatively saw and heard prompted by a previous suggestion. The first volunteer started the ball rolling and, in turn, the game went something like this:

"We see an old Chevy pickup making its way up a steep, winding drive north of Sunset."

"There's a tarp covering the truck bed, flapping open by the tailgate and a girl is at the wheel."

"She's got honey-blond hair, wears bib overalls and has a wild look in her eye. She's obviously lost. A farm girl, maybe, come all the way down from Salinas or something."

"How do you know?"

"By the license plate."

"Right. So she comes to a screeching halt at the bottom of one of those serpentine, hidden driveways that lead up to some Bel Air mansion. She turns off the motor and starts to amble up the driveway. It's very quiet, sunshine streaming down. We hear some strange sound coming from the back of the pickup."

"Yeah, and at the top of the drive, we see the Vegas plates of an expensive Jaguar. We look back and catch sight of the girl, inching her way forward around the curving wall till she suddenly stops. A close-up of the girl, her eyes darting back and forth. She reaches into the pocket of her overalls, snatches out a cell phone and dials."

"Behind the wrought iron fence, a suntanned hand reaches down and answers the call."

"We see this other girl now and her whole bronzed body. She's lying on a chaise lounge on a veranda. Except for the tan and the lip gloss and eye shadow, she's the spitting image of the farm girl. We hear someone playing a trumpet badly from inside the Spanish- style mansion. This other girl glances back over her shoulder, then leans forward in the direction of the front of the shiny Jag just behind the fence. She suddenly jumps up, fumbles for her cigarettes and starts cursing."

"We cut back to the farm girl who pockets her cell phone, keeps advancing and yanks open the gate."

Perhaps the game goes on. Perhaps it reaches a dead end. Perhaps it stops because it reminds everyone of a sequel to a sequel. Or, like many a storytelling problem, the fault is traced back to the beginning and the game starts over with a new or completely different opening shot. At any rate, a few years back, two classmates picked up on one of these imaginary sequences, kept switching the storyline around and eventually went on to shepherd a few drafts through channels until the story was finally made into a movie.

This isn't to say that every successful venture always starts with compelling imagery. But it is safe to say that an eye for motion pictures is a sine qua non (without which not)—an essential element.

It's also safe to say that the medium relies on imagery as the most efficient way to tell much of the tale. In Antonioni's *The Passenger*, there is a moment when the actress Maria Schneider, seated in the back seat of a speeding convertible, glances back at the receding tree-lined sun-dappled road. No amount of dialogue could compare with this vibrant image of a young woman fleeing from her past.

There are also times, of course, when compressed dialogue does come to the fore or a host of other factors. But more about that later. For now it's fitting to remind ourselves that *North by Northwest* came about when the director Hitchcock confided to screenwriter Lehman, as cited in Joel Engel's *Screenwriters on Screenwriting*: "I always wanted to do a chase across the faces of Mount Rushmore." Hitchcock also said, "I always wanted to do a scene where our hero is standing all alone in a wide open space and there's nobody and nothing else in sight. And then along comes a tornado. No place to run." Thus was born the famed crop-duster sequence when Lehman substituted a plane for the tornado. And Hitchcock's prompting sent Lehman crisscrossing the country scouting locations to generate a suspenseful "movie movie." He eventually wound up halfway to the top of Mount Rushmore and peered down dizzily.

Working on a much lower key, writer-director Cameron Crowe looked back on his experiences as a high school journalist covering a famous rock band. He began by picturing modest point of view shots like one of a teenager mesmerized in front of a plate glass window at a long-haired disc jockey wearing a red promotional T-shirt. Soon "vinyl was flying everywhere, the sound of Iggy Pop's rendition of *Raw Power* audible through a small overhead speaker above the empty sidewalk" (*Almost Famous*, 2000).

And everywhere you turn, no matter what the style or fictional world, if the photography is highly suggestive, you can trace it back to someone's notion of a story fit for the screen. In Todd Field and Tom Perotta's adapted screenplay *Little Children* (2006), a man with a cadaverous face suddenly appears padding toward a public swimming pool. It's a sweltering afternoon in an affluent Boston suburb; the man is wearing black flippers on his feet and carrying a snorkel. (This is the same face on the posters from an earlier shot distributed by a concerned father warning that the man was just released from prison.) As soon as this town pariah drops into the water, pandemonium breaks out, children scramble out of the pool scooped up by their parents, and a policeman approaches as if warily coming upon a monster who has slipped in from nowhere and claimed a new lair.

Prompted by Iris Yamashita's original screenplay (*Letters from Iwo Jima*, 2006), the camera catches moments like the flash of a Japanese lieutenant's sword seen from a low angle. The viewer is then drawn inside a darkened cave, dug out as a defensive position against the advancing marines, the lieutenant's figure a silhouette backlit by a sliver of daylight. Shot from this enclosed space in which a figure is framed against the natural light, we're reminded of John Ford's signature images from one of his classic westerns. We're also reminded of cinematographer Nestor Almendros' insistence on natural lighting and nothing else. Like the way he captured the magic hour during harvest time in the Heartland of yesteryear: the twilight afterglow holding perfectly still as if suspended between the end of day and the beginning of night (*Days of Heaven*, 1978). And we're also reminded that while the writer indicates, it's always a collaborative enterprise as the director and cinematographer take it from there.

In short, if a writer has an appreciation of this process and collaborative history, so much the better. At any rate, there's no question that the desire to prompt a range of moving images is indispensable.

2. A Knack for Juggling

Transporting the Audience

It's been said that the spiritual roots of film can be traced to the illusionist. Early on, things appeared, disappeared, dissolved and reappeared on a flickering screen. During this same silent era, audiences leaned away from the sight of an oncoming train. By the year 1916, D.W. Griffith's *Intolerance* carried them away to four interlocking centuries. By 1920, the tricks included a neutral shot of an actress' face followed by any number of shots like a baby, a carriage, a gun, another woman on tiptoe and an empty park. As a result, the audience assumed the woman's baby had been kidnapped at gunpoint, even though the shots were taken separately, days apart and unrelated. By simply switching the images around, the audience was led to believe that the woman on tiptoe was escaping from the heartless gun-toting woman with the blank look on her face. Pushing the possibilities even further, F.W. Murnau created *Sunrise* (1927), mixing the central characters' hazy daydream imagery with shots from contemporary reality as audiences continued to go along, identifying with these fleeting moments as if they were their own wishes and dreams as an escape from everyday life.

And all the while, writers added these devices as if stocking a screenplay toolkit.

When sound was introduced, audiences continued to fill in the gaps. In *Public Enemy* (1931), the script called for gun shots to be heard off-screen, prompting moviegoers to imagine the bad-guy's horrific comeuppance. Soon after, off-screen prompting was commonplace. By the time the low budget thriller *Cat People* (1942) came out, unseen threats suggested by ominous shadows were more effective than any attempt to show the actual menace. What an audience could imagine was more terrifying than anything anyone could come up with to shoot. Relying on viewers to fill in any gaps completed the experience. It gave them a sense of participation and enabled the dream machine to appear seamless as it continually shifted from illusion to illusion.

A glance at any segment of Lehman's script for *North by Northwest* shows that the manipulation of time and space had long been taken for granted. When Roger Thornhill finds he's trapped inside the henchmen's car, there's no need to follow him all the way to Glen Cove. And there's no need to track his trip from Chicago to the isolated cornfields. Intuitively, moviegoers expected a cutaway to the devious phone call between the vamp on the train and that selfsame henchman. They worried and delighted in being let in on knowledge superior to any and all the characters. By now it came with the territory; it was a given. Time after time they'd relished the fact that they alone were privy to, say, the cavorting ghost with her flowing wild hair dancing barefoot at the cove in the dead of winter. Besides, in order for a suspenseful movie to be effective (as Hitchcock pointed out), they needed to become so involved it was all they could do to refrain from crying out to warn the unsuspecting victim.

So ingrained was this interplay that the seasoned screenwriter could sense when audiences could piece things together and when they needed flashbacks or additional information. At the outset of *The Painted Veil* (2006), moviegoers are shown a misty terrain, shaggy foothills and a forlorn young Caucasian woman transported by cart by equally forlorn-looking Chinese peasants. Another Caucasian, presumably the young woman's husband, treats her with disdain as they wend their way. Clearly, at this point every viewer was wondering what brought this unhappy, sophisticated-looking Brit to this remote, forsaken place and how did her relationship with her spouse deteriorate so badly. Presently, the scene shifts back to a soiree in London, circa the 1920s, when the couple first meet and the young man in question becomes smitten with his future bride.

In *Casablanca*, the flashback comes much later. At the outset, the audience presumably is interested in Rick's malaise. Why does he forbid the entertainer to sing that particular song? Why is he so cynical about obtaining letters of transit for displaced persons so they can flee and make a new life? Why isn't he doing his best to thwart the local Nazi officials? Then, at long last and of all places, Ilsa appears in Rick's café and the narrative whisks us back in time to Paris just before the occupation. At this juncture, as if it were happening for the first time, the audience vicariously experiences their relationship at its height; followed by Rick's unbearable anxiety when Ilsa doesn't show up at the train station and he's forced to go on alone. The way the narrative is set up, there is no other way for this subplot to reveal itself. In the jaded state he's in, Rick would be incapable of confiding in anyone during the intrigues and goings on at his Moroccan gin joint. And even if, in some moment of drunken remorse, he were to reveal an inkling of what was troubling him, it would leave the audience still hanging and uneasy. It would throw the viewer's participation off-kilter.

In this way, the writer continues to take into account a collaborating audience. Potential changes and input from others in the development process aside, he works for the future benefit of ready and willing participants. He doesn't worry about steps down the road as dailies are transferred to videotape and onto a hard drive, shots called up, and a great deal of pasting, trimming and junking. As he puts together his blueprint, he is the sole editor, in tune with a way of telling a story made up of bits and pieces that, when joined in an appropriate way will, in a sense, work its magic like a satisfying musical score.

Finding the Right Tempo and Tone

As noted in the case of *North by Northwest,* Lehman set out to both please Hitchcock and find a springboard for a thriller that would fulfill his own desire to do a "movie movie." That is, a movie-going experience that was at once witty, sophisticated, suspenseful and propelled from east to west—New York to Chicago to the Great Plains. He naturally began with the hustle and bustle of midtown Manhattan which set up an establishing rhythm and a definite tone. It also set up a disorienting odyssey: taking a flippant Madison Avenue executive out of his element and pitting him against the machinations and arbitrary actions of an unknown enemy—a force which, for no reason, was out to get him. From the outset, he set the wit and non-chalance of a Cary Grant-like rhythm against the erratic counterpoint of lethal gamesmanship: sometimes subtle, sometimes volatile, pressing in on Thornhill, letting go a bit, altering Thornhill's own rhythm until he himself began to press, the pace picked up and the stakes became higher and higher. The lull as the woman on the train invited Thornhill into her compartment was like a slow, soft passage, then giving way to a faster, more urgent tempo. This kind of teasing variation kept building and releasing until the counterpoint played itself out and a new quietude took over, the jazzy beat of 1950s Madison Avenue a distant memory.

Switching to a more lyrical piece, made during the same era but set back in time, we can turn to a real-life figure the complete opposite of Thornhill: the humble, illiterate and dedicated Emiliano Zapata. In one of his agrarian odes to the common man, John Steinbeck wrote the screenplay *Viva Zapata* (1952) in honor of this tenant farmer turned Mexican revolutionary leader and martyr. The catalyst: the struggle for land and liberty from 1910 to 1919. Capturing the slow rhythms of the Indian peons of Morelos (shot in black and white to evoke an abstract, nostalgic quality), the opening sequence establishes the tone. Patiently, as is their custom, a delegation from

Morelos comes to petition their father figure, General Diaz, to return their land which has been usurped by men who have been given political favors. Diaz advises his children to go home, wait and go through legal channels. Quiet, unassuming Zapata, standing among his people, suggests that Diaz's advice runs counter to the planting cycle of raising corn and feeding the hungry. Zapata holds back until the pressures of injustices back home are too much to bear, until the natural life patterns of the land have to be acknowledged.

Now Steinbeck's narrative rhythm changes. In one telling sequence, the clicking of stones expands into the slow but irrepressible gathering of white-clad Indians flooding the imagined screen, joining Zapata as he is led off by foot by his Federale captors. His crime—coming to the rescue of an elderly peon who dared trespass on his own land. As an underpinning to the screenplay, you can almost sense a plaintive folk melody slip in and well up with the tide of followers, culminating in a laconic exchange as Zapata's captors reluctantly release him. Even as he fights his battles against Huerta and Carranza and the other despots, joins up with Pancho Villa and quits the capital, even as his fortunes ebb and flow, there is always a pull toward the land and its unhurried pace. A longing to court and marry Josefa, to gain lasting reform and peace—a rhythm often interrupted by the wily Fernando, who keeps stirring up intrigues, and Zapata's restless, wild brother, Eufemio, who literally looks for trouble, even to the point of claiming other men's wives as the spoils of war.

Somehow, once a writer has found the right key, a rhythmic pattern and counterpoint slip into the script as a matter of course. But when this factor is disregarded, there's a sense of sputtering or discord. A prime example is *The Rock* (1996). Written, by all accounts, by a committee of three and others who weren't given screen credit, there are no shadings of color, tempo and textures; no compositional unity, counterpoint or flow. In an early interlude, a biochemist in the name of law and order pursues an escaped convict and commandeers the first car at hand which happens to be a yellow Ferrari. Never mind that he has never driven the car before and has no business leaping into it in the first place, he proceeds on a high-speed chase. The convict, in turn, steals a new Humvee, a vehicle the convict has never encountered before having spent the past thirty years in Alcatraz. At the same time, colliding with a row of parking meters, a truckload of bottles in blue crates, risking countless people's lives and limbs on the busy daytime streets of San Francisco, the biochemist casually decides to drive straight through a wall after offhandedly remarking to himself, "Well, why not?" It's not just the fever pitch, the flaming cable car that comes hurtling sideways into the scientist's path, and the cartoonish nature of the whole experience that's at fault. Nor is it the fact that characters do and say things for no reason except to keep the silliness and barrage of sensations going. It's the climax after climax for its own sake, gratuitous clash and mayhem following on top of one another. It's the breaking of the unwritten bond that allows space for the audience to think, feel and imagine. And it's the total absence of any musical sense that makes it into a composition without a score.

For a corrective, all you have to do is switch over and back a few decades to *Bullitt* (1968). On the very same streets of San Francisco, writers Alan Trustman and Harry Kleiner also dealt with a convict or two and the pursuit of law and order, but in their narrative there is a definite sense of composition. Granted, like any script, the rhythmic patterns were suggestive, relied on editing and cutting and then underscored by added sound effects and music. Still and all, through the springboard of the material, the pace ebbs and flows, builds to each climax and eases off. During one turn of events, things take off again at a higher pitch during a famous chase sequence that's in sync with the rising and plummeting streets, the shifting gears of Lt. Bullitt's Ford Mustang and the interweaving stop and go of the traffic, slowed down by a motorcyclist's spill and Bullitt's momentary inspection to make certain the man was not hurt, and then shifting from low to high again after the hit men's speeding car further ahead on the thruway.

For a closer look at this innate sense of appropriate rhythm on the page, there is the opening beat of William Goldman's shooting script for *Butch Cassidy and the Sundance Kid* (1969). Though, like Zapata, the subject is a legendary outlaw-hero plus a sidekick—even more distant in time (1880 to 1908) and covering a greater swath of territory from the old West down to South America—the tone and rhythms are quite modern. Steinbeck was greatly affected by the locale, the times, the nature of the struggle and the life rhythms of the people. For Goldman, the tone is whimsical, the rhythm syncopated, and the whole design is consistently apt:

> Cut to
> BUTCH stopping by a window, giving it a glance.
> Cut to
> THE WINDOW. It is heavily and magnificently barred.
> Cut to
> BUTCH scowling briefly at the bars. He moves in toward the window to look through, and as he does, there begins a series of QUICK CUTS. His eyes flick from place to place probing for weaknesses.
> Cut to
> A DOOR. It is thick and solid metal and strong.
> Cut to
> PAPER MONEY being counted by ten skilled fingers.
> Cut to

A GUN IN A HOLSTER belonging to a MAN in a guard's uniform.
Cut to
A WINDOW HIGH UP ON ONE WALL. It is, if anything, more heavily and magnificently barred than the first.
Cut to
THE DOOR OF A BANK SAFE. It is behind shining bars and it is the kind of safe that has a time lock.
Cut to
BUTCH, eyes expertly flicking from place to place. Then he starts to walk around the bank again and he isn't happy.
Cut to
A BANK GUARD. It is closing time now and he is slamming metal plates into place, the sound loud and sharp and final.
PULL BACK TO REVEAL
BUTCH watching the GUARD work.

> BUTCH
>
> What was wrong with that old bank this town used to have? It was beautiful.

> GUARD
>
> (continuing to slam things shut)
> People kept robbing it.

Cut to
BUTCH, who starts to walk away across the street toward a barn of a building with a sign outside: "Macon's Saloon." In the middle of the street he turns and stares back at the bank. It is new and ugly and squat and functional and built like a tank.
Cut to
BUTCH, CLOSE UP.

> BUTCH
>
> (yelling back to the Guard)
> That's a small price to pay for beauty.

Without laboring the point, what we have here is the feel of jazz instruments playing off each other. It's as if Butch was a lead cornet, the facets of the bank a whimsical drummer answering him back, the Guard weighing in as a slide trombone, the cornet ending this opening riff on a bright note. Surely the real leader of the Wild Bunch and Hole-in-the-Wall-Gang didn't case a bank in this cool, offhanded way. And surely bank guards were more wary and no one used this clipped dialogue in the waning days of the Old West. Moreover, the classic westerns of John Ford, Howard Hawks (see *Red River*, 1948) and the like are more ponderous, as if carrying the weight of some great epic. Their films had moments of humor and comic relief—a bit of predictable joshing, horseplay and the usual barroom brawls before the next hard-won struggle against great odds. But there was no syncopation. Jazz hadn't been invented till years later; there was no sign of George Gershwin, let alone the jaunty licks from the silver cornet of Bix Beiderbecke.

What marks this script is Goldman's antic sensibility as it merged with his subject and each happening. Added to this mix is the contradiction between Goldman's lack of affinity for westerns and his great affinity for Cassidy himself, plus holes in Cassidy's story which Goldman found irresistible. In other words, there is no way to separate what drew Goldman to the material, Goldman's unique imagination and wit (see *The Princess Bride*, 1987), and the ensuing tones and rhythm of the screenplay.

For Goldman, it all started with the fact that Butch was the head of a great outlaw gang without being a gunman. Arrogant, brutal men followed him only because he was likeable. He could talk himself into and out of just about anything. When things got too dicey, when he heard about the territory's half dozen finest lawmen banding together to track him down, he was long gone. He and Sundance and Etta Place spent a few days in New York and went on to lead a frolicsome life engaging in more robbing, hustling and rustling and taking on various aliases. Ironically, as famous as they were in the West, they became even bigger legends in South America as "bandidos Yanquis." In Goldman's own words, "Recapturing the past is something we all wish for; they made it happen."

Consciously or unconsciously, it is this release from a conventional beat—the same release no doubt members of a Dixieland band enjoy as they take off on a melody line—that gives this particular work its devil-may-care variety of tempos. Compare it with David Newman and Robert Benton's screenplay for *Bonnie and Clyde* (1967) as the tone shifts from comedy to violent tragedy, from a light and airy beat to a throbbing, escalating intensity, and you find a different pattern. One based on different circumstances, different outlaws, a sometimes harsher, sometimes lighthearted brush with changing times. As a result, when the soundtrack was added, *Bonnie and Clyde* was provided with rambunctious dueling banjos as a counterpoint to impending doom, while *Butch Cassidy* was scored with pop tunes of the day like "Raindrops Keep Falling on My Head." (To what extent the screenplay prompted this silly number as Butch teeters on a bicycle is anyone's guess.) But again, once the key was established—consistently playful or out of kilter with reality—the framework held together. Even though Butch and Sundance were gunned down just as violently as Bonnie and Clyde and their two sidekicks, Butch and Sundance end in a sweet freeze-frame like the last quiet notes of an old refrain, while the Barrow Gang end their lives abruptly like the rat-a-tat-tat of a dozen military snare drums.

The musical pattern, of course, is totally dependent on the project. In Clare Peploe and Bernardo Bertolucci's screenplay for *Besieged* (1998), the restrained stylings of a reclusive, classical pianist play out against the sensuous, freely emotional rhythms of his housekeeper. Set mainly in the pianist's equally reclusive Roman villa, the rhythms are slow and contemplative as the pianist searches for some unobtrusive way to woo his comely servant. As a counterpoint, the authors furnish the busy Roman street scenes, rush of the transport systems, rhythms of African dives, haunts and markets, and the backstory of the housekeeper's flight from her husband's incarceration for anti-government demonstrations in her tribal homeland. Slowly but surely the pianist's compositions begin to take on the beat of his beloved until the counterpoint and the pianist's hopeless quest begin to merge and the scenes, in turn, quicken with the approaching arrival of the housekeeper's husband who has been freed.

In Michael Arndt's shooting script for *Little Miss Sunshine* (2006), the life patterns and unfolding action dictate the tempo, the given circumstances and offbeat characters who set the tone—e.g., a depressed suicidal brother, a deluded but irrepressible self-help marketer, a loose-living granddad, a stage-struck optimistic little girl, a teen brother biding his time seeking escape, a harried mom who is also a sister and a wife—all tooling along, playing their individual riffs off each other in a dilapidated van across the arid desert to the promised land of Redondo Beach, California. Adjectives like slow, boisterous, hesitant and still intertwined with jumpy and erratic would be more apt than musical terms as this dysfunctional collective pits itself against our loopy celebrity culture. (Much more about this model in Chapter 12.)

Testing the Limits

For some, none of the patterns mentioned so far will do. They're just too conventional for what a writer has in mind. One of the best examples of what some call "pushing the envelope" is Christopher Nolan's final draft for *Memento* (2001). The central character's mind-set requires a harrowing bit of time-traveling due to the fact that he can't make new memories. As a vengeance-seeking insurance investigator suffering from a neurological malady, he's forced to keep reminding himself that he can't remember anything he's told anyone. Finding himself dressed in an expensive silk suit, he cruises a Southern California landscape of anonymous motels and abandoned warehouses, as bleached-out as his mind, in a desperate search for the man who murdered his wife. Yes, he does retain a clear memory of his life before the crime and flashes back repeatedly, but his life since is a series of disconnected, forgotten and, by necessity, repeated images. Unable to experience time passing, he has to rely on a sheaf of photos. When he is convinced that any piece of information is vital, he has it tattooed on his body.

As a result, the unfolding sequence goes something like this: starting with a killing and its aftermath in reverse (an instant photo fades to white, a bullet flies out of someone's head and back into the chamber of a gun), segments lurch back in time, a scar or a bruise in search of the punch that put it there. Scenes in color alternate with black-and-white; meetings take place with a cheerful, teasing male and a weary female bartender who may or may not be using the protagonist's amnesia for ulterior purposes. Their seemingly normal lifestyle plays off the darting, clueless yet fanatically certain motions and daydreams of a person who can never get used to anything except endless first impressions which he tries to turn into facts. As another counterpoint, this pattern is intercut with bouts of melancholy and panic on the part of our hero.

Clearly, Mr. Nolan is an inventive screenwriter with a supercharged cinematic intelligence, playing with Mobius strips of disoriented time and information. Clearly, Mr. Nolan's kind of juggling act requires a more quirky sense of pace.

As another offbeat example, Guillermo Arriaga's original script for *Babel* (2006) may seem less experimental but more daunting in scope in its attempt to weave multiple story lines across three different parts of the world, loosely and, then again, tightly. Promulgating a global theme, his plan was to link the passing of a rifle and its repercussions on children who, at first glance, have nothing in common. In effect, the almost painfully slow rhythms of a desolate village in Morocco are juxtaposed against the pulsating beat of a Mexican wedding and the relentless, high-tech agitation of modern day Tokyo. In the Japanese segments, the noise level and insistent pounding are so intense at a local hangout that a deaf teenage girl can dance to it. In Arriaga's scheme, the footloose teenage girl is not just lost in her own world but somehow connected to her neglectful father who, unwittingly sold the rifle in question to a guide in Morocco. Almost simultaneously, the rifle is handed over to a Moroccan boy who thoughtlessly fires it, seriously wounding an American tourist traveling in a bus. The woman, in turn, has trusted her longtime Mexican caretaker who, also in turn, has thoughtlessly taken the woman's two little children across the border to the aforementioned wedding only to wind up lost in the desert hunted by the border patrol. A far cry perhaps from *Besieged*, where the rhythms dovetail intentionally. But, then again, with a little stretch of the imagination, the disparate patterns collide as the wounded young woman and her frantic husband encounter the unhurried medical practices of the Moroccans; the gayety of the Mexican wedding gives way to the botched border crossing and the timeless empty desert; the emotionally-spent deaf-mute finds solace on the rooftop of her father's high rise in the dead of night as the neon signs finally shut down and the overwrought city comes to a momentary rest.

There have been other models of multiple juggling. The trick seems to be to find some way to link the crosscutting without becoming too obviously schematic. As a case in point, Paul Haggis' script for *Crash* (2005) may, arguably, have crossed the line into contrivance. Here he manipulated a cross section of Angelinos according to race, class and life-style whose only connection centers on a minor accident. Each one of these characters are somehow isolated and prejudiced (a Hispanic woman climbs out of her car and confronts an Asian-American woman; on the previous day a hot-tempered Iranian shopkeeper is insulted by the owner of a gun store, etc.). Adding to this interplay is the grafting of two opposite sides to each character—e.g., a racist white police officer turns out to be physically courageous; a young black man who rails against racial profiling turns out to be a carjacker; a wealthy, mild-mannered man pulls out a gun and starts screaming. And somehow in this vast, sprawling city, the same characters keep running into each other.

Perhaps in some ways through the efforts of Haggis and others we've come a long way since D.W. Griffith's *Intolerance* and cross-cutting innovations. Then again, despite the fact that *Crash* won an Oscar for best picture, something vital can be lost in the shuffle. Like any magic show, it's all a matter of balance and slight of hand. Like the great screen musical star Gene Kelly, the inventiveness, sense of rhythm and sheer agility, perfectionism and discipline, and the countless hours of rehearsal are in service to the illusion that none of this was scripted. It was just a guy the camera happened to catch at a peak moment when he just felt like dancing and singing in the rain. Leaving audiences free to fill in the rest of the street scene with admiring onlookers and shopkeepers nearby.

3. A Touch of the Actor

For some reason, the vital link between screenwriting and acting is usually tucked away somewhere, hidden beneath sketchy character descriptions and exchanges of dialogue.

In Hollywood, the subject is often sloughed off by comments like, "Whatever happens after a script is purchased is out of a writer's hands." Carrying on, recalling the old studio system and the age of contract players, some members of the industry have been known to point out that most movies were simply cranked out to meet the demand and resulted in wide scale miscasting. For example, there was Edward G. Robinson, snarling as though playing yet another Chicago gangster in his stint as an Egyptian pharaoh; the non-actress, glamour queen Maria Montez's inept portrayals of Scheherazade, the Cobra Woman and the Siren of Atlantis; the slightly cross-eyed showgirl Virginia Mayo's token appearance as Cleopatra; Tony Curtis, a former member of a street gang, employing his Bronx accent as a noble rising through the ranks of knighthood in *The Black Shield of Falworth*; John Wayne's ludicrous turn as Genghis Khan in *The Conqueror*, and so on.

Along these same lines, despite scripts like Lawrence and Lee's stage tour de force *Inherit the Wind* (1960) with an equally fine screen adaptation by Nedrick Young and Harold Jacob Smith, the production was compromised by Fredric March's doddering impersonation of the legendary statesman and orator William Jennings Bryan. And Terry Southern's script for *Easy Rider* (1969) was made a mockery of by the principal actors as they ad-libbed at will and did whatever they pleased.

More blatantly, stars like Robert Mitchum have gone on network television and passed off screen acting as a lazy way to make a living by simply doing what you're told and playing yourself (which is what fans rely on when they line up to the box office). Pushing this problematic notion, American movie critics have referred to the commercial practice of banking on pop celebrities, athletes and other non-actors as saleable commodities. They've also written about stars with muscle who demand that roles be tailored to suit their needs.

There are also those claims that, by their very nature, screenplays are blueprints that have to be fleshed out, containing scenes that are switched around and altered according to shooting schedules and the desires of directors. In mainstream movie making there are always script changes that are called for along the way—even changes in casts and directors—plus the test marketing that takes place leading to different endings to please the public, and all kinds of manipulations before the final product reaches distribution. So why bother delving beyond serviceable character descriptions and dialogue?

All these arguments notwithstanding, there are countless examples of films from various venues based on material from writers who clearly understood the movie actor's art. These films would never have been fully realized if the scripts hadn't attracted gifted actors, and even those who were not so gifted, who had respect for what was implicit on the page and recognized a challenging opportunity. As a result, actors from different quarters who truly want to act, are always open for scripts that strike a chord, packages are put together on the basis of roles that draw actors together, and discerning directors sign on to become part of the venture.

Not that this is the special province of writers who are also actors or have taken acting from noted teachers, or feel they are especially attuned, or count themselves among the few who work in optimum conditions. It's the province of any writer or writer-director who appreciates what it takes to bring characters to life on the screen and the type of source material actors need to draw from.

For starters, consider the work of the writer Buck Henry and the contributions of the director Mike Nichols on *The Graduate* (1967). Instead of the obvious casting indicated in Charles Webb's novel of stock Southern Californians and the likes of Ronald Reagan and Doris Day as the parents and young, handsome Robert Redford as Ben Braddock, Buck Henry saw the part of Ben quite differently. Recalling the work of diminutive, wiry and decidedly non-glamorous Dustin Hoffman off–Broadway and the way Hoffman totally inhabited a role, Henry and Nichols came to a decision. Casting Hoffman would bring a unique, sympathetic quality to the leading role and alter the entire tone of the story. Originally it was a tale about the foibles of a golden-boy surfer who gets mixed up with his father's law partner's wife and then tries to win over her attractive daughter, Elaine. Henry, however, was taken with the plight of a confused, anguished Hoffman-as-Ben, fixated on his impossible love for Elaine, going to any lengths to win her back. And rather than a wholesome Doris Day as a benign seductress, he envisioned the conflicted menacing turns of Anne Bancroft (also a trained New York actress) as the notorious Mrs. Robinson, thus greatly adding to the range of emotional colors. When Nichols suggested that Ben rescue Elaine a moment after Elaine's wedding ceremony, the end of the movie became that much more compelling and the rest, as they say, is movie history.

Space to function—like the indications in Henry's script for Ben's private moments of anguish, longing and confusion—are cues a professional actor relies on. If the actor has a helpful director, so much the better. Taken together, the well-crafted script with actors in mind keeps everything reverberating: the camera seeking and focusing, the rhythmic scenarios unfolding, the actors capitalizing on all incentives and contributing something extra, something unexpected.

Those Telling Moments

The screenwriter Bo Goldman once said that when writing a screenplay, you have to imagine everything that's on the screen, especially what's between the words. By extension, this means what the actors say and don't say, do and don't do leading them on. Or, put another way, the writer intuitively knows that actors can't play the result, can't just be. There is no way to be happy or sad or angry or take on any other state. Bad actors will strike poses or attitudes, make faces and modulate their voice. True actors are always becoming. They have an intention as they work around obstacles. Though they know basically what's supposed to happen in the script, as the character they have no right to know. As the character they can only play the moment, so that what's supposed to happen is open to many shadings.

Given the fact that the camera penetrates and never lies, and by the nature of any tale it's never just another day, the stage is then set for the camera to capture unusual responses under pressure. Added to this pressure is the fact that ultimately moments have to be captured now. Whatever is produced as a result on the dailies will be all the director and editor will have to work with, a factor that only adds to the value and spirit of the moment. A factor that, ideally, a writer always has in mind as he continues to hone his script.

Delving a bit deeper, we can examine Budd Schulberg's Academy Award–winning original script for *On the Waterfront* (1954). We can point out some of the cues that led to Marlon Brando's Academy Award–winning performance as the ex-boxer, Hoboken longshoreman Terry Malloy, as well as the intensely believable work by the entire ensemble. One-third of the way in, because Schulberg provided relevant information (things other characters said about Terry, things he had done), Brando had all he needed to get into this phase of his unfolding saga.

At this point, Terry is more conflicted than ever. At the outset, he went along and called Joey Doyle out onto a rooftop where they both raised pigeons as a hobby. After all, John Friendly, the racketeering union boss who runs the docks, only asked for a little favor and Terry's brother, Charlie, is Friendly's legal advisor. In fact, Terry has been going along for years, gullibly believing that Friendly and Charlie backed him as a fighter until that night he was asked to take a dive. Unknowingly however, as a result of calling Joey out (believing that Friendly's henchmen were "just going to lean on him a little bit" and talk him out of "squealing" to the authorities, Joey was shoved off the roof and killed. Now, a short time later, Terry has rescued Joey's sister, Edie, from a clandestine church meeting in protest over Friendly's strong-arm tactics and kickbacks; rescued Edie, in effect, from Friendly's goons who just attacked the protestors. As it happens, Terry was in attendance as another favor to Friendly to learn about the protestors' plans which, inadvertently, put innocent Edie in harm's way.

As Terry and Edie linger for a moment in a rundown park, Brando-as-Terry has to keep hidden the fact that he called her brother out on the roof. He is evidently becoming attracted to Edie (a stool-pigeon's sister on the enemy side) and feels he is not good enough to be in her company—all at the same time as he learns that she's presently in a college run by nuns and is in training to be a teacher. Added to Brando's mercurial state is Edie's insistence that everybody loved her brother, Joey. Changing the subject, Brando-as-Terry reminds her of the times he used to see her when they were in parochial school. How funny she looked with her hair in braids, wearing braces. Trying to disarm her and keep her from leaving, he asks if she remembers him and how he was in trouble all the time.

"It's a wonder I wasn't punchy by the time I was twelve. The rulers those sisters used to whack me with. They thought they could beat an education into me—I foxed 'em."

In response, Edie says, "Maybe they didn't know how to handle you."

"How would you've done it?" asks Terry. Edie answers, "With a little more patience and kindness. That's what makes people mean and difficult. Nobody cares enough about them."

At this juncture, the actress playing Edie (Eva Marie Saint) also is called on to become conflicted, more interested in Terry than what just happened at the church. In this state, she inadvertently drops one of her gloves. Brando picks it up while they continue to talk, keeping his distance but still trying to hold her there. He can't touch her but he can slip his hand into her glove, something fine and delicate, something he has never been close to. None of this is in the script, but because Schulberg set this up, and because Brando had the talent to blend toughness and vulnerability and play the moment, the camera was able to capture this interplay "between the words" as Bo Goldman put it.

Visualizing these possibilities, not precisely but knowingly, sensing something appropriately surprising will happen as a natural emotional overflow, is the hope of the screenwriter in tune with the art of acting. So much so that he may very well be in the same heightened state as he writes and empathizes with the action.

Moving on and closer to the escalating crises between Terry and John Friendly, we can recall the famous taxi scene between Terry and his brother Charlie, the one where Terry says, "I could've been a contender. I could've had class and been somebody."

To force Terry into swearing that he won't rat on his boss Friendly, Charlie pulls out a gun. A stock actor would have simply gotten angry at his brother and shoved the gun away. But that wasn't what Schulberg had in mind. In that same hopeful way, Schulberg set up the conditions. And sure enough, Brando came through again, rolled his eyes and consoled the actor playing Charlie, gently pressing the gun away. In that moment, despite the fact that Charlie had led him astray all those years and was now threatening him with a loaded weapon, the bond between them, all the unspoken affection came through. During the shooting phase, the camera caught the moment just before Charlie gives up and lets his brother go.

Gaps, prompts and spaces, hopeful for telling responses on the part of the actors.

Leaving the realism of the New York scene and turning back to sunny Southern California and the comedy-drama world of Buck Henry's *The Graduate*, we continue to find these open-ended opportunities. As a result, Dustin Hoffman-as-Ben intuitively walks into an upscale hotel looking stunned as he approaches the lobby for his initial assignation with Mrs. Robinson. According to the storyline, at this point he's just celebrated his 21st birthday, is bored and lost and, seemingly, has no idea how to handle this middle-aged, neurotic woman. Preceding her up to a single room, Hoffman enters as if he's passed through a door into the unknown, warily working the blinds, peering around, looking for a last-minute way out. He makes a whimpering sound when confronted with Bancroft-as-Robinson's offhanded way of undressing, once even going so far as to spin away from her and banging his head against the wall. Sometimes these reactions are comic and sometimes they're slow and painful like the time Hoffman intuitively presses his forehead against a wire fence as Elaine drives off and away, headed back to Berkeley.

On the other side of the unraveling relationship with Ben, Bancroft-as-Mrs. Robinson is furnished with gaps that allow the sadness and emptiness of her life and her failed marriage to seep through. Judging from the lazy rhythm of the scene, Henry gave her ample time to light a cigarette, pause and reflect on how it all went wrong as Ben casually prods her about her past. In this same hotel room, as the affair winds down and becomes perfunctory, Bancroft becomes hurt, despite an attempt to hold onto her cool, calculating façade, and reveals a certain fragility and hesitancy between her lines. Apparently no longer the predator, but a woman whose youthful opportunities have been lost and passed her by.

Bancroft was able to do so, not only because she was a talented actress, but because there's an underlying subtext. Although the script has a much lighter tone than the starkly real *On the Waterfront*, there is often that self-same difference between what characters say and what they do, what they feel and what they say. It's at these moments that something slips out, like Hoffman's whimpers and head-nudging; and Bancroft's grimaces as she starts to lose control, snatches a cigarette and recovers. A writer of actable scripts understands the tension between the inner and the outer—the usual tactics and the unusual impulses—counts on them to produce something that will keep things percolating up on the screen.

During the last beat, as Ben snatches Elaine away from her wedding and they hail a passing bus, Ben and Elaine rush through the aisle past the curious passengers. The onlookers have doubtless never seen a gleeful bride in a wedding dress accompanied by a sweaty, disheveled young man dashing toward a rear seat. The script doesn't tell the two actors what to do. But there they are, on their own, free to let the realization sink in that the rush and immediacy of foiling a wedding and leaving everyone in the lurch may have consequences. Free to ponder their lack of funds and plans. Free to let the glee subside and allow the camera to record the gradual drain of energy and something totally unplanned to take over.

For an even more remarkable result from an open-ended opportunity, there is Krzysztof Kieslowski's script for *Heaven* (2002). In preparation, the story action finds Phillipa, an English teacher in Italy, planting a bomb in a wastebasket in a drug lord's office. She does so, we later learn, in frustration over the failure of the corrupt carabinieri (Italian police) to stop the culprit from selling drugs to children at her school (one of whom subsequently died). She does so because the same dealer's drugs led to the death of her husband.

The actress playing Phillipa (Cate Blanchett) is later interrogated by the carabinieri. She learns that a cleaning lady emptied the contents of the basket into her cart which she then wheeled onto an elevator carrying a man and his two little girls. When Blanchett-as-Phillipa is confronted with the fact that she inadvertently killed four people including two children, her expression goes from incomprehension to disbelief, to shock and to grief that is so overwhelming that she crumples up and faints. After supplying this hint, Kieslowski could have imagined all kinds of responses including sobs, writhing and a great deal of head shaking. But the fact remains that there are no lines for Phillipa to utter. Blanchett's sense of shock and release broken into distinct emotional stages is only one way the realization could have played out. But it was perfectly consistent with the space between the accusation and the stage direction calling for Phillipa's prone figure on the interrogation room floor.

Going even further afield, we can apply this same between- and under-the-lines gauge to Emma Thompson's work on *Sense and Sensibility* (1995). Granted, in adapting Jane Austen's early 18th century novel she had many advantages. She was an accomplished actress and a writer with a clever British television series to her credit. She was educated at Cambridge, extremely well read and well versed in Austen's writings. All told, she was able to think in that sophisticated, witty way and was a romantic to go along with her keen intelligence and sense of irony. But the principle is still the same. She needed to write efficient and appropriate dialogue leading to silences that said more than the spoken word.

In the following sample, lovely but newly impoverished Marianne Dashwood (Kate Winslet) has been pining away over the absence of handsome, dashing Willoughby. Though he never openly expressed his intentions, his amorous behavior led her to believe he was on the verge of asking for her hand. Now, inside the grand ballroom of a great country estate, Marianne is beside herself in anticipation, knowing that any moment she will be reunited with the love of her life. Instead, this is what happens:

> WILLOUGHBY sees MARIANNE. At the same moment the music pauses. MARIANNE looks up. In the brief moment of relative quiet, her great cry rings across the room.
> ### MARIANNE
> Willoughby!
> Everyone turns to look as MARIANNE rushes toward him with both arms outstretched. MARIANNE reaches him but WILLOUGHBY stands with his arms frozen at his side.
> ### MARIANNE
> Good God, Willoughby. Will you not shake hands with me?
> WILLOUGHBY glances toward a group of very smart PEOPLE who are watching him closely. Central to this group is a SOPHISTICATED WOMAN who frowns at him proprietorially.
> ### WILLOUGHBY
> How do you do, Miss Marianne?
> ### MARIANNE
> Willoughby, what is the matter? Why have you not come to see me?

Were you not in London? Have you not received my letters?
WILLOUGHBY
Yes, I had the pleasure of receiving the information which you were
so good as to send me. I am most obliged. If you will excuse me, I
must return to my party.
He bows and walks away to join the SOPHISTICATED WOMAN.

During this brief exchange, the actress playing the gushingly romantic
Marianne has been given much to play on the surface and beneath the lines.
Much to take in and much to go through as her whole life turns upside down
and Willoughby turns into someone else; someone who has jilted her for a
woman of higher station and wealth.

This brief exchange also points up another source of stimuli that writers furnish and actors rely on. One that, so far, we've indicated but need to
underscore.

The Pull of the Ambiance

It seems that writing with actors in mind also inspires everyone else
involved creatively, like the costume designer, production designer, art director, set director, cinematographer and, in the case of Thompson's script, the
music director and choreographer as well.

For instance, though in the beat before Thompson only penciled in the
words EXT. GRAND CRESCENT LEADING TO BALLROOM
ENTRANCE. NIGHT., she expected the creative people to fill in the gaps.
In this way, the actress playing Marianne is sure to be flush with excitement
as all the carriages enter the Crescent to deliver the guests. Thompson also
assumed Marianne would be dressed for the occasion, surrounded by women
dressed in greater finery, with the men, no doubt, following form. Once
inside, the costume will affect her behavior, as will the gay music of the
period, the dancers performing their mincing steps circling around her, plus
all the genteel bowing, greeting and shaking of hands. Added to this are the
bounds of propriety of the time, what Marianne is allowed to do and say
and not permitted to do and say. Losing her self-control for a moment and
calling out Willoughby's name naturally would cause the gentry (perhaps as
many as one hundred people) to stop and stare at her. The proprietary look
on the sophisticated woman and, in turn, the disapproving look of her set
will greatly add to the actress-as-Marianne's tension.

However, even though she's losing her composure, custom dictates that
she can't show it. The time, place, heat of the crowded room, glinting candlelight and everything else coupled with the quickly deteriorating situation
and the inner and outer nature of Marianne's character were all designed to

affect what happens to Miss Dashwood. Take away this attention to the potential, cumulative effect, and the likes of Kate Winslet and the rest of the stellar cast—let alone the distinguished director, Ang Lee, etc.—would not be needed. Emma Thompson and her Academy Award for best adapted screenplay would have never come to pass and neither would this spirited take on the social mores of the time. The result would be a standard take on one of Austen's work, quickly consumed and easily forgotten.

To go on making the case for the pull of the ambiance, we can return to some of the built-in stimuli contained in the source material from Budd Schulberg.

Take Edie, the once-sheltered college girl determined to learn the circumstances behind her brother's murder. Apart from the frigid cold, her visit to the Jersey docks making inquiries finds her surrounded by rough longshoremen as she scrambles for a tossed dock worker's tab to help out her father. This act forces the actress to drop her demure upbringing and holler at Terry to hand over this last tab so that "Pop" can get a day's wages which he desperately needs. Apart from this, the unsettling experience at the clandestine nighttime meeting at the church (a place where she should feel safe) where she is forced to flee as Terry pulls her away, there are many more locales and circumstances that pressure the actress, whoever she may be, to respond in new and different ways.

To cite one more instance, there is a scene in the middle of the script that takes place in a waterfront dive. It is ladies night. Terry has convinced Edie to have a drink with him after showing her his pigeons on a rooftop (her brother Joey used to raise pigeons and Terry seems very gentle with his). The actress-as-Edie now has to deal with the unfamiliar sights, smells and the incessant noise in this seedy riverfront saloon: the blare of a ball game, the blowsy women, the bartender yelling over at Terry about last night's prize fight, the presence of John Friendly's henchmen. In turn, we have what the atmosphere is doing to Brando-as-Terry who swaggers, dropping the tenderness he showed on the rooftop, claiming that in this life "you've got to get him before he gets you," leaving Edie shaken when he intimates that it's better to live like an animal on the Jersey docks than wind up like her dead brother.

Shifting gears once again, for the actor playing Ben in *The Graduate*, the atmosphere changes from the solitude of his room with his bubbling tropical-fish tank in the background, to the knowing glances of the hotel staff and the sterile hallways and rooms, to a sleazy strip joint where he tries to pretend he is as cocky and jaded as the place itself in order to dispense with Elaine. Though the place works to keep up his crass façade, the actress-as-Elaine's resultant tears as she runs out of the place have the same comparable effect on Hoffman-as-Ben as it does on Brando-as-Terry when his bravado in the saloon gives way in the face of Edie's sadness and bewilderment over his crass posturing.

And so it goes. Blanchett-as-Phillipa in *Heaven* goes to pieces when confronted by the hated carabinieri and the oppressive confinement of the interrogation room. Her plight touches her interpreter who becomes involved and mistranslates her story from English to Italian. His familiarity with the warrens of the jail cells and immediate vicinity combined with her unfamiliarity intensifies her response patterns. She later parlays her familiarity with the nearby countryside into an escape route that soon becomes alien territory as those who would befriend her and her new companion (the smitten interrogator) are caught in the carabinieri's dragnet and everything begins to go downhill.

Charting a Full Through-line

Soon, writing with actor-characters in mind dovetails with the shot flow, change in locales, and the variety and rhythm of the assembled bits and pieces. At the same time, you can pull back and isolate leading roles in terms of their arc from beginning to end as if telling separate and interwoven tales. In the shooting script of *The Graduate*, you can start to follow Ben Braddock, listless and adrift at his graduation party. At this point, he is barely acquainted with Mrs. Robinson and her daughter, Elaine, and, even then, only in passing. As things progress, thanks to Mrs. Robinson's machinations and then Ben's father's matchmaking, Ben becomes involved with Mrs. Robinson sexually and, in turn, truly falls in love with her daughter, Elaine. The contradictions between what Ben does and how he actually feels and the complications that ensue begin to proliferate. As a result, his relationships with Mrs. Robinson and Elaine follow the same roller coaster. By the time everything plays out, each of the three has drastically changed and switched positions. The role of Ben offers a full emotional and behavioral arc and the same can certainly be said for the roles of Mrs. Robinson and Elaine.

By the same token, you can chart the emotional, behavioral and relational arc for the roles of Terry Malloy, Edie, Charlie and John Friendly; Marianne and Willoughby; Phillipa and the interpreter who becomes her lover and guide in her flight from the Italian police. Given all the opportunities provided in the source material for transformation, creative moments, interplay with each other and the changing ambiance and given circumstances—given the gamut of emotions and obstacles they each have to work through, around and by, these roles would surely be coveted by anyone who loves to act.

Henry's and Thompson's work are adaptations, Schulberg's and Kieslowski's are original scripts. They represent a wide range of time, place and style; box-office mainstream hits, a trans–Atlantic success and a critically acclaimed European venture. The attention to the art and craft of acting is, for all intents and purposes, virtually the same.

By and large, good writers have always followed suit and taken good screen actors into account at every turn.

4. A Storyteller's Vision

A few years back, the American Film Institute (AFI) polled 1,500 people from the film industry, asking them to name the best one hundred movies. There is no way of knowing what criteria the voters used. Individually they may have been influenced by any number of things like, which movies received nominations as Best Picture? which won Best Picture in a given year? which mainly American features have received the most critical praise over the years and been seen by the most number of people? At any rate, Orson Welles' *Citizen Kane* (1941) garnered the most votes followed closely by *Casablanca* (1942). Whether you agree with the list or not, what's interesting for our purposes is the fact that the great majority of films in the top ten — *The Godfather* (1972), *Gone with the Wind* (1939), *Lawrence of Arabia* (1962), *The Wizard of Oz* (1939), *The Graduate* (1967), *On the Waterfront* (1954), *Singin' in the Rain* (1952) — and those not far behind share the same underlying characteristics. Distinctions that, in a sense, set them apart from the AFI's top film and "great" foreign films like Fellini's *8½* (1963), Antonioni's *L'Avventura* (1960) and the legendary films of Ingmar Bergman like *Scenes from a Marriage* (1973).

The Auteur Mode

In general, films like *Citizen Kane*, *8½*, *L'Avventura* and *Scenes from a Marriage* center on the highly personal vision of writers and writer-directors. At the outset of Welles and co-author Herman Mankiewicz's tale there are the dying words of a 75-year-old man ("Rosebud") in residence at Xanadu. But we have no idea who the man is. Some may know the movie is a take on the newspaper tycoon William Randolph Hearst's life, and Xanadu is a fictional replica of his tourist-attraction castle in San Luis Obispo. To fill the viewer in, there is a quasi documentary; reporters then discuss the mystery behind Charles Kane's dying words, one reporter sets out to discover the key to "Rosebud" and, thereby, the meaning of Kane's life. Presently, a flashback tells of Kane's mother who wanted her son to be rich and successful and entrusted his guardianship to a powerful banker. This is followed by an interview by the reporter-detective with Kane's mistress (an alcoholic failed opera singer who Kane abused and who finally left him). Next, there is Kane's rise and fall politically, shots of him filling Xanadu with artworks that he never unpacks, more flashbacks and inquiries leading to Kane's isolation (estranged from his wife, sans family, friends or love) and the announcement of his death. The viewer never learns exactly what Kane wanted out of life nor what the word "Rosebud" actually meant. Since "Rosebud" is the name of a lost sled, it may signify the loss of childhood innocence after a misguided pursuit of power and the American dream.

As an innovation, the project featured the deep-focus photography of Gregg Toland enabling Welles to show the foreground and background of Kane's world with equal clarity, plus a variety of novel shots like the one swooping down through a skylight in order to reach Kane's pathetic former mistress as she lounges in a seedy nightclub. We also have a circular narrative structure that challenges the viewer to guess what scene is coming next, flashbacks through the eyes of many witnesses so that the question of the meaning of anyone's life becomes unanswerable. Through this kind of narrative device the viewer is also given a certain history of an era, covering a great deal of ground from 1895 to 1941 in a relatively short span of time. And though fragmented, Welles was provided with an acting tour de force in the title role. On the basis of this freewheeling storyline, Herman Mankiewicz and Welles received an Oscar for best screenplay. As a model, all storytelling elements were in service to a highly personal, cultural point of view: the storyteller as auteur or author of the work whose voice and signature are ever present.

In another variation, harkening back to Antonioni and touching on Fellini, the style of authorship changes. As indicated earlier, in *L'Avventura*, a group of rich Roman couples take a boat trip to a rocky, unpopulated island off the coast of Sicily. At one point, Anna, one of the young women, tries to interrupt the dreary leisure of the boat trip by pretending a shark is after her. In the same half-hearted way, she engages in a brief tryst with her lover, Sandro. Presently, Anna wanders off and vanishes. The others search for her but then give up and drift back into their self-absorbed and empty lives, finding no faith in love or anything else for that matter. At one point, Sandro utters lines like, "I saw myself as a genius working in a garret. Now I've got two flats and I've neglected to become a genius."

As also indicated earlier, the viewer can never tell where the camera is going as it passes over the barren, rocky terrain or who or what the camera is going to follow. In this story pattern, since the characters are astray, the tempo and rhythms of life are all that are meaningful. The rest is a mystery. Another kind of personal vision, another way of telling a tale.

Fellini's fantasy in *8½* revolves around a director who has no idea what he wants to do next. In the process he engages in dreams, memories, episodes with a wife and mistress who collide in the same location at a spa near Rome, and he stages lots of parades. The producers in the documentary segments insist on rewrites in view of the money spent on an elaborate science fiction set the director insisted on but abandoned. At one point, the fictional Fellini engages in another fantasy as he floats up in the sky away from the movie set, only to be pulled down by a rope at the hands of his associates. In this writer-director's hands, everything is cinematic, a celebration of pure film and imagination in conflict with the demands of his profession.

With Bergman and works like *Scenes from a Marriage*, intimacy, emotional depth and passion come into the foreground along with the deeply personal. In his storytelling process he took an honest look at bittersweet and embattled relationships, sexual transgressions and the difficulties of communication. In other works he tackled spiritual crises and mortality, and the trials of his own childhood. Fittingly, often evoking the chilly winter light of his native Sweden in search of the sun, he took risks in trying to come to terms with these issues that, in each instance, doubled back on his life.

Like Murnau's silent classic *Sunrise* (1927) well before (the one where illusions and dreams mix with everyday reality) and countless films after, the world filtered through the eyes of the writer or writer-director who has a special story to tell is always an option, especially for those immersed in the indie world (more to follow in due course).

The Traditional Style

In contrast, and on the basis of the more traditional narrative form, we have the invisible storyteller, the one who, in a sense, disappears so that viewers can lose themselves completely in the illusion. One of the most telling examples is *Casablanca*, drawn from Julius and Philip Epstein and Howard Koch's Oscar-winning screenplay (number two on the AFI list, widely cited in many audience polls as the greatest film of all time and Oscar winner for Best Picture).

With this unfolding change of events, there is no underlying self-expression to be found. As it happens, in addition to the Epstein brothers and Koch, three other un-credited writers worked on the scenario, not to mention the creators of the original springboard, a play called *Everybody Comes to Rick's* by Murray Burnett and Joan Alison. At this juncture at the height of the old studio system, there was a rule of thumb that nothing should take away from the expectations of moviegoers everywhere to be carried away.

With the balance tipped in favor of the viewer, all six writers were continuing in the tradition of the international fairy tales of yesteryear, trying to captivate people in the same universal way. By extension, the ideal of the big screen was to insure that there were no distractions, nothing between viewers' identification with the characters and total involvement. Everything in *Casablanca* was geared toward drawing them into this particular world. They, in turn, gladly consented, safe in the realization that this was a place and a life that bore little resemblance to their own. Vicariously, they went through the experience, one that, if only they had the courage or wits or spirit, they would've gladly undertaken. An escape that became all the more gratifying because there were no repercussions.

Which brings us back to Rick and Ilsa. As we've seen, at the most optimum moment when viewers wanted to know why the owner of Rick's Cafe Americain seemed so cynical and disenchanted, moviegoers were swept effortlessly and seamlessly into the past and the couple's idyllic romance just before the Nazi occupation of Paris. Just as effortlessly and seamlessly, they were brought back to the present, doubtless hoping that the two can get back together. At the same time, viewers learned that this wish was seemingly impossible because Ilsa had a husband, Victor Laszlo, a legendary hero of the Resistance who reappeared after Ilsa had given him up for dead. A man who now, more than ever, was dedicated to the fight against Nazi tyranny. Ilsa couldn't possibly leave him. Or could she? Once more, at the optimum moment, the dialogue became as appropriately effortless and unshakable as everything else, as though this is what Rick should say to resolve the dilemma as he insisted that Ilsa board the plane with Victor before it was too late:

> RICK
>
> Last night we said a great many things. You said to do the thinking for both of us. Well I've done a lot of it and it all adds up to one thing. You're getting on that plane with Victor where you belong.
>
> ILSA
>
> Rick, no. I've—
>
> RICK
>
> Now you've got to listen to me. Do you have any idea what you'd have to look forward to if you stayed here? Nine times out of ten we'd both wind up in a concentration camp.
>
> ILSA
>
> You're saying this only to make me go.
>
> RICK
>
> I'm saying it because it's true. Inside of us we both know you belong to Victor. You're part of his work, the thing that keeps him going.

When that plane leaves the ground and you're not with him, you'll
regret it. Maybe not today, maybe not tomorrow, but soon and for the
rest of your life.
>ILSA
But what about us?
>RICK
We'll always have Paris. We didn't have. We lost it until you came to
Casablanca. We got it back last night.
>ILSA
When I said I would never leave you.
>RICK
And you never will. But I've got a job to do too. And where I'm going
you can't follow. What I've got to do, you can't be any part of. Ilsa,
I'm no good at being noble. But it doesn't take much to see that the
problems of three little people don't amount to a hill of beans in this
crazy world. Someday you'll understand that.
>(pause)
Now now. Here's looking at you, kid.

As emotionally involved as the audience, Ingrid Bergman's eyes are full
of a sad longing, her voice soft and hushed. It's not in the stage directions;
it doesn't have to be. And neither is the moment when she looks down and
Bogart gently tilts her chin up before he says, "Now now." Not wanting to
lose his resolve but barely hiding the sense of imminent loss just the same.

There may be a message having to do with sacrificing love for a higher
cause, but it's never telegraphed, never spelled out. Fittingly, there is a cast
drawn from 34 nationalities including Bergman from Sweden, Paul Hen-
reid from Vienna, Bogart from the U.S. and Claude Rains from London,
but there is never an instance that capitalizes on any performer's international appeal. The film is guided by a world-famous director from Hungary
(Michael Curtiz, Oscar for Best Director) but nowhere does he flaunt his
art or his expertise.

Underneath it all, like all great love stories, there are obstacles that can't
be overcome, two people who can't get together and a resultant satisfying
sadness. But it isn't derivative, isn't a variation on some tried and true formula. Moreover, it's not like one of those countless tales that take place in
some watering hole where interesting types conveniently run into one
another. During World War II, French Morocco was a crossroads for spies,
traitors, Nazis and the French Resistance. The exit visas that Rick hands
over to Victor are the couple's only means of escape to Lisbon and embarka-
tion to freedom and the Americas where Victor can gain support to carry
on the fight. Rick wanted more than anything to use the visas for himself
and Ilsa, but it's this dilemma that kept the tension and the story going. If
it were formulaic, there would have been a happy ending. The story goes

that Ingrid Bergman's complex responses came about because the writers hadn't decided on the resolution. She, like her character and the audience, was never certain how things were going to turn out. If it were formulaic, all the attention would have been heaped on the two stars. In this case, echoing the complexity of the time and situation, there are scenes with rich supporting characters: a corrupt club owner, a sniveling thief and murderer, an ingénue who will do anything to aid her naïve gambling husband, a piano player and Rick's loyal friend, a smooth-talking Nazi officer who is determined to snare Victor Laszlo, and an ambivalent French chief of police who finds himself doing something totally uncharacteristic—making a moral decision.

In this same rich tradition, the background moves in at the most opportune moments and becomes foreground. In one memorable scene, we find a French woman of easy virtue hobnobbing with the Nazis at Rick's, reluctant to interfere as the Nazis break into their anthem. However, when Victor and other compatriots retaliate and sing *La Marseillaise* backed up by the resident band, it's almost impossible not to root for the French woman to risk everything and join then. And so she does, impulsively, raising her voice with the others in defiance.

From *Casablanca*'s regard for the audience's involvement and its rock-solid narrative, we can look backwards or forward and find innumerable screen stories in the same mold. Perusing other examples atop the AFI list, there they are storylines in this same tradition, drawing the audience inside the central characters' world, enabling them to see it the way the characters see it from their emotional point of view.

The Godfather gives us a unique perspective of family loyalty and bonding in contrast with other crime families who are much more ruthless and corrupt. From this vantage point, despite his wild, crazy temper, Sonny attempted to protect his sister and didn't deserve to be duped and ambushed at the toll gate; the godfather himself didn't deserve to be gunned down for refusing to go along with the mob bosses who insisted on going into the narcotics trade. From his emotional perspective, Michael, the college graduate and forthright war hero, had to stand guard immediately afterward the shooting, stand by the hospital bed and utter, "I'm with you now, Pop." From this standpoint, Michael made a difficult but necessary moral choice.

We've noted the predicament Terry Malloy was in and the built-in rooting interest in having this ex-fighter fight again, but this time for something worthwhile even if it meant going against his brother. In this same light, it's only natural that audiences would root for Edie to put aside her sheltered ways and seek justice for her slain brother.

Ben Braddock's sad-comic plight, given his everyman characterization by writer Buck Henry—tentative, bewildered and then desperate—falls under the same umbrella. As do the escapades and tribulations of Scarlett O'Hara (if you can go along with the notion of the Old South as a Camelot of "cavaliers and cotton fields," a lost idyll of plantation life). Here we have a free-spirited, willful woman far ahead of her time, taking on Rhett Butler, devastation and whatever comes her way, undaunted throughout the Civil War as the storytelling maintains interest for almost four hours. The literate script by Robert Bolt and Michael Wilson of Lawrence of Arabia's adventures holds audiences for almost the same length of time. Even though the character, as played by Peter O'Toole, is highly enigmatic, the chance to be drawn into this vast canvas, caught up in Lawrence's epic task of uniting the Arabs against factional strife and fate as he claims "nothing is written," proved to be irresistible.

In a much lighter vein, for moviegoers of all ages, Dorothy's adventures with her transformed old pals from Kansas, overcoming low self-esteem as well as the forces of the wicked witch, seems to be continually captivating. The same goes for the yarn fashioned by Betty Comden and Adolph Green of what is generally regarded as the greatest movie musical of all time, *Singin' in the Rain*. In this instance, Kathy Selden, a perky, 19-year-old tyro, bucks the odds. Through sheer talent and determination, she makes it into the talkies, keeping up with the veteran song-and-dance men, Don Lockwood and his irrepressible sidekick, Cosmo Brown, every step of the way. The book of boy-meets-girl, boy-loses-girl, boy-gets-girl-back may be old hat and would certainly be flimsy without the song-and-dance numbers, but in this case, the book keeps everything fresh, spirited and original as it plays against the backdrop of vaudeville and the growing pains from the silent era to the talkies.

If you add in the backdrops—World War II Morocco, the heyday of mob corruption on the East Coast, the Civil War, Arab–British–Turkish interests in Arabia, Oz and the heartland—the great appeal of these narrative structures becomes even richer and clearer. But before this all starts to seem prescriptive, we need to widen the focus a bit.

Variations on the Theme

There's a danger of making too much of a distinction between auteur explorations and engaging storytelling, as if one form was limited to writers and patrons of art houses and cinematheques while the vast majority of scriptwriters and moviegoers were ensconced in the mainstream and never the twain shall meet. A glance at Jean-Pierre Melville's *Le Samourai* (1967) might help loosen that notion. Apart from the fact that this film is also on some best movies of all time lists, Melville's tale utilizes a Felliniesque reliance on imagery. At the same time, Melville submerged it all in realism with no interruptions or flights of fancy, allowing nothing to stand in the way of the audience's involvement with the fate of Jef Costello, a contract killer. For moviegoers everywhere, there is constant suspense over the seemingly implacable coolness of this anti-hero with his samurai-like code of honor to finish each job no matter what. There is always the question, How far should this loner go in this shabby of world of compromise and betrayal? In his dingy room with only a gray, caged bird as a companion, he maneuvers beneath and above the rain-soaked streets of Paris, gets shot by someone he trusted, counts on the loyalty of a young woman who loves him, foils the manipulations of the police but is caught between his code and both his unscrupulous employees and the law. Throughout, the audience is with him, never knowing how this story will play out, having all the room in the world to worry about what will happen next.

One more thing. Melville was greatly influenced by the best of American crime movies. By adding his own unique take to the genre, he influenced a host of writers and directors. Echoes of the cool, crafty way Jef Costello operates can be found in a great number of other films. Following in Costello's footsteps, there are the painstaking preparations of a hired assassin who went Costello one better, switching identities and tactics on his single-minded quest to kill the French war hero Charles De Gaulle (*Day of the Jackal*, 1973). Moving well beyond the streets of Paris, this tale of a professional loner takes us on a picturesque cat-and-mouse chase throughout Europe.

The yardstick of identification and empathy can also mean entering into an unsettling situation or set of circumstances just to see how far it will all go. Through the writer's tale, audiences can follow the exploits of the disenchanted drifter Fast Eddie Felson as he works his way into position to take on the legendary Minnesota Fats (*The Hustler*, 1961). Though the pool hall scene and other grungy locales lead to some depressing consequences, there is still something mesmerizing about following an expert at his trade or one who has a chance to be as good as they come, if only. There is something inviting about entering that selfsame world far different than ours, especially if what's on screen is not the same-old same-old. This kind of walk on the wild side can draw viewers into the strange plight of an outsider who had no intention of becoming a duplicitous murderer, only a paid companion. In screenwriter-director Anthony Minghella's version of Tom Ripley's odyssey, Tom becomes so enchanted with Dickie Greenleaf's privileged lifestyle on the Italian Riviera, it wasn't long before he accidentally did away with Dickie, then Dickie's snooping friend, and even someone Tom was falling in love with as he became determined to stop at nothing to maintain his new identity (*The Talented Mr. Ripley*, 1999).

In conventional terms, perhaps Billy Wilder put it best when he declared that the only rule was, once you've grabbed an audience's attention, don't let them go. Don't alert them to the fact that they're watching a movie. Like Herman Mankiewicz and Welles, Wilder went so far as to begin the tale of our failed screenwriter Joe Gillis at the end, floating face down in the decaying swimming pool of his crazed employer, former silent film star Norma Desmond. He let the newly deceased writer start his own tale and kept the audience enthralled. It's almost impossible for moviegoers not to wonder, What happened? Isn't there some way Joe can pull himself out this? Some way he can rejoin that sweet, script development girl from the studio whom he loves and who loves him? Some way he can start over and make good? (This Oscar-winner for Best Screenplay is listed at number 12 on the AFI popularity list.)

Following Wilder's general rule, the traditional storyteller is also free to start at the end, but center on a character no one identifies with, use a voice-over of a character few people can relate to, employ a great deal of dialogue and still keep moviegoers enthralled. The work in question is *All About Eve* (1950), another Oscar-winner and high on the AFI list at number 16. This tale was conceived by Joseph Mankiewicz, Herman's brother, about a decade after *Citizen Kane* and concerns an imaginary celebrity this time. There is, however, still a mystery. How did Eve Harrington climb to the top of the ladder? Turning the viewer's expectations about the wonders and glories of fame upside down, here is what the suave and knowing theater critic Addison DeWitt tells us as he surveys the hall at the opening of the film, just before the lavish awards dinner:

> DE WITT
> Eve. Eve the golden girl, the cover girl, the girl next door, the girl on the moon. Time has been good to her. Life goes where she goes. She has been profiled, covered, revealed, reported—what she eats, what she wears and whom she knows. Where she was and when and where she's going.

Like all effective screen dialogue, there is a subtext. What is this critic really telling us? Who can we trust as this story unfolds through a long flashback? And then, back in time, how did seemingly young, warm and sincere little Eve get to this point? What about the seasoned Broadway star and her director husband? How did Eve get into their good graces? And the playwright and his charming wife? What about them? There is obviously much more here than meets the eye.

As for the crisp speech patterns, everyone in this world is articulate because they are of the Broadway theater which, by custom, lives and dies on the strength of its dialogue. All, onstage or off, rely on the ability to turn a phrase, memorize passages, quote from the Bard and exchange witty repartee. A young lady's choice between a flamboyant Greenwich Village novelist and a tried-and-true pickle salesman from the old neighborhood (*Crossing Delancey*, 1988) sparks a different kind of story and set of speech patterns. Jef Costello hardly speaks at all, careful never to tip his hand as he threads his way down the darkened Parisian streets and slips into a nightclub. Sundance, Butch's sidekick, speaks through his actions and his deft way with a six-gun. The garrulous Scarlett O'Hara is a product of the Old South during a distinct passage of time just before and just after the Civil War; the latter referred to as, "The war of Yankee aggression."

As the traditional storyteller weaves his tale, all remains seamless, nothing seems out of place. At the same time, traditional story-weaving also serves as a point of departure for the true movie buff. As the story goes, Quentin Tarantino once worked in a video store and had seen so many crime movies that he was able to fracture the narrative and the chronological order of time and create *Pulp Fiction* (1994), playing with three separate vignettes framed by an opening and closing diner scene that dovetail. All of this was accepted as another step in the ongoing process. To some discerning eye, it might appear that Tarantino's effort was also somewhere in the vicinity of the time warp of *Memento*, within striking distance of *Le Samourai*, and, perhaps, even touching on the perceptions of the likes of Welles, Antonioni, Fellini and Bergman, which would blur any hard and fast distinction between auteur and the invisible traditionalist.

For all intents and purposes then, if you decide to take off, you have to take off from somewhere. Ernest Lehman, who, in addition to *North by Northwest*, wrote the screenplays for *Executive Suite*, *Sabrina*, *Somebody Up There Likes Me* and *The Sweet Smell of Success*, had this to say in Engel's *Screenwriters on Screenwriting*:

"I try to be aware of whether the audience understands what the characters are thinking and intending; whether the dialogue is more than mundane; whether something is being communicated. Audiences should never say, 'Wait a second, I don't understand that.' I'm interested in how to be brief and how not to stay in a situation too long. The camera should take the place of dialogue whenever possible. I'm always aware of the audience: Do they still want to know what comes next?"

That said, it may all come down to an appreciation of the basics and the best, and even the worst, of all that has gone before. Some just call it "a feeling for the medium" or "a keen movie sense" which somehow has become second nature. But however you put it or acquire it, it's the basis for more pertinent and pressing questions like, What kinds of films am I drawn to? What kinds of stories would I like to tell and how would I like to tell them? What are the possibilities?

II—OPTIONS AND METHODS— RUNNING THE GAMUT

5. Genre as a Niche

As it happens, a prominent screenwriter once dashed off a first draft and sent it to four colleagues for a critique. Briefly, the scenario was set in and around Manhattan and revolved around an attempted kidnapping, intrepid double rescues (a private detective rescuing a perfect young woman and later the young woman rescuing him), a marriage between this intrepid duo, complications as it turns out that the perfect woman is irrevocably far above the detective's station in life, time passing, precocious children who are taken with their dad's detective work, and a final breakup of the couple after the kids, on their first case and initiation, run into a robbery and shootout. This is followed by a second act as things go from bad to worse: the perfect woman becomes engaged to an insufferable man of her own class, the offspring become despondent, the detective takes to drink, one of the kids gets kidnapped. And it goes on from there.

What is interesting is not so much the setup and sequence of events but the response. All four script doctors wanted the sketchy draft revised into a format they could relate to. One wanted it to focus solely on a daunting case involving the detective father and his two offspring. But first he wanted to know the characters better, who they were beyond the indicated types and attitudes so that he could care what happens to them. Another reader not only opted for a different storyline, he reminded the author that readers and audiences alike make critical decisions at the opening moments. Exactly what kind of investment was being asked of him? Was this a family thriller, a noir comedy, a romantic spoof or a gothic farce? Then and only then, right at the outset, could he decide whether or not to go along. The third critic revealed that she was interested only in the relationship between the detective and the woman in his life, past, present and future. The fourth critic wanted the story to be about the clash of social worlds with a custody battle hanging in the balance.

From this example, and by extension, certain expectations apparently arise at the outset. Intentionally or unintentionally, the writer has made a promise or posed an enticing question that will be answered in due course. If the setup is too loose or fuzzy and remains that way, this implicit bargain falls apart and readers and audiences alike have to then shift for themselves. Thinking back over the top-10 list in the previous chapter, each film can be classified according to type, even if it's just a simple tag like a biopic. And each one establishes a certain tone and carries it through to the end. This certainly makes a case for deciding on a coherent pattern at the very start and sticking to it, or risking disappointment for those on the receiving end who thought they were in for a high adventure or domestic triangle or whatever.

In effect, the sketchy draft in question was only a harmless probe. There was nothing at stake, except perhaps some hurt feelings on the part of the writer. Incoherent story arcs turn into cautionary tales when they reach the production phase of a major film. For instance, unlike *Casablanca*, with its clear-cut love story against a backdrop of World War II intrigue, the French Resistance and Nazi malevolence, the scenario of *Charlotte Gray* (2001) waffled back and forth. It was never established what kind of World War II drama this was going to be, not to mention a sustained main concern.

At first it seemed the heroine, a young Scottish woman who travels to London during the Blitz, was going to do everything in her power to join a Royal Air Force pilot with whom she'd fallen madly in love. It was her determined mission the moment she learned he'd been shot down over occupied France. Fully believing her pilot may be sheltered by the Resistance, and because she was fiercely patriotic and spoke fluent French, she then joins a cadre of secret agents, goes through a grueling training period, assumes a false identity and drops by parachute near a village. She presupposes the site is not far from her fallen lover. She also realizes the local Vichy government is collaborating with the Nazis. But after she hears her lover may be dead, she becomes involved with an ardent Resistance fighter whom, at one point, she protects to keep him out of harm's way. Soon after another incident, the ardent young man threatens to shoot her, convinced she has betrayed his fallen comrades. It takes the Resistance fighter's father to finally bring him to his senses. The plot shifts again as she tries to shelter two young Jewish boys whose parents have recently been deported. Her basic training is never utilized; her attempts to shelter the boys are in vain when the hideout of the two brothers is exposed by a collaborator. Except for a letter she types to give the pair some comfort, it's not clear how much good, if any, she has done. She subsequently departs back to London, discovers her lover is there, alive and well, but no longer cares for him. And so it goes. Whatever film, viewers may initially have had in mind is left to their own imaginations.

There is no problem with the genre; it's immediately recognizable. And somewhere there may be a fresh underlying theme beyond the standard-issue rescue attempt behind enemy lines. The dilemma a woman faced operating under cover, skirting between spying collaborators and her attempts to hide Jewish children, is filled with possibilities. Moreover, acting as a liaison between the Resistance and the home office in London with the added threat of Nazi reprisals offers further opportunities to keep an audience wondering what will happen next within this same framework.

It's often been said that writers can express themselves easily once they've settled on a form that frees up the imagination. The main focus within the parameters of this playing field may have been dealt with time and again, but not in this way or under these circumstances. In this sense, it becomes a matter of selecting the right umbrella or a suitable variation.

The Romantic Comedy

A closer glance at *Singin' in the Rain* reveals the conventional meet-cute format that was in vogue when talking pictures took over the industry. In this particular scenario, opposites are attracted when Kathy, the young chorine, pops out of a cake at a Hollywood party and Don Lockwood, the famous star from the silent era, becomes instantly smitten. It's all a lighthearted take on old routines buoyed by winning song-and-dance numbers. The appeal of the book stems from the comic possibilities when Don's old co-star, Lena Lamount—grating voice and all—is hell-bent to continue her career by starring in the talkies. Adding to Lena's obstacles is Don's new love interest and threat to her plans: the young upstart Kathy, brimming with those two dreaded ingredients: youthful energy and talent.

In short, this is obviously a musical comedy with a touch of romance. If we put romance solidly in the foreground, the aims and expectations change. Now we're focused in the same light breezy way on some larger truth about the present state of courtship rituals and the battle of the sexes. This calls for characters and a situation that a modern audience finds credible.

To add another cautionary tale, in recent years a screenwriter decided to skirt over the rules of the game. Though his movie was made, it all came to naught. In this scenario, thanks to a single mother's Internet dating machinations, one of her daughters winds up with two choices: a well-to-do fastidious architect or a single dad who takes everything in stride and shares a cozy bungalow with his adorable son and his own single dad. But where is the conflict beyond an obvious wrong choice on the daughter's way to the right one? Where is the emotional ebb and flow apart from a few giggles, tears and hugs? How can there be accelerating complications as Mr. and

Ms. Right keep missing each other? And what are the physical comedy possibilities beyond a few obligatory sight gags like mom struggling with her computer?

This particular genre centers on cycles of believing in love and not believing in love and each era's take on the battle of the sexes. And since fascination with courtship rituals is timeless and ageless, any fresh wrinkle has a built-in recognition factor—something new in light of the parade of old standbys.

Back in the 1930s, audiences wanted to escape from the dreariness of the Depression into a sophisticated world of champagne and caviar, a life where money was no object. Where the myth prevailed that you will find the right person for you somewhere soon and, once found, that love will last forever. The fun came about as these ultra-handsome duos kept missing each other: a basic facet of the game and the ever-operative, What's going to happen next? The game, like all games, required obstacles that kept falling in the couple's way. It was called screwball comedy in reference to a baseball pitcher's pitch that came at you in the opposite way from what you, the batter, expected. The plot kept twisting in on itself. The women were bright and strong, wild and free-spirited and gave as good as they got. Many times they were from the upper classes while the men were butlers or of a lower station. At times the male leads took on the clichéd women's roles, not quite as bright, finding themselves at the short end of the stick, defensive or in over their heads. It was a comedy of inversion. The world had delightfully turned upside down.

It was also a world of high and low comedy as Hollywood of the silent era provided the pratfalls and writers from New York who were adept at playwriting and wordplay came west and provided the witty repartee.

There was also something erotic about all the squabbles and fights under the strict production code, all that was hidden and imagined. This is in contrast to the promiscuity and filthy patter running through some 21st century comedies that leave nothing to the imagination, eliminate much of the tension as to will they or won't they ever get together and, as a result, are neither witty, sexy or engrossing.

In general, the desire in this world is to see gender conflicts worked out in different ways, animated in different ways with different kinds of resolutions.

To illustrate the evolving plot line, in light of the new, wilder, unpredictable woman of the 1940s, the writer Preston Sturgis centered his screwball comedy on a lady con artist. Here she is on an ocean liner, after a wealthy amateur naturalist returning from the Amazon who spouts lines like, "Snakes are my life." Witty repartee, a male dolt if there ever was one, a wily young woman, a clear-cut comic premise, and innumerable proliferating complications that keep the couple apart. The con artist unwittingly falls in love with her prey. He proposes marriage. She confesses her past life of sin, no longer able to live a lie. He rejects her because of her criminal past. He is heartbroken, she is heartbroken. She decides to impersonate a wealthy British countess, insinuate herself into her loved one's rich Connecticut set and win him all over again, thus reverting to her old chicanery. Now what? What about true love and honesty over and above money, position and revenge on her part and foolish pride on his? What next?

Another illustration. During this same period, there was the one about the breezy newspaper woman who spars verbally with her managing editor and ex-husband. A third party, a mild-mannered businessman, offers to take care of her if she will only consent to be his wife. Though the woman thinks she can have it all—career and a life as housewife and mother—in reality, the verbal sparring match with her boss and ex takes place in a rhythm nobody else can match. No one else speaks this language or is as exhilarated when hot on the trail of breaking news. It seems that, no matter what, they were always meant for each other.

Later on, in the late 1980s, the triangle was updated. This time it was high-profile television, the woman as the brains and the boss with the drawback that she's socially inept. She's even given to crying jags when no one is looking. There is the good-looking anchorman who is much more attractive but insensitive and can't match his rival for brains. The nice-guy rival is much more articulate, witty and sensitive but can't measure up as either a newscaster under pressure or lover. To compensate for his shortcomings, the anchorman, through some high-handed editing, fakes a seemingly sensitive interview on the air. In disdain, our heroine turns away from him but can't accept the love of the nice guy whom she just sees as a friend. As a result, all three miss their chance and have to settle. Our heroine has to pay the price for being too bright and scrupulous. The anchor has to live with his underhanded ploy, and the nice witty guy has to give up network news and find a second-best life in suburbia. A bit sad perhaps but, overall, whimsical, in tune with the times, and firmly within the parameters of the game.

Flipping back to the late 1950s when psychoanalysis was still in vogue and the notion that no one was purely male or female, Billy Wilder came along testing the staying power of the genre with two struggling band members fleeing from the mob after witnessing the St. Valentine's Day Massacre in Chicago. In disguise as young women (virtually their only ticket out of town) the two guys join an all-girl band in a train headed for a gig in Miami. In keeping with the theme of inversion, Joe the sax player, is in love with Sugar, another band member, and is in a quandary. How can he tell her his real gender, keep the job and remain incognito with the mobsters in hot pursuit? His pal Jerry, the bass player, finds he needs to keep playing his role as Daphne and relishes the courtship and protection of Osgood, a rich older man who owns a yacht. The yacht also provides Joe with the opportunity to switch disguises and pursue Sugar as a blasé millionaire. In turn, confronted with a marriage proposal, Jerry finally confesses, whips off his wig and declares that he's really a man. No problem, all is well as Osgood declares, "Nobody's perfect."

The next variation on the screwball gender twist came about in the 1980s as the New York writers Larry Gelbart and Murray Schisgal et al. came up with an irreverent stage actor who couldn't find work as a male but secured a triumph as an actress and feminist on television and, as a result, became a better person.

In the late 1980s, women screenwriters like Nora Ephron were empowered to tell their side of the continuing story, creating characters and situations they could relate to, like the difficulty of men and women ever becoming friends. These writers told women something they didn't know about the tricks men employ in relationships and visa versa. Other themes that were later explored were the fruitlessness of waiting for Prince Charming; the plight of traditional housewives seeking their opposite, a devil-may-care kindred spirit as a model in order to change their lot and gain renewed passion, then finally realizing they are simply seeking their true selves and a bigger truth about gender and identity.

In all of this, there is only one certainty: the genre has staying power. And so does another genre and its offshoots for those who seek the total opposite side of the coin.

Film Noir

A decade before Billy Wilder was toying with the gender-bending scenario about the two struggling musicians eluding the mob by joining an all-girl band, he was in a more cynical mood. A decade before, he was charting the downward spiral of our down-on-the-heels screenwriter Joe Gillis. Little wonder after fleeing from Berlin when the Nazis came to power. Little wonder after experiencing a cultural-political climate that offered only a pervasive anxiety. And little wonder that the French entitled all films generated by this sense of imminent gloom film noir, dark film.

Appropriately, Joe Gillis surveys the Hollywood pool and the rest of the decaying estate and says, "It was all very queer. But queerer things were yet to come." Here is Norma Desmond, Joe's benefactor with a mad look in her eyes, long claw-like fingernails, drawing and exhaling smoke from a long cigarette holder. Joe and Jerry, the down-on-their-heels band members, found love and playful joy cavorting around with Sugar and Osgood and playing hide-and-seek with the mobsters. But there was no Sugar or fun to be had in the entertainment world for Joe Gillis, no financial security without a price. And when he stopped paying that price, stopped putting up with Norma's twisted notion of love, he wound up shot in the back, face down in that same blighted pool.

Writers who work in this vein, or use aspects of it in their storytelling, are drawn to the seductive danger, irony and hard-boiled reality as are audiences who continue to flock to its many forms.

In the detective story, the P.I. can take you anywhere. You gain access to any level of society high and low—areas audiences are curious about, different aspects of society the writer can continue to mine. In this motif, the femme fatale is a continuing figure, one who takes on many guises. In one prototypical scenario, Sam Spade seeks after the person who killed his partner. The comely woman who hired his partner to tail a man in the dark of night later uses her feminine wiles on Spade himself. But Spade soon realizes she isn't who she says she is. Madcap Jerry and Joe aren't who they say they are either, but that's all in fun. This woman, like Norma Desmond, has no scruples. Whereas in the screwball comedies, the new breed of woman who made her own rules is a positive figure, here she is known as a spider woman, capable, like Norma, of murder and deceit.

Unlike wary and cynical Sam Spade, many storylines feature men who are duped into killing the seductress' husband. Or committing any number of disreputable acts under the delusion they're doing it for love or other enticements the woman is offering. It's been claimed that psychologically, men are both endangered and lured by a powerful female sexual figure who is uncontrollable, who alone can provide the thrill of living on the edge.

This scenario is so enduring, there seem to be endless remakes. Not long ago, another take on real-life lonely hearts killers was released (a couple who preyed on wealthy, weak and lonely single women). In this version, the femme fatale is a demented predatory beauty and a victim of childhood incest. Her partner is a small-time gigolo who is easily manipulated, and one of the lead detectives is perplexed and depressed.

Back in the early 1970s, *Chinatown*, engendered by Robert Towne's Best Original Screenplay, moved the genre into wider territory. Towne's tale had its beginnings while he was reminiscing about the lost L.A. of his childhood. He began reading about the destruction of the Owens Valley by corrupt politicians who were placating speculators who wanted to bring water down to irrigate the San Fernando Valley. This time, in Towne's tale, the cynical detective returns. But unlike Sam Spade, who won't compromise his ideals and do divorce work, this P.I. ex-cop thrives on it. And unlike the lonely-hearts killer and victim of childhood incest, this victim of incest is purely a victim and there are no femme fatales. But the P.I. doesn't remain cool and wary. Nor is he duped by women; not for very long, that is.

Both curious and angry after being manipulated by an attractive woman who isn't who she said she was, he delves deeper. The downward spiral leads him to unsettling truths as a pillar of the community high up in the socioeconomic ladder turns out to be disreputable and guilty of an incestuous act with the very attractive woman the P.I. has fallen for. As an upshot, the incest victim and object of the P.I.'s affections unjustly loses her life as the result of a stray bullet during an incident in Chinatown, the pillar of the community carries on in custody of his disturbed and distracted daughter, and the P.I. who, in the process of solving the case and rescuing the woman he loves, is left devastated.

In yet another variant, the motif of the innocent man who finds himself unwittingly slipping into the dark secretive world can be traced from Cary Grant's forced exit from the Plaza Hotel in *North by Northwest,* over the Atlantic to Graham Greene's exploration of black market profiteering in watered-down penicillin in post World War II Vienna. In this one, an ingenuous American writer of pulp Westerns is played for a patsy, caught between loyalty and morality, hopelessly in love with his old school chum's languishing girlfriend. He eventually winds up literally underground in the Viennese sewers, forced to do away with his friend.

The locales (usually in and around actual, claustrophobic urban settings) are authentic and part of the stylistic web. The form is often shoehorned into what are now called noirish thrillers and crime stories with noirish undertones. As for the latter, they can involve anything from hustlers who fall deeper into debt, to policemen working both sides of the street, at once double-dealing with each other and organized crime. As for the former, the dark side of human nature involves scandals and cover-ups, ruthless power brokers, double agents, high-tech spying and goings-on in the corporate world, inside governments and beyond.

As long as the escapade generates a sense of unease and distrust of the safe, predictable and reasonable we're basically in the same territory. For the purist, classic noir always centers on someone unwittingly caught in a web of deceit and murder from which there is no return. It also calls for an environment of sparseness: deep shadows, light and dark contrasts, a sense of isolation, the only source of illumination from the glimmer of a street light through the gaps in Venetian blinds—that sort of thing.

However, though styles like romantic comedy, noir, war stories and wartime romances continue to evolve and have great staying power, other patterns become so mixed they're hard to identify. One influential critic spoke of a movie called *First Snow* (2007) as a "moody paranoid metaphysical thriller." New trends come and go or are reclassified. Satirizing Hollywood studios and their insistence on coming up with a marketing label according to type, Michael Tolkin gave us this exchange in *The Player*:

> WRITER
> It's a funny, political thing. It's a thriller too. All at once.
> EXEC.
> And what's the story?
> WRITER
> Well, I want [a certain high powered star] because it's a story about a bad guy senator.
> EXEC.
> Sort of a cynical, political, thriller comedy.
> WRITER
> Yeah, but it's got a heart. He has an accident and becomes clairvoyant.
> EXEC.
> So it's kind of a psychic, cynical, political thriller, comedy.
> WRITER
> Yeah. Sort of like *Ghost* meets *Manchurian Candidate*.

Still and all, and recalling the response to the opening rough sketch—"What is this, a family thriller, a noir comedy, a romantic spoof, a gothic farce?"—genres still serve a convenient purpose and we might do well to note at least a few more recognizable patterns.

Standbys and Spin-offs

The Western: This foray into wild, uncharted territory centers, for the most part, on the years of the Civil War in the U.S. up until the turn of the century and a little beyond.

What gave Goldman's take on the Butch Cassidy legend its appeal was a second chance to reclaim a whimsical freedom without restrictions. When law and order begin to close in and the wide open spaces were no longer wide and open, outlaws could always head south, ride with their sidekicks and even let a woman tag along (Etta in this case) as long as there was no threat of an entangling relationship.

Another issue deals with the pursuit of a code in a lawless region under threat of marauding Native Americans who resent encroachment on their land in the name of westward expansion. Other issues crop up revolving around cattle drives, range wars, gunslingers, unscrupulous lawmen, prospectors, rustlers, railroad barons, merchants, speculators and the like. The self-reliant loner and gunfighter might temporarily slip into a social setting and help some embattled homesteaders, but his way of life has no place in settled society. By the same token, a group of gunfighters may band together temporarily when down on their luck to take on bandits ransacking a powerless Mexican village. But only the lone caballero has the option of returning to his roots and staying behind to make a life for himself and a village sweetheart.

The form has been stretched to include a one-time crazed killer, long since reformed, who comes out of retirement as a farmer to take on some cowboys, hired by prostitutes who want revenge for one of their own. The lawman in this ironic tale wants no part of this. He's content to work on his house and be left in peace. Thus villainy and the restoration of law and order have been turned inside out. The form has also included a small-time braggart who comes into a wintry boom town in the great northwest and goes into business with an enterprising madam. A bordello thus becomes the center of joy and happiness until it is threatened by mining interests and their hired guns bent on taking over this new, thriving enterprise.

There is also the one about middle-aged worn-out outlaws on the eve of World War I who are confronted by one of their old partners. He has reluctantly become a lawman and stands in their way only because of the threat from the railroad barons who will put him in jail if he refuses. The hired guns provided by the barons are shifty and unreliable and don't understand the old code of freedom—e.g., stick with your partners, rob the railroads and whatever source of ready cash you can find, hope too many civilians don't get in the way and move on. After the carnage, when the lawman hears a new gang is forming, there is a glint in his eye and the hope that the days of yore aren't entirely gone.

And then there is always the remake. There is no better illustration of changing times and perception than *3:10 to Yuma* (2007). In the original, fifty years earlier taken from an Elmore Leonard short story, an outlaw by the name of Ben Wade is escorted by a rancher by the name of Dan Evans to the prison train in Yuma, Arizona. Dan, it seems, needs the money to keep his ranch going. Ben is very soft-spoken, his children are young, his wife is stalwart, sweet and concerned for Dan's safety. The only source of tension is whether or not Charlie Prince, Ben's second in command, along with the rest of the gang, will arrive in time and thwart Dan's quest. But all is well, as the train arrives, Dan succeeds in getting Ben on board, one-dimensional Charlie is shot or winged in a failed pursuit, and Dan waves to his wife who just happens to be seated on a buckboard in full view as the train passes by.

In the new version, Charlie Prince is a sociopath. The character has become so enigmatic that the actor had to do research till he discovered that gunslingers were like rock stars, wore outlandish outfits and perfected a unique swagger. From an army veteran the actor learned that the eyes become dead while killing because there is no time or place for second thoughts in the heat of battle. The killing is rationalized out of duty and loyalty to the squad and, in this case, to the boss in an ambivalent world where there is no right or wrong, just expediency. Ben Wade himself has become a quixotic figure who knows the Bible inside and out, is a bit of an artist with a jaded sense of humor and tells tales of how his father and mother died at the hands of unscrupulous townspeople. Dan is now a limping Civil War veteran with a troubling backstory and an older son who continually faults him for his apparent cowardice. Dan continues to change and becomes more intrepid and volatile as Ben goads him. Ben entices Dan with promises of money and regales him with more tales and philosophizing about the amoral nature of the world. Through the screenplay by Halsted Welles, Michael Brandt and Derek Haas, the viewers themselves, ostensibly, become equally as ambivalent as the level of violence is ratcheted up, the Pinkerton guard is revealed to be a man who indiscriminately killed innocent Indian woman and children while in the employ of the Southern Pacific Railroad, the good citizens at the railway depot readily accept Charlie Prince's offer of a reward to gun down anyone holding his boss, Ben Wade, prisoner, and the marshal and his deputies abandon Dan in the face of these overwhelming odds.

Which brings us to another touchstone: ironic recognition. Or, to coin a phrase from GIs during the Vietnam War, a striking sense of "there it is." If something unpredictable happened but was patently true (because under those particular conditions anything was possible), the soldiers would invariably look at each other and say, "There it is." Like the time a Vietnamese rock band in Saigon was impersonating The Grateful Dead while an oncoming monsoon whipped up as a light plane circled overhead, brandishing a streaming banner that read "the devil's music" attacking the concert below. As one witness tells it, a cluster of rear-echelon troops gave each other a knowing look and said in unison, "There it is." It was the payoff to the day's events—another revelation.

Ideally, all takes on any genre are more effective when moviegoers can nod to themselves as if saying, "There it is." And delving into these old standbys like the wartime romance, screwball comedy, film noir and the western, and giving any one of them a fresh twist certainly has its advantages. The parameters and rules of the game are clear with more than enough room to play. If adopted, they also eliminate the problem of the disjointed noir comedy, romantic spoof and gothic farce and the cynical political thriller comedy.

Moreover, some old favorites may be out of vogue, new combinations may not be at all clear cut, or have been taken over by old and new television series or relegated to cable. Some categories have become franchises and are overblown with special effects and pyrotechnics. Because of all this, the sample list that follows is offered as a further springboard in the search for a potential stamping ground.

Crime: More Spin-offs

1. The mystery. This tightly woven pattern depends a great deal on the ability to write intriguing puzzles that draw an audience into a conundrum with all its red herrings and twists and turns. Aside from the puzzles, there's also the task of coming up with engaging investigators (amateur or professional) and fascinating suspects, ones we haven't seen over and over on the *Mystery* series from the U.K. An example might be the reinvestigation of a haunting 30-year-old unsolved murder or disappearance like the true-life abduction of two young sisters from a shopping mall in Baltimore that left a family shattered. Some new lead or sighting of an alleged accomplice or even the appearance of a distracted woman who claims to be one of the victims but refuses to talk could add to the proliferating suspense. Unlike the downward spiral of the noirish tale, this style of detection is an antidote to wrongs that are never resolved, and the accounts of people falling prey to random or planned malicious acts.

A much lighter offshoot is the mystery-comedy, like Woody Allen's homage to the old *Thin Man* series and Hitchcock's *Rear Window*. Instead of the reclusive murderer who ostensibly chops up his wife across the way in the Manhattan apartment complex, this time the suspect is very amiable and lives in the same apartment building. And instead of a sophisticated Nick and Nora who blithely sip martinis while coming to the aid of the hapless New York police, Allen offered a hapless neurotic husband and his loopy wife, hell-bent with the aid of their over-imaginative writer friends to solve what may or may not be a juicy murder (*Manhattan Murder Mystery*, 1993). In scripts of this kind, the dialogue is witty, there is some degree of tension, not over the eventual fate of the reckless investigators but, somewhat like the romantic comedy, in terms of how close they come to harm but still keep missing. There is also the built-in recognition factor, the fresh-but-familiar situation and allusion to other films. In this double-spin-off, Allen also managed to bring it all to a climax in an old movie theater while a vintage crime movie flashes on the screen.

2. The gangster film and the police procedural. Ever since William Monahan garnered an Oscar for Best Original Screenplay (*The Departed*, 2006), two genres have merged and may continue to subdivide. When you have undercover agents on both sides of the law, upright and corrupt members of the state police, factions of the Irish mafia double-crossing the rival Italian mafia, and the head of the Irish mafia looking for a mole within his mob, it might seem to be quite enough. However, Monahan also added the ploy that the head of the Irish mafia was surreptitiously working undercover for the F.B.I., and his own mole was working for the police searching for the mole who infiltrated the Irish mob—all of this liberally doused with dark and raunchy humor, non-stop profanity, violence and bloodshed, psychiatric care and a sexual liaison for the undercover cop.

3. *The hit-man film and the serial killer.* The conventional difference here is the fascination with the adventures of a loner with a code (*Le Samouri,* etc.) whose exploits are both ingenious and criminal on one hand, and the ventures of a sociopath whose methods are new and frightening on the other hand, and whose deeds may or may not be curtailed.

4. *The heist or caper film.* This format features a tightly orchestrated robbery by either a mastermind with a provocative cache in mind (with the aid of a group of criminal experts) or, in a light-hearted vein, a caper undertaken by one of society's losers and his colorful gang. In its more serious form, the cache, unbeknownst to the experts in their field, may be integral to a political plot involving rogue elements of a small nation trying to throw their government into turmoil or for any number of reasons. In any case and in all likelihood, the trove is located in some inaccessible location and is virtually impossible to steal. As always, it would take a study of all that has gone before in order to come up with a fresh take on either of these genres.

5. *Dishonor among thieves.* In this variant, criminals or would-be criminals betray each other wittingly or unwittingly, trying to outsmart one another, hiding their true motives like poker players; or through anxiety and bungling ineptitude throwing everything off as the whole enterprise spins off into surprising directions.

It's been claimed that in all of the above categories there is an awareness that we live in an age of untold criminal activity, corruption and violence. Since the average person may never encounter any of this personally, there is an underlying need to deal with every conceivable development through movies, as if to be able to say, "So that's what it's like." And again, "Ah, there it is."

Other Old and New Favorites

Though a further discussion of genres and subgenres would be endless, a writer could recall a few favorites and look them up on the Internet Movie

Database (IMDb). If it's a clear category like science fiction, the classification sci-fi/fantasy/whimsy might help to narrow the field to, say, Ray Bradbury-like tales where the technology or worlds beyond the reach of contemporary science are not the point. It's really some kind of universal longing, hope or fear with a backdrop beyond the confines of reality. A parallel universe where, perhaps, the pull of an endless childhood summer can be pitted against clocks and the middle-aged and elderly who hold the secrets of encroaching maturity.

A general list of memorable films and their plotlines can serve the same purpose: the struggles of farmers and the impending loss of a rural way of life; the joys and sorrows of small-town America as opposed to the lure of the ladder of success; the intricate maneuvers of spies and agents across the globe; historical epics and biographies of notable figures; parodies of our current foibles, mores and our celebrity culture; the politics of global warming, racial and gender issues, "the troubles" in Ireland. The trick is always the fresh take on the familiar.

However if the idea of staying within any set of boundary lines is too confining, there are other ways, other territories.

6. Alternative Routes and Strategies

Topical Issues

Some screenwriters prefer to first come up with a dialectic, a term borrowed from philosophy (Hegel), adapted by playwrights (notably Arthur Miller) and transposed for the screen. It pits a thesis or premise against an antithesis. What remains after the issue plays itself out is a synthesis, better known as a satisfying resolution. In simple dramatic terms, it's a high-stakes contest. In play form, the contest is usually verbal, as if the characters have so much on their minds and percolating underneath that they have to let it all out, here and now within this set. The screenwriter, with a much broader canvas at his disposal, looks for a contest that will take him and the audience anywhere and everywhere, holding still at times and taking off again, following the conflict wherever it takes him.

Referring to his screenplay for *In Bruges* (2008) during a *New York Times* interview, the Irish playwright Martin McDonaugh put it this way:

> One of the fears I had, being a playwright, was to write a playwright's film, to have it be about two guys talking it through for two hours. It was really good for me to have some kind of cinematic vision in my head for every single moment.

The spark for a dialectic can come from anywhere. An instructor at a Midwest college used to say that the best policy was to try not to write. Keep avoiding the issue until it goads you to the point where you can't help but work through it. In a conversation with this writer, Connie Congden, dramaturge of The Hartford Stage, phrased it a little differently: Wait until one of your basic assumptions is threatened, or something upsetting out there in the world comes to light. That's when you're ready to play it out.

In screenwriting, the process of working through an issue often goes something like this. Naturally drawn to the political arena, Rod Lurie found himself troubled by a particular concern. He began to shape *The Contender* (2000) with the realization that even in the 21st century there was a double standard for female politicians as opposed to men. A male senator's sexual adventures while in college would just be considered sewing wild oats, whereas allegations about a female senator's indiscretions would be taken as a moral outrage. And if this female senator was up for nomination for vice president to take the place of a man who has just died, she would certainly be fair game during the confirmation proceedings.

Underpinning this proposition, he had his dialectic: a lady senator who refuses to answer the charges (claiming the same rights to privacy as a male) vs. a self-righteous but secretly flawed chairman of the judiciary committee. By the time Lurie was through, his two leading roles were highly actable and laced with contradictions so there was no telling what either party might do or say under pressure. And there was another underpinning of classic films Lurie had studied which revolved around politics dating back to *Mr. Smith Goes to Washington* (1939), the one where a sweet, idealistic young man finds himself in an uphill battle, attempting to derail the corrupt plans of the old guard. And there were more recent films with a political bent Lurie was drawn to, informed by changing times and a growing sense of paranoia, uncertainty and controversy.

For Peter Morgan, the British screenwriter who was nominated for an Academy Award for the 2006 film *The Queen*, it's a matter of imagining opposing forces behind the scenes of defining moments in recent history. A duel of personalities. Real public figures thrown into unlikely relationships. The dialectic promises to move toward a telling closure because both parties are volatile, ambitious antagonists. Or so it seems.

In the real life scenario following Princess Diana's questionable death, we have a quasi mother and son conflict: media-savvy Prime Minister Tony Blair in tune with a liberal generation; the tradition-bound queen from an older, highly conservative way of being. Two different worlds, different Englands, different languages. And writer Morgan himself teetering politically between the extreme left and the extreme right. The queen is master of her public role and inept in her personal life. Mr. Blair is publicly on the side of his constituency who want their princess to be duly honored. But he is deferential in private audiences with his queen whom he looks upon with great respect in view of all she has done and stood for during her reign. In Morgan's screenplay sentiment and propriety continue to battle out of the public eye. The pressure grows on Blair to persuade the royals to publicly acknowledge this great loss and provide a suitable display of mourning and homage. The queen, in turn, is seen reflecting on a longstanding tradition which includes avoiding histrionics at any cost, retreating, reviewing the situation, conferring with the queen mother and so on. The final draft was based on a great deal of research which makes both the progression of events no one could have predicted and the imagined scenes plausible. The shot-flow includes the sounds of bagpipers that wake the queen in her Scottish retreat announcing her day and images of the rituals that define her life, along with invented episodes like Blair's press secretary advising him how to play the growing outcry of grief for all it's worth.

For Morgan, history and events furnish irresistible opportunities to explore all sorts of imagined contests behind the headlines. There is the encounter between British TV host David Frost and Richard Nixon, two explosive, contradictory opponents on the decline, looking for a visible way to redeem themselves and finding it on television; and the prison reformer and would-be-saint Lord Longford struggling to win a pardon for the child murderer Myra Hindley, who insisted that evil and murder on the moors "was a spiritual experience too."

If you push it a bit further, you could argue that the key for writers like Morgan is the two sides of their own personalities: ambivalent feelings about success and fame and being able to grasp opportunities, or being independent and maintaining their integrity. As he confided to journalist Charlie Rose, contrariness shows itself even when going to a movie with friends. "Who leads, who chooses the movie, who opens the door? Everything is riddled with complexity and rivalry."

Another way the setup for a dialectic seems to happen combines the personal, current events and synchronicity. The idea that quickly grew into *Lions for Lambs* (2007) stemmed from Matthew Michael Carnahan's practice of flipping channels looking for a Southern Cal football game. He had just gotten through ranting over how ridiculous the Iraq war was and a president who knew nothing about military history and blundered into sending troops to fight a war on two fronts. Carnahan paused for a moment at a story on CNN about some soldiers who had drowned when their Humvee turned over in the Tigris River. Then he continued searching for the game.

Later that night, it dawned on him that he himself was the same kind of hypocrite that carries on about the consequences of political and military incompetence and can be found flipping past the news for something more entertaining. To Carnahan, the best way to come to terms with this troubling behavior was to devise a screenplay and send it on to his producer who then hooked up with The Creative Arts Agency and packaged it with its clients Meryl Streep, Robert Redford and Tom Cruise.

Mr. Redford jumped at the opportunity, not only because of his liberal convictions but also in view of his past successes with the likes of *The*

Candidate, All the President's Men, and *Three Days of the Condor.* Without going into all the details, Mr. Carnahan's exorcism was accomplished by pitting a rising Republican senator trying to sell a new Afghan war to a skeptical but influential Washington reporter, and a college professor who runs up against his own ultra-conservative institution while trying to inspire one of his talented but tuned-out students.

Border Crossings

Sometimes the playing field has nothing to do with politics or current events. Sometimes it's more like a boundary line, physical or emotional or both, between here and there. It may evolve from a writer's background and time spent in a certain setting, then begin to change as other factors are imaginatively brought into play that rub against the norm. In the following example, it began with one person's experiences and progressed to include a partner from a totally different background who, as a writer, was primarily plot-oriented. It went on to be modified once again due to the input of a director and leading actor. As an open-ended illustration, we can look at what actually happened in the process that led to the shooting script for *Witness* (1985) starring Harrison Ford and use it as a point of departure.

For starters, the original writer spent a great deal of time studying the nearby Amish way of life in and around Lancaster, Pennsylvania. People were observed still driving a horse and buggy, eschewing modern conveniences and the conflicting and confusing influences of urban living. There were no phones, no computers, no distracting television programs or the web of useful and dubious information found on the Internet. The members of the larger community, which numbered over 7,000, were honest and hardworking, and strongly believed in nonviolence. Here the writer found both skilled carpenters whose furniture was prized for its sturdy, long-lasting quality and sold far and wide, and accomplished farmers. Their dress was traditional black; everyone spoke Dutch-German, and English during occasions when they had business in town or had to interact with the outside world. On balance, it was a close-knit community living close to the land and deeply religious. They led their lives, grew up, married and passed away in a natural, cyclical rhythm and by a clear set of rules, firmly upheld by the elders.

In other words, all of this was ripe for a disturbance. But how to bring a contradictory force into the picture—the hustling world of potential conflict, duplicity, incoherence and violence? The world where law and order is sorely needed and, to make things worse, may not be up to the task.

The solution. One Amish custom dictates that a young mother should marry within a year after the death of her husband. But what if she is not ready to wed? Even to a man deemed worthy, a man who ostensibly cares for her, is a bit older and able to provide for her and her young son, and is approved by her father and the community leaders? What if she needs more time to think it over? What if she decides to take her 9-year-old on a train trip to Baltimore where she can visit her sister and resolve her dilemma?

A young mother (whom we will call Rachel), can set off soon after the funeral. Her state of mind can lead to contact with the problematic outside force that will hook into things and set them in motion.

The creative problem. How to keep some action-thriller recipe from taking over?

What awaits Rachel and her son (now called Samuel) in the train station in Philadelphia would normally be a connecting train to Baltimore. But since the boundary lines have to cross in order to ignite the story, the pacifists and the mean and worldly have to meet.

Waiting in the wings there can be an undercover urban police officer investigating police corruption and involvement in drug trafficking, but this tack has become standard fare. So has the notion of an official in the department who is in on the take and will stop at nothing to keep the undercover cop from blowing the whistle. And so is the idea of this same diligent detective (call him John Book) finding himself unpopular with his fellow officers because he will stop at nothing to bring a perpetrator to justice, even if that perpetrator is one of his own (see *Serpico*, 1973).

In the final draft of the actual screenplay, the train is late, Samuel asks his mother if he can go to the men's room, she nods, Samuel witnesses the slaying of an undercover detective from behind the stalls, and the story has begun.

If, at the police station, shy and docile Samuel somehow indicates to John Book that the killer was one of John Book's colleagues, the story becomes John Book's; the pressing question: will John catch the perpetrator and save Samuel and Rachel from great harm? If so, Rachel becomes secondary, which is a problem because it detours from the expectations that were raised at the outset.

To leave the options open and retain the dramatic possibilities of crossed boundaries, the storyline has to move back to the Amish farm and heighten Rachel's dilemma: not only are she and her son in grave danger from the perpetrators inside the police department, but she needs the security of her community. John Book is still on board and, ostensibly, has to protect the two of them from the machinations of his colleagues.

But now we have two problems: not only whose story is it, but also how to incorporate the original spiritual dimension and, at the same time, allow the interplay of forces to unfold? It's a matter of balance and emphasis.

Incorporating Mythic Threads

One answer would be to deepen the focus in favor of a universal path. Anyone brought up under strict, authoritarian rules as Rachel has, must find some way to actualize her own uniqueness. Otherwise there can be no growth and she will have nothing authentic to give to the world. Anyone stuck in a hard-bitten wary mode like John Book (which is plausible given his circumstances), will remain a loner and never tap his own inner resources. Or as the renowned psychiatrist and mythologist Carl Jung put it, the key to your wholeness requires the release of the part you're not using—e.g., your spiritual side, intellectual side, connection to nature, nurturing, masculine, wild shadow side, etc.

In fantasy films like *Star Wars* (1977), Darth Vader hides under his mask, a bureaucrat frozen in the system and, in later episodes, as Luke Skywalker's father, he is the shadow side in the fight between good and evil. Skywalker, the prototypical innocent, humble young man is called on to embark on a great adventure to find himself and save his galaxy. In Tolkien's stories brought to the screen like *The Lord of the Rings* (1978, 2001, 2002, 2003), Middle-earth and its range of fanciful characters are a timeless mirror of our own world.

In the case of John and Rachel, mythic elements could be introduced without bringing in archetypes like sages and wise old mentors, tricksters, stand-ins for dragons, faithful companions, pixilated helpers, guardian angels and the like. An underlying mythic quest could also be eased into the screen story, like Rachel's need to heal her inner wound due to the loss of her husband. If she could find love again, lose her own concerns by healing someone else who is, say, physically wounded, then the age-old transformation could take place. For John, if he had to put aside his rational, macho self-reliance, if he was the one physically wounded and had to be taken care of, if something more mysterious and intuitive within him was tapped, if he reconnected to a community, he too could transform.

As for Rachel's close-knit family and community of farm, father, elders and neighbors, if they could allow John Book in their midst and allow him, after he regains his strength, take part in, say, a barn-building, perhaps they too could grow.

Propelling us back to Rachel's world, one of Book's duplicitous colleagues (the killer Samuel identified) could try to eliminate Book. Wounded, concealing this fact, Book insists on driving Rachel and Samuel back to the protective cover of their isolated Amish home. Then, unable to drive off, he and his car, of necessity, are hidden, the story centered on the healing-transformative, placing the threat of discovery by his nefarious colleagues on hold.

But then what happens to John Book? Is he transformed? Does he have a change of consciousness, fall in love with Rachel, the one who nurtured him and insisted that he be sheltered? What happens to Rachel after all she's been through? Is it still her story or is it both their stories? What happens to the rules and traditions of the community and Rachel's relationship with her father and the elders if she does fall in love? Won't she receive warnings that unless she breaks off with this man and his weapons, she will be cast out and shamed? And, after all, what is the person Rachel was to marry, an integral part of the community, doing all this time? Last but not least, what of the crime, Samuel as material witness, and the nefarious drug ring within the highest echelons of the Philadelphia police department? Surely they are not just sitting still all the while.

Perhaps the mythic and the transformative can serve only as a rich, universal counterpoint.

Favoring the Character-Driven Tale

Deferring to the actor-characters, the writer can bring them to the forefront. The operative question then becomes, if I were this character, with this background and temperament in this pressured situation, what would I do? Or better still, what would the character do? Under stress, what would he be capable of? If it's Rachel's story, then it all may come down to a sacrifice—giving up John to protect her child, convincing John to move on to prevent any chance of the murderer and his cronies closing in, convincing John to return to his world to bring matters to a close. Or putting off any decision about herself and Samuel for the time being and any kind of future she and John might have, she could face up to her father and the elders and the man who was set to marry her. Given her ambivalent feelings, she could come to terms with things, return to the fold if that's how it plays out, or forced to live her own life, she could wait till all this witness business is resolved and then carry on.

In this case, switching the focus to John, what would happen if he tried to return to his Serpico-like existence, with other detectives wary of him because he has no qualms about turning someone in, and a problematic relationship with his partner who is caught between doing the right thing and peer pressure. What is John like in these circumstances: putting on a cool front but about to explode? What effect does this have on his relationships outside of his job? How would he try to zero in on the man who shot him, to protect Samuel and Rachel from any harm, put an end to things and eliminate any further violence or gunplay?

In the movie, John stays on after he is healed, borrows Rachel's deceased husband's clothes and rides out on a wagon with the others headed to town to make a phone call. His objective is to check back with his partner to see how close the crooked captain and his underlings are in their pursuit of Samuel, the key witness. But how plausible is this? Would Rachel simply let him go? Would the others risk it? In the movie, John is goaded into retaliating when troublemakers, assuming him to be a docile pacifist, begin to taunt him. But would John really strike back knowing full well that the manhunt is on and all the local police have been put on alert for any kind of suspicious behavior? And even if his "fellow Amish brothers" do let him go along for the ride and warn him not to react to any teasing, would they then just excuse his behavior, telling the local policeman investigating the incident that John is just a cousin from a sect that does things differently?

Given a three-dimensional John Book with a past, tendencies and experiences, in tandem with a healing, loving Rachel out to protect Samuel at any cost, what would he truly do? What would Rachel do and, under the volatile circumstances, what would be the inevitable result step by step?

Finding a Comfort Zone

Leaving the alternate high stakes possibilities of the Amish tale, we can turn to a less ambitious project focusing on the simple plight of a pie-making waitress in a tiny Mississippi town. In Adrienne's Shelly's script for *Waitress* (2007), Jenna, our heroine, is saddled with an abusive husband whom she loathes and an unwanted pregnancy. This, in a nutshell, is the problem that hooks into Jenna's life and sends it spinning. No high stakes confrontations, no forays into corruption or the complications of urban life, no newsworthy events. Just a playing field that's both familiar and fresh at the same time with little traveling required.

At the same time, within this homey setting, Ms. Shelly also provided the waitress's fantasy of winning a pie-making contest as a means of garnering enough money to leave her husband and start anew. Which, in effect, is a semi-mythic feminist quest for independence from the machinations of dominant males who use all manner of means to control their mates—e.g., "give me all the money you make because I am your main means of support.... Now that I've made you pregnant you will have to stay under my roof forever and bring up our child.... Promise you will always love me more than the baby.... If you dare cross me in any way I will have to discipline you as is my right by tradition" (all of this according to the strictures of many a small community in the Deep South).

Along with the fantasies and semi-mythic underpinning, Ms. Shelly also provided the life of a waitress in a diner that features homemade pies, narrow and confining options, and the pure reality that we often don't know what we truly want and what the response from others will be if we try out various schemes to escape from intolerable circumstances.

To illustrate. Right after the inciting incident (learning of her pregnancy), Jenna is convinced that she doesn't want the baby and will make a terrible mother, that hiding money from her husband will eventually bring her salvation and a ticket out of town, that the difficult owner of the diner is just a cranky person she has to put up with and has no bearing whatsoever on her misery and her life, and that an affair with her affable obstetrician who has just come to town from the far reaches of another world (Connecticut) will bring her love and happiness and a way out of her dilemma.

Jenna's voice-over fantasies brush up against a backwater southern man's world at odds with a powerful underlying feminine sensibility. Her assumptions that something has to come into her life by chance (the young married doctor from Connecticut) or that happiness can only be found "out there" are at odds with the way things actually happen; what she thinks she wants is at odds with what she needs; her fears about her abusive husband are at odds with his private fearful fantasies; and her offhanded ploys are at odds with her intuitive responses.

Moreover, having established a highly actable set of circumstances within an easily manageable framework, Ms. Shelly was free to imaginatively let her actor-characters go and see what happens in the spirit of the moment. These moments include Jenna's response when she learns she is pregnant during the breakfast shift and is about to take the order of the crusty owner sitting alone in his usual booth; how she responds when later that same day her loathsome husband picks her up and asks for her wages and cloying words of affection or else; later still as she fantasizes how to explain to a baby girl that she is totally unfit for motherhood; and the moment she is on the verge of breaking down when all her plans of escape have fizzled.

In this freewheeling see-saw and ebb and flow, Ms. Shelly always had a re-energizing happenstance at the ready: the crusty owner beginning to come out of his shell as he comments on Jenna's distracted or wistful behavior, Jenna's husband's outrage when he finds money stashed away in the cupboards of his home, the arrival of the doctor's wife and his urgent proposal that he and Jenna run away together.

At each low point, Jenna could be empowered by coming to the aid of one of her coworkers who has spurned the attentions of a hapless nerd who may have redeeming qualities. At the same time, her other coworker could always bolster Jenna's spirit by keeping her apprised of her own plans to spice up her life by taking matters into her own hands.

Along these same lines, it certainly didn't hurt that Ms. Shelly was an accomplished New York actress who was adept at improvisation and knew full well how to keep a situation fresh and moving.

The Partially Unscripted Ploy

Following Ms. Shelly's lead but going even further, there's a way of working that relies a great deal on the actors themselves. Admittedly, it also requires a connection with a director and even, as the example below indicates, a creative collaboration between an actor and a director, then a screenwriter and a group of actors. At any rate, taken together, it certainly qualifies as an alternative playing field.

In this particular case, a seasoned American actor once contacted a seasoned American director, toying with the idea of doing a kind of Upstairs, Downstairs British mystery through the servants' perspective on location in the U.K. The mystery would be secondary. What would be primary were the private agendas of each of the servants as they may or may not relate to those they are attending to above stairs. As the idea evolved, it all centered on the way the hierarchy of the underclass (the butler as king and the head housekeeper as queen, etc.) mirrored their counterparts above (the master of the country estate, the lady of the manor and so on), and how the servants were also repressed or exploited. In other words, what was important was the behavior of the 35 actors who, except for the instigating actor and one other supporting player, were from the U.K. and totally familiar with the given circumstances. It was assumed that their interplay and happy accidents would reveal the truth of their individual storylines during a weekend at an English country estate circa 1932. The happy accidents that occurred included a matronly guest who, in character, found herself unable to open a thermos and had to rely on her Scottish maid; a footman who, in character, had to find some way to conceal his lit cigarette and finally settled on hiding it and himself behind a pantry door; a patronizing butler and wartime deserter who, in character, saluted his mirror image when alone in his quarters.

The dialogue for *Gosford Park* (2001) was scripted by Julian Fellowes, who subsequently won an Oscar for Best Original Screenplay. As for all the rest, the director (Robert Altman) furnished the actors of the downstairs staff with authentic instructors who had been in service during the times in question. He created a relaxed environment so that every player was free to live through the series of events as the camera roved about, capturing telling bits of behavior during scenes of arrival, assignment of duties, times when the upper class guests chatted away in the drawing room while being served refreshments, during dinner scenes, preparations for a shooting party and the like. For the more focused scenes and the advancement of the story, which eventually evolved into a murder due to the past abuses of the country squire, Fellowes' plotline and dialogue came prominently into play.

On a much more flimsy note, for their mockumentaries co-writers Eugene Levy and Christopher Guest first determine a topic to satirize. They then come up with a detailed outline of the scene progressions and character backgrounds, hand it to a favorite troupe of actors and give them free rein. The result depends on the tastes and sense of humor of the actors and the viewing audience. In one send-up called *Best in Show* (2001), the improvisations exposed the foibles of judges and pet owners at a prestigious dog show whose very lives, relationships and well-being seemed totally dependent on the outcome.

On the other side of the coin, writer-director Paul Greengrass prompts his company of actors to improvise around provocative historical events with *Bloody Sunday* (2002) serving as a prime example. Greengrass's aim here was to unlock a believable truth, leaving things open, specifying only the key points that were known about the events that took place in Derry, Northern Ireland, in 1972. In this British-Irish production, the preliminary happenings and awful aftermath took place between British soldiers and Irish civil rights workers during a clash that was intended to be a peaceful protest. In effect, Greengrass's effort was a documentary-like chronicle, pro–Irish but an expose of faults on both sides, brought fully to life by the inventive work of the actors within this framework.

The same strategy was used for *United 93* (2006) in an attempt to explore the passengers' behavior—who might have done what, how and why—on that fateful flight leading up to the confrontation with the hijackers just before the plane crash.

Relying on actors to contribute insights and flesh out a character's through-line goes at least as far back as Budd Schulberg's dependence on actors like Marlon Brando to live moment-to-moment through Terry Malloy's odyssey in *On the Waterfront*. Greengrass's explorations using real-life events as a springboard are somewhat different than Peter Morgan's imaginings behind closed doors during real-life topical episodes. Carnahan's screenplay was also prompted by real-life events but with a liberal bias, and Lurie's *Contender* was prompted by a real-life bias but extended to a what-if political situation. The seeds of *Witness* began with William Kelley's research on the Amish but then took off thanks to the imaginative plotting of Earl Wallace. Fellowes' screenplay was based on highly familiar social rituals adding an imaginary secondary plot to go with the improvised behavior of the actors. Ms. Shelly's screenplay for *Waitress* was totally a figment of her imagination. All of these screenwriters, each in his or her own way, devised an accommodating playing field. But, not unlike genres, playing fields that mainstream moviegoers could easily accept.

7. The Indie Option

The term indie is relative and a matter of degree, depending on how you define it, how you wish to work and how independent you want to be.

Looking at it another way, at the yearly Sundance Film Festival in Park City, Utah, the chosen few have, theoretically, produced a low-budget, privately financed film that's modestly scaled. A low-key exploration much in the same vein as the offerings of Antonioni, Bergman and Fellini but without the European sensibility and built-in support system. By and large, the storylines here are in no rush to get anywhere and feature imperfect characters, bits of life nicely observed with stretches of evocative imagery.

Sometimes the films are disturbing or challenging as a writer or writer-director makes certain viewers will not be reassured or transported into another world they can easily dismiss. Just the opposite.

Indie films can also be formless, paying little or no attention to the quality of the storytelling, professionalism of the actors, camera work and production values. As such, they too qualify on a scale ranging from highly accessible to enigmatic and obscure.

As for the highly accessible efforts, of late, big studios send some of their scouts to festivals like Sundance to shop for films, future projects and possible franchise hits. Early on we touched on Edward Burns' *The Brothers McMullen*. Writing, playing a leading role and directing this unassuming tale, shot on 16mm film at a cost of $28,000 in and around his house and working class neighborhood in Long Island and bits of Greenwich Village, Burns' project went on to win the Grand Jury Prize in 1995 at Sundance, became a hit as a romantic comedy and grossed over $10 million at the box office. It also won the Independent Spirit Award in 1996 for Best First Feature. In this tale that's anchored in Burns' real-life family home with its breezy, upbeat Irish Catholic perspective that Burns knew so well, he tackled the riddle of love, sex, marriage, religion and family according to his own experiences, aided and abetted by his imagination.

In terms of storytelling, this piece is not in the formless category. There's a disturbance in the lives of each of the three brothers centering on their relationships with women. Throughout, viewers can certainly keep asking, What happens next? But, then again, there isn't a great deal of imagery and movement. Because of the close bonds of family and lifelong friendships, the brothers are able to discuss their feelings frankly and openly. The oldest brother (Jack) finds himself in a marriage that has gone stale and is under pressure to start a family. The middle brother (Barry) is caught between a film career and the search for what he considers true love. The youngest (Patrick) has just left college and is caught between his religious beliefs and pressures from his longtime Jewish girlfriend. From the outset, after a brief interlude between Burns (Barry) and his mother—she's off to Ireland and her own true love after finally ridding herself of her husband who has just passed away—the film segues to another conversation on the steps of Burns' family home:

> JACK
> Let me ask you, what's up with you and Heather? You've got a new one now and you guys are all done?
> BARRY
> I don't know. I just don't like any long relationship.
> PATRICK
> Long relationship? You were with her for six months.
> BARRY
> That's a long time, you know? I mean the mystery was over, man. I don't know why that happens.
> PATRICK
> It's God's way of testing you.
> JACK
> You're failing.
> BARRY
> He loves to torture me.
> PATRICK
> So you believe in God now? This is your story?
> BARRY
> Yeah yeah, on his good days.
> PATRICK
> Then you're not a Catholic any more?
> BARRY
> No no, I'm still a Catholic. I guess. You know, kind of.
> JACK
> Catholic? Who are you kidding? You haven't been in church since the tenth grade.
> BARRY
> Yeah, but who can deal with all that repression anyhow?
> PATRICK
> Hey, repression is not such a bad thing. Okay? Especially for a savage

> like you. So, when did this happen? What did she do because I'm positive it was her fault completely.
> BARRY
> You know. She started talking about getting married.

In no particular hurry, it soon becomes obvious that there are going to be many casual talks like this with little camera movement. As the next scene moves to the dining room table and those assembled talk about JFK, the fabled Irish Catholic president, cheating on his wife, Jack (whose house it is) comes to JFK's defense and toasts his own wife, Molly, on her 30th birthday.

Another young woman makes eyes at Jack. Remarks are made about the brothers' deceased, abusive, cheat of a father, and a scene in the kitchen follows, washing dishes as Patrick confides in Barry about the pressure he's under from his Jewish girlfriend who wants to get married.

In comparison to a work like *Waitress,* the stakes are relatively minor, the visuals are minimal (no intermittent fantasies or the like), and there is no significant underpinning or universal quest for empowerment. Its low-budget, easygoing homemade style continues as it takes its own sweet time getting to its destination. For audiences who can relate to questions about adultery and other temptations, especially among the 20– 30-year-old set with a religious background, this story can be taken as a slice of life that satisfies because of its amiable nature. A way of working that can serve as a model for writers who prefer to explore some aspect of life as they know it, for the benefit of their peers, on the same modest, easygoing scale.

Switching gears, the spare, hyper-real, off-kilter style of Hal Hartley offers a different perspective for those who take a more jaundiced look at life. In *Trust* (1991), we're still in a working class section of Long Island, but there is nothing reassuring here. At first glance the characters may look familiar, but their behavior is bizarre. One morning a teenager tells her father that she's pregnant. Like a black-humor take on an old saying ("If you break your father's heart it will kill him") the father slaps the girl's face and drops dead. The boyfriend dumps her and goes to football practice; the mother throws her out of the house for killing her father. She finds shelter in an empty house where she meets Matthew, 10 years older, on the run from a sadistic parent. He carries a hand grenade with him "just in case." She asks him if he's emotionally disturbed and he answers, "No." In what one reviewer calls "Planet Hartley," the girl and Matthew keep bumping into characters who seem normal but turn out to be just as quirky. As viewers continue to wonder what will happen to this loopy couple in terms of trust, the behavior patterns continue to be filtered through Hartley's outlook.

To reinforce this notion of quirky, offbeat storytelling, there's Hartley's

Henry Fool (1998), another film with a lower-middle-class Long Island back-drop. Here this one-man-band (writing, directing and producing) contin-ues on with his signature minimal resources. In this tale, a taciturn garbage man, who takes a great deal of abuse from his neighbors, heavily medicated mother and dithering, slatternly sister Fay, is accosted by a complete stranger (Henry Fool). Out of the blue, Fool barges into the basement apartment and takes up residence. Not only that, but he urges the garbage man to write down his secret thoughts and points to his own unpublished work as "my opus and confession," a literature of protest that will remain private because his writing has been blatantly rejected. In due course, the garbage man, whose name is Simon Grim (like Henry Fool, another bit of black-humor parody), finds that the poetry Fool urged him to write is so reviled that, once posted on the Internet by his sister Fay, it winds up winning the Nobel Prize. Just as ironically, this send-up of literary celebrity won the prize for best screenplay in 1998 at Cannes.

It appears that Hartley, like Henry Fool, went out of his way to sati-rize conventional writing, normal human behavior and the laws of attrac-tion. Clearly, his films are an acquired taste and offer those, who may themselves have a jaundiced view of life, a refreshing look at so-called norms. And so it seems that the screenwriter who is one of a kind, whose approach and arch characters are unique, can take Hartley's method as a yardstick miles apart from the Sundance future hit.

Which, paradoxically, brings us back to Adrienne Shelly.

Ms. Shelly's career includes her stint writing and directing plays in New York and the pair of films she wrote and produced before *Waitress* that were screened in numerous festivals across the U.S. She also starred in twenty independent films including a few by Hal Hartley. In point of fact, she was the self-deprecating pregnant teenage outcast in *Trust*. The character of her sister was a flirty, gum-chomping waitress, not far removed from one of Jenna's two colleagues at the Mississippi diner. The character Ms. Shelly wrote for herself, Jenna's other fellow worker, is not far removed from the self-deprecating teenager in *Trust*. Jenna is also pregnant at the outset of the tale.

The point of departure is what's interesting here. Instead of a Hartley-like deranged, hand-grenade-toting lover from *Trust*, the love interest she devised for herself to play against in *Waitress* was a sweet salesman who dotes on her and writes spontaneous ditties and odes. Instead of a seedy section of her native Long Island and dubious relationships a la Hartley, she trans-ported her characters to a homespun southern hamlet, one that comes very close to a benign sitcom world.

In different circumstances, unlike anyone populating Hartley's turf,

Jenna could have easily become the ideal debutante, prom queen, model of success and all–American girl. Moreover, Jenna is married, not a rejected waif, and is provided with a Hallmark Cards resolution to her dilemma. Around the time of Shelly's tragic demise, *Waitress* was featured at Sundance. Fox Searchlight acquired the theatrical distribution rights which led to its great success as yet another highly accessible comedy hit. You could still make the case that Shelly owed a nod to the quirky characters on a Hartley set piece, but she endowed her work with an endearing quality and compassion for the situations the eccentrics of this world find themselves in. And she certainly wasn't out to show how oddball we all are underneath.

The same goes for Michael Arndt, a product of NYU's film school, whose *Little Miss Sunshine* (2006) is another modest entry chosen for Sundance. *Sunshine* went on to win two Oscars: the first for Best Original Screenplay; the second for Best Performance by an Actor in a Supporting Role. The latter went to Alan Arkin for his portrayal of little Olive's quirky grandfather who choreographs Olive's number for the beauty contest. (More in greater detail in the final chapter.) *Sunshine* is also another instance of a Hartley-like satiric eye at cultural foibles presented in a winning way.

Taking stock up to this point, you might conclude that visual elements and the camera are secondary, giving way to situations and characters from true to life to quirky to bizarre, with either a view toward acceptance by Sundance or some other major festival and on to wide distribution. Or possible recognition at Cannes and the life of an enigmatic art-house figure.

But there's a band of indie practitioners, not unlike the ones who subscribed to the tenets of the counterculture of the 1960s, who've drawn an invisible boundary line, one that rules out acceptance by major festivals that might lead to sales to mini-majors or what-have-you and commercial success.

Pure Indie

These purists shy away from anything that smacks of creative interference down the road from studio execs who, they feel, will treat their original work as a product. They foresee test marketing by a mixed crowd of moviegoers from L.A. who fill out score cards resulting in reediting, re-shooting and even recasting. In these filmmakers' eyes, any work they considered finished will be treated as a nice try, much like a promising first draft. In their view, the price you pay for integrity and creative freedom is making do with less money and, on the plus side, less risk for other people's investment. On the minus side, limited funds also means foregoing any storyline that calls for traveling expenses, marked changes of location, reliance on the weather and days of re-shooting.

Less money also means doing without seasoned actors who work for scale and whose calendar will probably not jibe with location shooting any distance from places where they usually find work (like L.A). or have previous or impending commitments. Anything involving cast, crew, preproduction, production and postproduction that can't be easily financed has to be scratched from consideration.

In other words, a limited budget has a great influence on the kinds of stories you can tell.

Looking back, most purists would agree that John Cassavetes was the spiritual father of this movement (if you can call it that). A jobless, drifting, aspiring New York actor, he put aside all thoughts of entertainment and appeals to either a mainstream audience or patrons of the art-houses in favor of raw, personal explorations of the meaning of his life and those around him. Working on *Shadows* between the years 1956 and 1959, writing, starring in, directing, shooting and editing his footage—struggling for money to get the movie made and then into movie theaters—he attempted to strip away personal secrets and facades and expose what was most vulnerable and volatile beneath people's behavior. Realizing that he himself was trying to pass for something he was not, always acting, essentially lonely, he bore into the nighttime, wandering side of his personality.

He also mirrored the relationship between himself and his older brother Nick, mooching off him, frequently looking for temporary shelter. Rather than a narrative arc, Cassavetes used his script as a starting point and a handheld camera as a relentless voyeur, capturing whatever he and his fellow actors—schooled in the same pursuit of organic, emotional release—could pry loose. As a result, each scene went well beyond the typical rule of coming in late and leaving as early as possible. In a Cassavetes film, the camera never leaves a scene until every last drop of feeling is squeezed out, no matter how embarrassing it gets. Instead of any concern over an advancing plot, actors, camera crew and viewers are in it for bare, unvarnished moments of no return.

As an example that moves from self-exposure to the exposure of others in Cassavetes' life, we can turn to *A Woman Under the Influence* (1974). In this effort, Cassavetes seemed to be seeking the point where neurotic behavior lapses into madness. Focusing on an emotionally vulnerable woman named Mabel, using his wife, Gena Rowlands, in the lead role, he followed her progression through a few rituals of her life. Here the cracks and fissures that begin to surface are the focus, the episodes of instability that cause people to withdraw from Mabel the main point of interest. In one instance,

Mabel imposes herself on one of her husband's coworkers, prodding him to dance with her during breakfast one morning, succeeding only in embarrassing the baffled guest. Another time, she forces her reluctant husband to play one of her children's favorite games. Later on, she tries to convince her family that despite her anxiety spells, she is in control. But it's her isolation from people and her desperate attempts to gain their approval, the extremes to which she goes before she's eventually institutionalized, that Cassavetes served up for those who wished a brutally honest examination of how far alienation can go.

Critics have referred to his work as cinema verite (catching life as it happens) as his panning camera caught the unpredictability and chaos of a situation and searched for more. After sending Mabel away, for instance, Cassavetes doesn't let it go at that, as the husband instigates an argument that leads to an unfortunate accident. And even in the end, after an awkward homecoming, as the couple try to bring some semblance of order and come to terms with their failures, there's a sense that something else could fall apart if Cassavetes wanted to linger a while longer.

Using less of a confrontational style, in *Love Streams* (1984) Cassavetes continued his search for the bitter truth beneath the façade. This time he plays a dashing, successful writer of lurid romance novels who encounters a number of flighty female companions while supposedly researching what exactly constitutes a good time. Eventually, what's revealed is his incapacity to invest in the complexities of love. His own vacuous lifestyle and casual affairs are as empty as his flashy attire and best-selling romances.

Granted, like Hartley's quirky slice-of-life social commentaries, Cassavetes' relentless psychological exposes are an acquired taste. But he established a set of rules and stuck to them: no evasions or compromises, no concerns about popular appeal.

Years later, Jeff Lipsky, one of Cassavetes' admirers and a 28-year veteran of the indie world, created a film called *Flannel Pajamas* (2006). Though this effort is comparatively flimsy and lightweight, it too is preoccupied with what Lipsky called "the slipups and cracks in the sidewalk" and what is really going on beneath the games people play. His characters, however, are unable to let go of their feelings, let alone vent their blown anger. They constantly talk things out or deflect by fetching coffee when a moment becomes too stressful. As if compensating for the lack of raw emotion in this work, Lipsky added a mentally unstable brother who infuriates the wife (though she can't express it openly) and holds loud, no-holds-barred encounters with other women while staying in the couple's apartment.

Initially, Lipsky found himself pondering over what went wrong with a perfect courtship and marriage that ended in divorce 10 years prior. Armed with a photo album and a journal (in lieu of Cassavetes' exhaustive background material), Lipsky went on to work in retrospect, trying to discover the incremental slipups that, taken together, led to the end of his relationship. He recalled such things as his mother-in-law's feigned forgetfulness while, at the same time, letting her blunt anti–Semitism slip out. In this way, he incorporated Cassavetes' insistence that what people say is not at all what they're really thinking or feeling. Lipsky also discovered that people's professions play a large part in the way they deal with others (like Cassavetes' façade as a dashing romance writer). By assigning careers to his characters, he felt the persona would amplify what was missing from real connection— e.g., the husband, a cocky promoter of Broadway shows who can make love and talk his way out of anything but can't feel any empathy toward his wife. The wife, who hails from the wilds of Missoula, Montana, and whose Irish Catholic family has a history of alcoholism and prejudice, hides behind a bright, cheery veneer as a successful Manhattan cookbook writer.

Following in Cassavetes' footsteps, Lipsky tried to get by with serviceable and somewhat kinetic camera work and production values. He also relied on a loose, almost haphazard structure and improvised lived-in performances.

In between Cassavetes and Lipsky, as an experiment in just self-indulgent talk, there was Wally Shawn and Andre Gregory's *My Dinner with Andre* (1981). Spliced from hundreds of hours of taped conversations between Shawn and Gregory and partially fictionalized, in this outing we have a struggling playwright and actor (Shawn) winding up in a posh New York restaurant to have dinner with a now-failing Off–Off Broadway director. During a voiceover Wally tells viewers he's not looking forward to the encounter but only consented because a friend came upon Andre weeping after being moved by a line in an Ingmar Bergman film: "I could always live in my art but never in my life."

What follows is nearly two hours of Gregory rattling on, captured by a static camera. Gregory talks at length about such things as his search for himself in the forests of Poland, the dunes of the Sahara, among the giant vegetables in Findhorn, Scotland, the mountains of India and other exotic locales. Wally gets to express amazement in his role of sounding board and mild-mannered, ordinary guy. In what may have been a climactic moment, Wally exclaims, "I really don't know what you're talking about."

Whether or not this is really a film, it still passes under the true indie rubric.

There's even less at stake in a typical entry at an indie film festival in Woodstock, New York. Apparently attempting to be as offhand as possible, John Dorrian and John Gallagher's *The Deli* (1997) simply set up shop in a

New York delicatessen and seemingly waited for colorful characters from the neighborhood to drop by. Somehow the creators felt it was interesting to allow a parade of various minor characters to drift in and out and improvise excitably.

For anyone looking for any trace of a storyline here, there is Johnny Amico's gambling habit, his mother picking a lottery number and Johnny forgetting to place the bet. Johnny's outspoken mother has a minor fit during this purely slice-of-life hit-or-miss daily ritual. Nothing is sharply observed, an impromptu dance sequence is tossed in and the camera has little to do. Arguably, its merit rests on pushing off-handedness to its limit.

Making a complete 180-degree turn from Dorrian and Gallagher's work is the unique approach used by the twin brothers Mark and Michael Polish in their creation of *Northfork* (2003). Coming from northern California, adamant about the freedom to follow their free-ranging imaginations in search of an alternative world, their process is as far from *The Deli* as you can get. If you had to make an analogy it would be like leaving the Ash-can school of painting with its portrayals of scenes from daily life in urban neighborhoods, and suddenly switching to abstract expressionism.

The incubation of *Northfork* began with a fantasy of wings that had been cut off an angel and salesmen going door to door selling angel wings to townsfolk as religious symbols. Continuing with this pattern of free association, they decided the film should be set in northern Montana "where the buffalo had roamed. So, why not a herd of angels?"

Next, to ground their work, the theme of angels took them to a biblical study and the realization that most religions had the story of a flood that held great moral value. Carrying on with their free associations, they recalled that their grandfather was a construction worker on the Hungry Horse Dam that was built in Montana in the 1950s. They also recalled that black-and-white photos hung in the interior of the dam, reflecting the story of the land and the lives that the lake covered over. Visualizing the dam as a massive headstone commemorating all that had been lost, the brothers merged the angel-wing notion with the events centering around the construction of the dam and the effect on the surrounding community. For a working title they considered the names of all nearby rivers and settled on *Northfork* "because the prefix *north* fit in well with the angelic theme."

As noted in the unwritten pure indie code, money is always an operative factor. With a shooting schedule of 24 days and a limited budget they also had to cut down on location shooting. Two main settings to be exact: an orphanage and a hippie-like gypsy house. Between the two they envisioned a father and son driving through the mountainous landscape, thus giving two storylines "some breathing room" with a visually epic suggestion without the expense. The first storyline was now generated by a trio of salesmen hired to evacuate holdout residents before water submerges them and their town' s history. The second story centered on a dying orphan boy searching for his wings and a way out of his earthly confinement.

The combination of free-association and research continued.

In time, they came upon the first *Life Magazine* cover of Fort Peck Dam in Montana, the enormous cement spillway symbolizing a monument to a fully industrialized America. A book on angel wings disclosed the parable of God granting each angel a choice: leave with him to heaven or remain behind without their wings. Thus the metaphor for people on earth as a group of wingless angels.

Eventually the decision was made to use several key characters, 15 in all, with separate functions that only indirectly related to each other so that the actors would rarely share screen time. It was thought that this strategy would create a larger picture of the community and enlarge the scope while remaining economical at the same time. These characters included a religious zealot with two wives and a homemade ark, a shaggy minister, and the young, chronically ill orphan boy who encounters what may or may not be a band of visiting angels dressed in late–Victorian medicine-show costumes. The boy would claim he is an angel himself, displaying the scars on his back as proof his wings had been amputated. Dark suited men would join in the dilemma as to what to do about the boy: offering immaculate white wings if the boy becomes reluctant to leave. None of the characters are fleshed-out; they have no inner life, contradictions, back story or range of emotions.

In pure indie terms, there have been projects that are even more obscure or puzzling. In fact flights of fancy and personal musings have become so commonplace that they've even turned up in *New Yorker* cartoons. In one of these panels, framed like a movie still, two stranded motorists are shown waiting it out in an area as desolate as a moonscape. Undaunted, digital movie camera in hand, the man turns to the woman and says, "Let's make a low-budget movie till help arrives."

In all of these endeavors, it seems that the environment a writer finds himself in is a strong determining factor. There would be no talky dinners with Andre without the Manhattan theater scene, or boisterous denizens of a neighborhood deli, psychological probings or peculiar street characters were it not for the cultural history, constant buzz and cross-fertilization in and around the port of New York. Likewise, it would be hard to imagine a preoccupation with Americana coupled with the pervasive influence of the Bible were it not for the American heartland and the pull of the West.

But apart from this and the whole notion of pure indie, if you delve a bit further, the imaginary line that separates the purists from the marketplace doesn't always hold. Cassavetes appeared in big budget hits like *Rosemary's Baby* (1968). The money he made from his leading roles in mainstream films helped pay for his personal projects. Lipsky put in a great deal of effort, especially in the L.A. area, promoting his film as a tale anyone could relate to who was concerned about sustaining a relationship. Wally Shawn and Andre Gregory employed Louis Malle, the French director who worked on mainstream movies like *Pretty Baby* (1978), *Atlantic City* (1980) (starring Hollywood stars like Burt Lancaster and Susan Sarandon) and *Crackers* (1984) with Donald Sutherland. Dorrian and Gallagher were not above billing their effort as a fun-loving comedy, and paid veteran actors like Judith Malina and up-and-coming stars like Gretchen Mol to appear in their portrayal of daily life at a corner of the not-so-mean streets.

And let's return to the brothers Polish who, as it happens, sought the feedback of an agent in shaping their surreal script. The cast featured such well-known A-list Hollywood actors as James Woods, Nick Nolte, Daryl Hannah and Peter Coyote. The brothers also had the advantage of a high-powered producer and were given backing by a well-to-do Texas businessman because of their cast and track record. Which leads to some more backtracking.

Their first film, *Twin Falls Idaho* (1999), was generated by their lifelong circumstances: close twins who wanted to know what it would be like to be conjoined. Watching an Oprah TV special—watched by millions of fans who are captivated by heart-tugging topics and sunny self-reinventions—they came upon conjoined girls who carried on intimate conversations and revealed that they didn't want to be separated. The brothers Polish also wanted to create an intimate connection with viewers over the universal bind of interdependence and never being allowed to be alone. Moreover, a great deal of time was spent looking for backing before they went past a first draft, moving on only with a producer's encouragement who loved the fictional relationship between the twins—one strong and the other sickly (a prototype of the sickly orphan in *Northfork*). More scouring for backing in L.A. until a second producer signed on because she too could relate to the universality of the dramatic circumstances. It turned out that her younger sisters were, just like the Polish brothers, identical twins. She then consented to finance the project as long as the brothers could keep the expenses down to a half-million.

On the indie low-budget side, the twins naturally starred themselves in the leading roles, with Michael directing, kept the setting to a minimum (mainly the interior of a room in a rundown hotel). As a story catalyst, they had a wild, gorgeous young woman enter their life and become involved with Mark. As a pivotal ploy, the young woman convinces the twins to attend a Halloween party to impress strangers with their marvelous costume (a two-armed, three-legged suit) and an opportunity to seem as normal as everyone else.

On the conventional side, the plot unfolds in a linear fashion; the sickly twin becomes seriously ill and the brothers have to face the strains of separation. Also on the conventional side, apart from the built-in audience involvement, a gorgeous professional model was cast as the gorgeous young woman, and another featured role was played by a well-known TV heroine, a regular on a popular series and a veteran of sixteen mainstream films.

Then there was the positive review in the *New York Times*, acceptance at Sundance, press screenings in an attempt to create a critical buzz, a sale to Sony Pictures Classics for distribution rights, and more critical affirmation. After that came Hollywood and writing assignments for Touchstone and New Line Cinema dealing with themes involving close brothers and mental illness—subjects considered to be in the brothers' bailiwick. This meant being caught up in the studio development system, conferences about story ideas and conflicting notes from studio execs, otherwise known as writing by committee. All of this provided enough networking and enough of a track record to go on to *Northfork* with its bigger budget and much greater risks to all concerned, especially to the careers of the brothers.

As the lines continue to blur between commerce and artistic integrity, low budget and marketable product, what it all may come down to is that selfsame track record and a promising calling card. Even if the project is as limited as a 20-minute short, if it's selected at film festivals and shows a certain film sense, it's a stepping stone. Seen in this light—formless, low-grade, amateurish flicks aside—it becomes a matter of consistently delivering fresh, engaging work.

And once you take on independent ventures on this level, it's hard not to consider the relative scope of your efforts. Hard not to admire those who have taken on a great deal more, even to the point of taking on Hollywood itself.

8. Intrepid Merchandising

In brief and in passing, the following examples touch on what some in the industry call "the new Hollywood." Although most screenwriters find the scale of these projects daunting, they also appreciate the advantages of complete development and control.

After reading about missing tourists in the back country, the Australian writer-director Greg Mclean wrote a spec script, incorporating some imagined violent incidents and turned it all into a horror film called *Wolf Creek* (2005). The movie was financed in part by a local distributor, based on its potential as a scenario his fellow countrymen could readily relate to. Encouraged by its commercial success, Mclean and his distributor decided to bring it to Hollywood and screen it for one or two studios. Their notion was that one of the studio heads would want to pick it up before others saw it; in effect, said studio head would have a jump on the competition. The notion worked and created a positive profile for Mclean and enabled him to approach the same studio for his next venture.

Writing again on spec, utilizing the tourist ploy once more, he centered his next scenario on the traditional Australian anxiety and curiosity about huge deadly creatures. In his imagination, the threat was the biggest crocodile conceivable, its lair the remote, lonely Australian outback known as the Northern Territory. The story involves a travel company that guides a handful of tourists to the croc's swampy terrain. Though reassured that it's all perfectly safe, the sightseers come up against *Rogue* (2007), a 24-foot crocodile so named because he'd been around for so long and had never been captured. The sightseers and their guides are not only attacked by the creature but find themselves marooned. The only way out is a narrow crossing where all manner of alligators and crocodiles lie in wait to pick them off one by one.

Accepted by the same studio and given the green light to direct and jumpstart the process and then buoyed by the scare factor in test screenings, Mclean was on his way.

Aside from his writing and directing and savvy about frightening movie-goers, what makes Mclean's approach noteworthy is the fact that he also acts as a salesman and entrepreneur. Predicated on his experience as a director of commercials in Australia, he makes two-dimensional renderings of some of the scenes as a trailer to show buyers how the movie will look and, in a sense, how it will feel to be in the audience. He may even add an animated clip.

All in all, he pitches his writing, his expertise as a commercial artist and filmmaker and his track record as a writer-director to a studio and whoever else he has to approach to get his work financed and is off and running. At the same time, he insists on making his own movies in Australia, independently, with full creative control including casting and final cut—thereby creating his own development studio, and retaining an agent in Hollywood to handle foreign sales and marketing rights.

You could say the prototype of this kind of venture packaging is New Zealand's own Peter Jackson. He began by making backyard movies like *Bad Taste* (1988) for approximately $50,000 financed by his fulltime job. It took him four summers using himself as an actor, whatever friends were available and a hand-held camera. *Bad Taste* is a horror-comedy about four guys who happen to come across an alien plot to harvest humanity as a fast-food source for the folks back home. The storyline was created by Jackson and his collaborators who, later on, relying on much more viable material, became Academy Award winners.

After a time, as a departure from his horror comedies, he made *Heavenly Creatures* (1994) based on the true-life story of two New Zealand girls who, in 1964, committed matricide. He and his co-writer, Fran Walsh, viewed the story from the girls' point of view in an attempt to understand how they were capable of committing this act. Another relatively low-cost movie to make, but this time it garnered him and his co-writer an Academy Award nomination for screenwriting.

With his foot in the Hollywood door, as a huge fan of Fay Wray and the 1930s *King Kong*, and with a background as a backyard special effects creator of stunts and animated models baked in his mother's oven, he made a deal whereby he would shoot an update of *Kong* in New Zealand, retain final cut and rely on the Hollywood studio to release it. In addition, the studio was bound to hire his special effects company to create the early artwork, animation and special effects, enabling Jackson to pre-visualize the film for himself as well as the studio.

From this point, the story evolves to J.R.R. Tolkien's *The Lord of the Rings* trilogy, a 20-minute mini-movie preview and sales pitch, replete with voice-over detailing some of the background—e.g. in a small village in the Shire a young Hobbit named Frodo is entrusted with an ancient, potentially deadly, ring and must embark on an epic quest to the Cracks of Doom to destroy it. Sketches of the fantasy creatures in this action-adventure-fantasy are incorporated in the preview along with computer animation of the battle scenes.

Like Mclean, the enterprising Mr. Jackson has gone far beyond the standard indie canon.

On a smaller scale, without all the graphic tools but still in the same vein, we can take a second look at Rod Lurie (the one drawn to political themes). With a background as a film reviewer, film critic for *Los Angeles Magazine* and talk radio host for KABC, you could say his screenwriting and filmmaking career started with his speculation about the true identity of Deep Throat (the pivotal source in the Watergate scandal). As a result, Lurie went on to make a short called *4 Second Delay* (1998), predictably using the device of a talk-radio show. As it evolves, viewers are afforded the sense that they too are on the phone with the person who brought down the Nixon White House.

For his next foray, full-length this time but still financed on a low budget, Lurie set his tale in a diner during a presidential campaign. The incumbent is snowed in, his campaign limited to the ten people snowed in with him with nowhere else to go. At the same time, there is a potential third-world-war crisis, all of this centering on the interplay with the diner patrons and the president on the phone (shades of the talk show) dealing with the perpetrators and anyone who can circumvent this dire emergency.

Which, moving past his one-set days, brings us back to *The Contender* (2000), financed independently again but with the look of a big-budget studio movie. It was shot in Richmond, Virginia, with its capitol dome and rotunda not unlike the nation's Capitol. The main sets were interior, with added coverage of other locales and appropriate film clips. He assembled an all-star cast including Gary Oldman, Jeff Bridges and Joan Allen.

In his scenario he blurred the lines between good and evil in American politics and his writing reflected sentiments like, "Principles only mean something if you stand by them when you're inconvenienced." Two of his leads, Jeff Bridges and Joan Allen, received Academy Award nominations. These nominations, in turn, led to interest from other A-list actors and studios. His stints as writer-director-producer led to a *Commander in Chief* series for network television (2005) with its behind-the-scenes look at the first female president. And on from there.

Though these examples take us beyond the usual scope of screenwriting or the range of the indie writer-director, they keep all possibilities and options open. They also bring up questions about risk, commercialism and the margins of creativity. No matter how complete these filmmakers were, *Kong* and the Ring cycle were taken from proven material: one from an old cult movie, the other from popular literature. The crocodile incident, *Heavenly Creatures* and the Watergate short were culled from newspaper accounts, which also qualify as high-profile proven material. Proven springboards like these can—graphic skills and all the rest of it aside—serve any writers looking for a safer route.

9. The Adaptation Chronicles

There's a long history of screenplays based on other writings. Just to name a few, *Casablanca* was originally a play, *The Godfather* (1972) and *Gone with the Wind* (1939) were sprawling novels, *All the President's Men* (1976) was originally an account of the investigative journalism that led to the downfall of the Nixon administration, *Dog Day Afternoon* (1975) was inspired by a magazine article and the British classic *Quartet* (1948) was taken from a collection of Somerset Maugham's short stories. Even *Adaptation*, the loopy Charlie Kaufman vehicle we touched on earlier, was a film about a failed attempt to turn a popular journalistic account about orchid mania and a certain South Florida orchid poacher into a movie that morphed into a Hollywood potboiler.

How any of these works grow in someone's mind as a possible film, let alone one that eventually gets made, depends on a number of variables including pure chance. However, while there are no rules of thumb, there do seem to be a few touchstones.

From a Short Story by ...

Dianna Ossana, the novelist and co-screenwriter of *Brokeback Mountain* (2005), was taken with Annie Proulx's short story. At the outset, she had a strong sense of who the two men were: very macho guys in the 1960s, lower-middle class working cowboys who just happened to be up in the Bighorn mountains doing their job. Then, all of a sudden, they were in a relationship. The tale tapped into Ossana's own sense of loss about incidents in her own life: loving someone who didn't love her back, or someone loving her that she didn't love back, the tragedy, lost opportunity and the regret.

In tandem with Larry McMurtry, the famed Western author and co-screenwriter, the pair put up some of their own money to obtain the rights from Proulx and began networking to get the project rolling. Aside from the provocative roles and themes that seemed sure to garner a great deal of buzz in the industry (at the time, the subject was trendy though traditionally taboo), they were also struck by the filmic quality of Proulx's writing, the abiding sense of place and landscape, the crisp dialogue and spare and precise prose. Because both writers felt that the world had become primarily visual—few people who read but go to the movies instead—the project was a natural.

In order to open up and expand the material into a feature-length film, the writers took the suggested domestic life in the story and amplified it. The offhand way the aggressive cowboy treated his more sensitive male partner, along with the pain he inflicted on his own wife, plus the underlying homophobia of the times were expressed visually in cinematic terms. This also applied to the way the sensitive cowboy was unable to juggle a family life (indifferent wife, overbearing father-in-law, passive child) and his need for male companionship. All this primarily nonverbal material was added by the screenwriters.

On a much smaller, experimental scale, writers have sometimes opted to place vignettes side by side in an urban setting with only a slight attempt to weave the little portraits together. Drawing from Grace Paley's collections and the vantage point of beleaguered yet independent women, screenwriters John Sayles and Susan Rice put together the three-part *Enormous Changes at the Last Minute* (1985). The first profile, Virginia, is deserted by a shiftless husband and allows herself to be courted by a former suitor who has his own family in New Jersey. Another woman, Alexandra, finds herself pregnant after a careless relationship with a cab driver almost half her age. A third, Faith, discovers that her father has decided to divorce her mother even though the pair of them live in the same retirement home and have never been married in the first place. Faith ponders why any of this is her responsibility but comes to no conclusion.

According to the story writer Paley, narratives have to have movement and change but not plot. Plot is too deliberate. Sometimes she ties up the knot, often she leaves it wide open for the reader—and in this case—the viewer to picture a resolution or "whatever they want to do with it." She further claimed that since all good writers explore, they have to come up with a new form with every piece they write. Sayles and Rice's screenplay of *Enormous Changes* was produced by ABC Video Enterprises Inc. in association with Ordinary Lives Inc. and had a limited release.

In this same vein, tired of sending out spec screenplays that may or may not get produced someday, Rebecca Miller tried her hand at a Paley-like series of intimate portraits and character sketches. At the time, she wasn't aware of the opportunity to transform short prose that she owned the rights to onto super-low-budget digital video (otherwise known as mini–DV) for the Independent Film Channel. But thanks to a friend in the field and his encouragement, it all came to pass. It went on to be released by United Artists in 2002 and was given screenings nationally and internationally.

Eventually the work became a triptych of three women of contrasting temperaments whose misspent lives begin to disintegrate. In simple terms, Delia, a working-class woman, is escaping from an abusive marriage; Greta, an upper-middle-class woman, is driven out of her stultifying marriage by her ambition; and Paula, an artist who doesn't produce anything, nearly gets killed in an accident and then tries to come to terms with the randomness of that event by rescuing a hitchhiker. Miller called the pieces *Personal Velocity*, each sketch running less than 28 minutes bridged by the voice of a male narrator. The piece was given a shooting schedule of 16 days and a budget of $250,000. The title comes from Miller's belief that we all develop at different rates depending on our personalities and circumstances.

It should be mentioned that what she brought to this venture, aside from her writing skills and sense of film, was her background as an actress. She knew her characters inside and out and what motivated their every action. Movement (in a Paley mode) traced the way thoughts move, one triggering another, sometimes flitting back and forth, the flashbacks in chronological order or a cut just before Delia is shoved into a table by her husband, as his way of expressing, "Wait, let me explain."

The mosaic is tailored to digital video and its reliance on medium shots, close-ups and very intense close-ups (wide shots and all other camera work literally out of digital video's range). Miller also kept in mind that memorable images were key and told much more than words. Among these visual moments were a battered Delia standing in front of a mirror; Greta crying behind her husband's shoulder as he reads her a bit of news from the *New York Times* (he's unaware that she's about to leave him); the image of a boy who is all cut up as Paula (the accident prone, faux artist) finally realizes what's happened to him.

As a departure from this kind of tight imagery and loosely connected themes on an intimate level within a limited venue, there is the short story that cries out for an expansive feature film given enough time and space and an unhurried approach.

Far from the urban hubs of filmmaking and the pressures of major film festivals, Ali Selim was residing quietly in his native Minnesota when he was taken with a short story by Will Weaver called "Gravestones Made of Wheat." The story takes place in post–World War I, Minnesota among immigrant Scandinavian farmers and centers on the relationship between Olaf and his mail-order German-born bride, Inge.

At the time Selim discovered this piece, he was directing TV commercials; it had been ten years since he'd taken a screenwriting class. All the same, moving past the central conflict in the story about the legality of burying someone in a wheat field instead of a cemetery, he was moved by the love story and the underpinning of heritage and the immigration experience. As it happens, Selim's father was an immigrant and his mother came from a Minnesota farming background. And as it so often happens, the story and his own background and sensibility began to merge and tap his imagination.

Sensing that he could reshape the material into an engaging film, he traced the rights to a local PBS affiliate and, when the rights lapsed, contacted the author's agent. He then worked out an arrangement whereby he would send a check every six months, keep the option going and take his time creating a screenplay.

Along the way, he was influenced by recollections of his grandparents' history and the photo database at the Minnesota History Center. A reference to feelings about God in the short story led to research into church-going circa 1919 and 1920 and whatever else was going on in that time and place. He discovered it was the end of the wheat boom and how it affected those who, like Olaf, hung onto their money and others who bought everything in sight and were always broke.

Perhaps most importantly, he came upon an old wedding picture which became a key visual element. Soon it became a story of memory, beginning with the present day and flashing back to the meeting and courtship of Olaf and Inge. Instead of any preoccupation with plot, it was always a matter of evocative imagery and feelings. How did it all begin and how did their relationship evolve? How did the community respond to Inge's presence in different ways, testing her spirit and awakening the stoic Olaf to his own, true underlying nature? Continuing in this reflective vein, Selim explored how, sometimes ally and sometimes foe, the character of Minister Sorrensen epitomized some of the era's prejudices. But most of all, as memorable film imagery, Selim created in Inge a character who doesn't speak English and yet still expresses alternating emotions of confusion, tenderness and trust as she tries to make a place for herself in this new world.

It became a bit more commercial when Selim found a line producer who also connected with the material and wanted to see it made. The parts of the story that gave the narrative a sense of progression were kept and larger scenes that would prove to be too costly were cut.

Luckily, Selim's naturally sparse writing style attracted actors (who fundamentally love to fill in the blanks). This led to development at the newly formed Cygnus Emerging Filmmaker's Institute in Los Angeles, staged readings and discussions as a result of what worked and what didn't: lines of dialogue that were necessary and lines the actors had trouble with or were superfluous; screen directions that were succinct and those that weren't immediate and in the active voice—e.g., Olaf sits as opposed to Olaf is sitting.

Sweet Land was finally filmed in 2006 by a small production company called Carbon Neutral Films. The lesson here, though the evolution was much more gradual, is basically the same as the three previous examples. If the potential imagery and given circumstances engage the writer, actors, producers and anyone and everyone up and down the line who want to see it on the screen, it stands a chance of being made.

Weighing the Stage Play

Turning back to the basis for that great favorite *Casablanca,* you might very well think that its springboard, the play *Everybody Comes to Rick's,* has something to tell us about the natural connection between stage and film. However, the play about Rick's place was never good enough to be produced. It even prompted one of Warner Brothers' top writers, Robert Buckner, to openly fault the synthetic storyline and cliché characters. Until the Epstein Brothers and Howard Koch got hold of it, all it had going was co-playwright Murray Burnett's recollection of a quaint café in the south of France circa 1938 with its eclectic mix of expatriates, Nazis and arty types who were drawn to the piano stylings of a gifted black entertainer.

In any case, it seems you can start with something as slight as Burnett's unproduced playscript and turn it into a memorable film. On the other hand, there are playscripts that only work on the stage and, as another caveat, require a particular type of audience. For a prime example, we can turn to *Luv* (1967) as a cautionary tale. When Murray Schisgal's play opened in 1965, it appealed to knowing Broadway audiences as a send-up of New Yorkers who were caught up in the trendy-at-the-time existentialism. This philosophy had become so commonplace that, as a pastime, everyone in restaurants, at parties, on subway trains and everywhere you went seemed to be questioning the meaning of life and the bankruptcy of traditional values. To dramatize this phenomenon, Schisgal devised an abstract bridge spanning Brooklyn and Manhattan, placed a pseudo-despondent Harry Berlin at its edge about to jump off, added Berlin's old wheeler-dealer college classmate Milt Manville and, presently, Milt's self-dramatizing wife, Ellen.

Without going into detail, Harry's fake suicide attempt, Milt's con job to shelve his wife in favor of a younger mistress, and Ellen's pseudo-attempt at doing away with Milt was just an excuse for a tour de force. Harry, played to the hilt by the outrageous Alan Arkin, was given the opportunity to rant and rave and spout garbled nihilistic philosophy; Milt, played by Brooklyn's own smooth-talking Eli Wallach, had ample space to talk himself into anything and everything relating to love and lust. One of his lines was, "Do you know, Harry, that I am more in love today than the day I got married? But my wife won't give me a divorce!" In turn, the over-the-top Ellen, played by the formidable Anne Jackson (and Wallach's real-life wife), took over the stage singing, dancing and recalling her wasted life with Milt. Nothing came between these semi-vaudeville turns—no traffic, no other characters, no reality that would impinge on this interplay between this ideal ensemble and appreciative audiences who clapped and laughed and kept the show running month after month.

The characters traded partners, went through moments of elation and despair—anything to keep the act going. Without these highs and lows and a wallow in angst, there was nothing else to sustain them. Any moment of calm would do each of them in and stop the show.

Whatever possessed producers to turn this two-act vaudeville turn into a movie is anyone's guess. Apart from the miscasting and extraneous gaggle of characters, the writers unwittingly shifted locales to suburbia, a luncheonette, a moving car, etc. It was as if the movie actors were told to recite their lines no matter where they were taken, to pay no attention to the external realities while the camera crew was asked to dutifully capture all this incoherence. Unfortunately, no one was aware that there was no need to leave the warm, intimate confines of the Booth Theatre, let alone scout locations, hire the camera crew, toss in as much gratuitous business as possible, involve an editor and project the final results onto movie screens.

Of course there have been worse examples of this kind of miscalculation, but for now, the film version of *Luv* will suffice.

As an aside and on a much brighter note, playwright Schisgal co-wrote the screenplay of the mega-hit *Tootsie* (1982) from a story by Don McGuire and Larry Gelbart. In this one, Michael Dorsey, a brash stage actor who has antagonized every New York producer, can only find work disguised as a liberated woman on a TV soap opera and subsequently becomes a better person. Or as Gelbart put it, "The challenge was developing the idea of how a man might view the plight of women after spending a period of time being one of them."

Working with actor Dustin Hoffman in the title role and director Sydney Pollack, the writers conceived a structure and Schisgal added his own inimitable wit with the additional help of that improvisational whiz Elaine

May. The results can be viewed as a variation on the universe of movie drag in the tradition of Wilder's *Some Like It Hot*: Michael as Dorothy Michaels falls in love with his beautiful TV co-star Julie and Julie's father falls in love with "Dorothy." The point here is that there is no way this character can be confined to a stage. Of necessity, it has to be a film as Michael is driven from point to point in a shot-flow that takes him up and down the streets of New York, to apartments and auditions, TV studios and out to Julie's father's place in the country and beyond. And not a bit of time for any extended dialogue.

For a quick glance at a play that was easily transformed into a movie, William Inge's *Picnic* (1955) furnished an intimate look at the impact Hal, a handsome drifter at the far edge of his youth, made as he entered adjacent front yards in a small Kansas town in the early 1950s. The occasion: the morning of the annual Labor Day picnic. As a result of Hal's entrance out of the blue, a single mother's memories of a failed marriage are rekindled; her older daughter, Madge, is no longer content to be the prettiest girl in town and promised to Alan, the scion of the local grain baron. Her younger sister becomes smitten—caught between wanting to get away and to fit in; Rosemary, the spinster school teacher in the boardinghouse next door, decides she has one final chance to land Howard, the storekeeper and confirmed bachelor, before school begins the next day and her life is entrapped forever. All the repressed feelings and sexual longings typical of this period in the American heartland are jarred loose by Hal's presence. Even the neighbor Mrs. Potts is prompted to say how good it is to have a man around as she offers Hal some breakfast in return for a little work.

As a playscript, it was all perfectly fine. But what it cried out for was Daniel Taradash's screenplay and Josh Logan's direction in providing the imagery the play only hinted at. A shot of the freight train as it rolled by, Hal, the drifter, hopping off, the train whistle signaling possibilities and dreams far away to points east and west. There is the grand picnic itself and all the rides and hoopla and Madge drifting down the river in her finery crowned as the "queen of Nuwalla." There is Alan's privileged home and the contrast between Alan's prospects and Hal, his old fraternity brother and once-upon-a-time football star, who barely owns the shirt on his back. When Hal is shown the silos and told he can work his way up from the bottom, there is the visual option of the cooped-up wage earner vs. the freedom of the open road. Rosemary's drunken tirade as she throws herself at Hal and tears off his shirt after Hall wards her off, can fully be appreciated only as the camera shows us all the onlookers peering down as the festivities begin to unwind. And how else to capture all this except through the cinematography of the legendary James Wong Howe and the final helicopter shot as

Madge's bus begins to catch up with the freight train carrying Hal away from her? Arguably, the screen story furnished moviegoers much more than they could ever derive from seeing the play.

In addition to the sketch that turns into a memorable film, the play that can work only on the boards and the play that can be expanded successfully, there are instances when a play and a film seem to merge. This was the case with Aaron Sorkin's adaptation of his own playscript *A Few Good Men* (1992). The play offers a stationary courtroom battle between Colonel Jessep's covert reign over his Marine station in Guantanamo Bay and what really happened to Private Santiago, who allegedly died at the hands of Pfc. Downey and Lance Corporal Dawson, who may or may not have been following orders.

The film opens everything up by taking us to the Cuban base, showing us the assault on Santiago as he lay asleep in his bunk, various scenes in and around Washington, DC, as the untested plea-bargaining prosecutor Lieutenant Kaffee goes through the motions. Then, through a series of mishaps, embattled conferences and encounters in various locales and much goading by a defense lawyer (Lt. Cdr. JoAnne Galloway) including a heated street scene late at night, Kaffee is finally induced, with great risk to his career, to put Colonel Jessep on the stand.

In screenwriting terms, the crux boils down to, Did Colonel Jessep order a Code Red (an unlawful hazing practice)? In short, if Jessep cracks under some underlying irresistible impulse to crow over his hard-bitten tactics, the case turns and it is Jessep who will be up for court-martial. Though the rule of thumb in screenwriting mandates that you cut all monologues, show don't tell, come in as late as possible and leave early, this narrative rests on what this egomaniacal character will do, after all this time, under pressure, in the spotlight, while perhaps secretly dying to tell the world and set the record straight.

On the page, as well as on the screen, the tension builds during this pivotal scene as Kaffee runs out of options. Jessup, smiling, about to leave the witness stand, holds all the cards. This is Kaffee's last chance but he has no material witnesses, no evidence, only suppositions. Jessup has remained cocky throughout his testimony and has coolly fended off all of Kaffee's intimations. More cocky and patronizing than ever, Jessep is about to slip away but Kaffee announces he's still not through with him. After a bit more thrusting and parrying—the camera holding, going nowhere else as if insisting, through close-ups, on penetrating Jessup's façade—Kaffee plays his last hand.

Kaffee revisits Jessep's contention that he ordered that Santiago wasn't to be touched and needed to be transferred off the base for his own safety. Thus keeping the onus for Santiago's death squarely on the shoulders of Kaffee's clients, Dawson and Downey, who claim they were only following orders and had no intention of harming Private Santiago.

Now, obviously miffed at Kaffee's continuing impertinence, Jessup responds:

> JESSEP
>
> You ever served in an infantry unit? Ever served in a forward area? Put your life in another man's hands?
>
> KAFFEE
>
> No, sir.
>
> JESSEP
>
> We follow orders, son. It's that clear. Are we clear?
>
> KAFFEE
>
> If you gave an order that Santiago wasn't to be touched and your orders are always followed, then why would Santiago be in danger? Why would it be necessary to transfer him off the base?
>
> JESSEP
>
> Santiago was a sub-standard marine.
>
> KAFFEE
>
> But you said he was being transferred because he was in grave danger. Why the two orders?
>
> JESSEP
>
> Sometimes men take matters into their own hands.
>
> KAFFEE
>
> I'd like an answer to the question. Colonel Jessep, did you order a code red?
>
> JUDGE RANDOLPH
>
> You don't have to answer the question.
>
> JESSEP
>
> I'll answer the question. You want answers?
>
> KAFFEE
>
> I think I'm entitled to it.
>
> JESSEP
>
> You want answers?
>
> KAFFEE
>
> I want the truth!
>
> JESSEP
>
> You can't handle the truth. Son, we live in a world that has walls and those walls have to be guarded by men with guns. Who's going to do it? You? I have a greater responsibility than you can possibly fathom. You weep for Santiago and you curse the marines. You have the luxury of not knowing what I know. Santiago's death, while tragic, probably saved lives. And my existence, while grotesque and probably incomprehensible to you, saves lives. You don't want the truth because at places deep down you don't talk about at parties, you want me on that wall. You need me on that wall. We use words like honor, code, loyalty. We use these words as the backbone of a life spent defending something. You use them as a punch line. I have neither the time nor the inclination to explain myself to a man who rises and sleeps under the blanket of the very freedom I provide and then questions

the manner in which I provide it. I would rather you just said thank you and went on your way. Otherwise I suggest you pick up a weapon and stand a post. Either way I don't give damn what you think you're entitled to.

KAFFEE
(shouting)
Did you order a code red?
JESSEP
You're goddamn right I did!

As with Goldman's *Butch Cassidy*, Joseph Mankiewicz's *All About Eve* and all other apt examples, not a word is wasted. The camera lingers because both the visual and the verbal are vital. As a screenwriter, Sorkin can offer moviegoers a greatly expanded view of all the ins and outs that led up to this climactic moment: an insight into the life and trials and tribulations on Gitmo, a quasi record that can be shown countless times as long as it remains compelling.

In terms of the highly verbal, no matter how apt a screenwriting rule seems to be—like avoid speeches at all costs—the answer always seems to be, "It all depends."

Looking at it the other way around, seasoned screenwriters like Stanley Weiser and Oliver Stone appreciated the theater and theatrical scenes, the power of necessary and compressed dialogue, and the expanded cinematic view, all at the same time. They reached a point about a quarter of the way into their original script for *Wall Street* (1987) when Gordon Gekko, the ruthless but highly articulate corporate raider, has to convince Bud Fox, the young and impatient stockbroker, to become a mole. In Gekko's mind, this tack is vital in order to get Fox to wheedle some inside information so that Gekko can bring down a rival corporate raider who is on the verge of beating him to a big takeover. But Fox is waffling, after getting a taste of the good life, fast money and fast women via Gekko but still under the influence of his honest, blue-collar upbringing.

The speech Gekko has to deliver, the amount of persuading he has to do to sway Fox would take at least 12 to 15 minutes on stage. It would also be limited by a single setting, say the living room of Gekko's upscale Manhattan apartment. On screen, it would take six minutes or less, provided that the camera has something meaningful to capture and an opportunity to move along.

The solution: break the scene up to a three minute shot-flow inside Gekko's private athletic club and the final 2½ minutes inside the back seat of Gekko's moving limousine, cutting to shots of a travel computer screen to illustrate his rival's portfolio, and cutaways to a high-rise Gekko has bought and sold for a huge profit, and other passing Manhattan street scenes as Gekko underscores his points. To demonstrate, we can pick up Gekko's ploy in the steam room right after Bud Fox has given him a bit of bad news. After being given a chance to work with Gekko after giving him a tip about confidential negotiations between his father's union and the airline, Fox lost some of Gekko's money in today's trading:

> GEKKO
> I guess your dad's not union representative of that company.
> FOX
> How do you know about my father?
> GEKKO
> The most valuable commodity I know of is information. Wouldn't you agree?

INT. LOCKER ROOM.

GEKKO and BUD FOX are getting dressed.

> GEKKO
> The public's out there throwing darts at a board, chum. I don't throw darts at a board. I bet on sure things. Read *The Art of War*. "Every battle is won before it's even fought." Think about it. You're not as smart as I thought you were, Buddy boy. You know why fund managers can't beat the S&P 500? Because they're sheep and sheep get slaughtered. Give me guys who are poor, smart and hungry and have no feelings. You win a few, you lose a few but you keep on fighting. If you need a friend, get a dog. It's trench warfare out there, pal. I've got twenty other brokers analyzing charts, pal. I don't need another one. See you around, Buddy.

BUD FOX runs up the stairs after GEKKO.

> FOX
> I'm not just another broker. You give me another chance, I'll prove that to you. I'll go the extra mile.
> GEKKO
> You want another chance? Then you stop sending me information and you start getting me some. Get dressed. I'll show you my charts.

INT. THE BACK SEAT OF GEKKO'S CHAUFFER-DRIVEN LIMO—DAY

At this point, Gekko's speeches become more intense as Bud mutters about possibly losing his broker's license and going to jail. Gekko reminds him that he's already divulged the facts about a court ruling on the airline company his father works for. Gekko then denigrates the ethic of hard work and points out what happened to his own father who played by the rules, worked hard and died of a heart attack at the age of 49. He goes on to declare that "if you're not inside, you're outside." He points out the car window at a well-dressed man on a street corner hurrying by a street vendor and says, "The difference between the two of them isn't luck." And the only status worth having is to be "rich enough to have your own jet, rich enough to not have to waste time. To be a player or nothing." Gekko continues for another brief moment until, at the immediate prospect of being dropped off for good, Bud gives in.

(As it happens, Michael Douglas earned an Oscar for Best Actor in a Leading Role for his bravura portrayal of Gordon Gekko and many other awards as well.)

Moving on, while we're at it and on a much more modest scale, there is another type of photoplay, even though, unlike the power and pull of *A Few Good Men* or the inherent theatricality of a role like Gordo Gekko, it may only potentially reach a limited number of screens.

The Personal Playscript

It may have been made on a shoestring, financed by house-party fundraisers and mailings requesting donations but, still and all, a small play that strikes a chord can be reconfigured and find a place in movie houses.

An example that comes easily to mind is Chuck Evered's *Running Funny* (2007), prompted by a time in his life when he was young, had just lost both parents and had no idea where he was going and what he was going to do. A degree from college supposedly meant he was ready to tackle any kind of career though, in fact, he was emotionally drained and there was nothing in the workaday world he could relate to. What is remarkable about all this is the 20-year hiatus between the play he wrote during that low period (which had a run as a non-equity project at Williams College in Massachusetts) and the making of the movie and its acceptance at a film festival. A test of the universality of his premise if ever there ever was one.

The 3-character play featured Paul Giamatti as the brooding and introspective Michael (who at the time had just lost his own father and later went on to become a noted film actor), and Eddie, the more hyper and positive of the two graduates. In tandem, they rent an apartment-garage from a blind veteran named Stan for a month as they, just like Evered himself, move away from home and try to figure out what to do.

Life, however, hits them broadside as they begin to realize just how lost they are. Again, borrowing from life, like the character Michael, Evered too was in limbo as he rented a room from an elderly man named Stan. Evered went on to set the play in his own middle class New Jersey home town eight miles from New York City because, as an aspiring playwright, living there gave him the abiding feeling he was on the other side of the river. This afforded him the perspective of always longing, wanting to belong and the feeling of constantly reaching. He also viewed New Jersey as a world where people are naturally quixotic and funny—perhaps because they are anxious and on the wrong side of things, perhaps for other reasons—qualities he drew on in while writing this play.

Later on, under Evered's guidance and his nephew's subsequent direction (who, some 19 years later found himself at loose ends and strongly relating to the play's premise), the play was opened out. Shooting on a Panasonic DVX 24P camera on a budget of $10,000, scenes were added introducing viewers to Eddie's home life that revealed why Eddie was so miserable under the thumb of a demeaning mother and a distracted father fixated on a life as a clown.

Totally confused, Eddie quoted his father, saying things like, "Doing nothing in this world is better than doing less than nothing because it's not getting you anywhere just as fast." Other new locales included areas around the blind man's home, interiors where the blind man talks to his imaginary wife (who is deceased), the neighborhood where Michael had been belittled for running funny, Michael's former childhood home, and job interviews in various Manhattan office buildings where Michael and Eddie are confronted with surly personnel managers.

As these kinds of small projects go, there is something to be said for the contemporaneous ploys and sorrows of youth. As a defense mechanism, finding they were all in the same boat, Evered and his college theater buddies took part in what they called standup tragedy instead of standup comedy. As a possible guideline, it can also be said that scripts of this nature, spawned from deeply felt experiences that are both poignant and humorous, have meaning for all generations. In general, it seems everyone remembers being at this point at some time in their lives.

Returning to the mainstream—short stories and plays that may or may not be serviceable aside—there is a type of narrative that producers find especially attractive with its built-in sales record.

10. Taking on the Novel

At times, finding scenes and devising a storyline from pages of exposition, descriptive passages, streams of consciousness and the like may seem daunting, no matter how popular the novel. Other times, depending on the book and the screenwriter, it doesn't pose much of a problem at all. As noted, Emma Thompson had a great affinity for Jane Austen's style and wit and had many successful screen and BBC adaptations of Austen's works to draw from as well.

There are also times when a screenwriter has both the makings of a provocative screenplay and a middling one and, for one reason or another, plays it safe and opts for the middling alternative. Sketching in stock characters and a central figure who "looks like the action-hero Harrison Ford," the author of *The Da Vinci Code* provided screenwriter Akiva Goldsman with a murder inside the Louvre that had great religious implications. The author also provided Goldsman with enough cat-and-mouse chase sequences over Europe to keep the camera busy until the final credits. By the time the movie version was released in 2006, the provocative notion of a religious mystery that would shake the foundations of Christianity was overshadowed by the shopworn ploy of keeping everyone running around. With the amiable Tom Hanks in the lead, hardly anyone noticed any spiritual implications at all, save for a "nefarious secret cult" that just happened to occupy a prominent midtown Manhattan skyscraper and took exception to the inaccurate depiction of its activities.

On a more meaningful note, Joel and Ethan Coen's script followed Cormac McCarthy's bleak crime novel *No Country for Old Men* (2007) beat for beat, scene for scene. What the Coen brothers sketched in and directed and what the camera work disclosed is a cinematic facsimile of what McCarthy described: a parched Texas landscape; incidents like the one where a hunted ex-serviceman (neither good nor bad, who has made off with a cache of drug money) sits in a dark room in a shabby hotel as his pursuer walks down the corridor, causing the floorboards to creak; shadows of the maniacal pursuer's feet flit by the glint of light under the door, footsteps move away and the glint of light dissolves with the squeak of the unscrewed hall bulb.

As another option, one section of a book will do the trick. In approaching John Irving's novel *A Widow for One Year*, which became the movie *A Door in the Floor* (2004), Tod Williams decided to concentrate on the first 183 pages of the 700-page narrative. In Williams' view, Irving's tale was written in a standard 3-act format with the first act (a prelude to what happens to a little girl later on as an adult) providing a satisfactory beginning, middle and end. Williams selected the chapter title "A Door in the Floor" knowing the ending gave him the sense he was working toward a definite objective.

The structure now evolved around a pivotal summer in the privileged beach community of East Hampton, New York. Ted Cole, a famous author and illustrator of children's books, has lost his inspiration and his driver's license after numerous DUIs. The DUIs are ostensibly due to the deaths some years earlier of his two teenage sons. His wife is also despondent; they now live in separate houses.

Their little girl, 4-year-old Ruth, was born after the car accident that killed her brothers, and the main house is lined with pictures of the boys, each one representing a story that Ted tells his daughter over and over again— the "door in the floor" of the movie's title.

Eddie, a boarding-school student who has come to spend a summer working as Ted's assistant and driver, is the catalyst that induces the wife to attach herself to Eddie as a replacement for her son and exacerbates Ted's drunken philandering. Eddie's arrival also leaves little Ruth at a loss between living in the here and now and her fixation over her lost brothers and her dad's illustrated children's story. In the resolution, it appears that the real child turns out to be Ted. Movie made, not much of a screenwriting problem solved.

Somewhat along these same lines (the continuum between childhood and maturity), we have Richard Russo's Pulitzer Prize-winning novel *Empire Falls*. Unfortunately, when given the opportunity to write the screenplay for HBO featuring major stars Russo decided to try and tackle his whole book. As he disclosed to members of the WGA East, he assumed he "might be able to find a visual equivalent of what he had told on the page and now realized had to be shown."

In his novel, the characters are introduced at leisure and all the conflicts that are slowly brewing take an equally slow time to pay off. Miles, the central character who is approaching middle age, doesn't arrive at a point of maturation until the lengthy novel's end. Mrs. Whiting, the main antagonist who has a stranglehold on this decaying hamlet in Maine, hovers in the background but disappears for long stretches.

A solution Russo devised in attempting to solve one problem for the film was to begin and end episodes with Mrs. Whiting's presence in the forefront. As for Miles' slow and subtle odyssey, Russo had to somehow show that he had gone from a passive, adolescent way of handling things to living up to his responsibilities like a man; to eventually realize that his purpose in life was to be a good father and save his teenage daughter (again the motif of competent and incompetent parents). To make this transformation visually compelling without shoehorning in the message, Russo had Miles return to the seaside cottage where, as a boy, he had vacationed with his mother and first met Charlie Mayne. Not realizing then that Charlie was his mother's lover (and a far cry from the wastrel he thought to be his father), Miles had been ambivalent about this man Charlie who occupied his mother's attention. Years later, back at the seaside, Russo decided the camera should focus on Charlie as he was way back then and pan back to Miles as he is now. Without missing a beat, Miles sits down, turns toward Charlie of old and says, "Okay, truce."

The trouble with all this tinkering is that it simply doesn't measure up to the reading experience. The novel meanders as though Russo fully expected the reader to put each chapter down and mull over what just transpired before reading on. The prologue alone takes a great deal of thought as you take in the history of Empire Falls and how Mr. Whiting, who married beneath his station, had no interest whatever in taking over the Whiting enterprises and quietly slipped away for more exotic climes.

Once past the prologue, there is so much space given to Miles running the Empire diner over a period of 20 years, and his mother's life as she fell on hard times and had to work for Mrs. Whiting (due in no small part to her ne'er-do-well husband and their strained relationship). Miles' failed marriage is another consideration; his loopy relationship with the wastrel he takes to be his dad; and his changing relationship with his brother and daughter and others in the town—all his past encounters and the slow evolution of his passivity. Not to mention his reluctant dealings with Mrs. Whiting's daughter and the daughter's accident, his own daughter's trials and tribulations, the fate of a bullied classmate at his daughter's school whom she alone befriends, and so much more, that it literally takes days of unhurried reading to take it all in. All this along with the reverberations in terms of the fate of many lost factory towns in the region, the hard-pressed lives of those who stayed on, still hoping that some new business venture will revive everything.

In other words, no matter how hard Russo tried, there was no way he could write a compressed script that would in any satisfactory way show what he had so artfully told.

On the other hand (somewhat like Tod Williams' *Door in the Floor* tack but much more meaningfully), if the times and circumstances are right, it doesn't matter how much of a novel is omitted, even one that encompasses a significant span of history. In some cases, what it takes is one special segment that can make all the difference.

Take John Steinbeck's *East of Eden*, published in 1952 to great acclaim. It was over 600 pages long and covered a period from the birth of the fictional Adam Trask in 1862 to World War I and beyond, touching on Chicago's packing house strike in 1886, Adam's bitter relationship with his brother in rural Connecticut, the perverse actions of an angelic girl by the name of Cathy who, later on, married Adam after a clandestine affair with his brother. Then there were the early days of farming in the fertile Salinas Valley of California, the life and times of a Chinese cook from San Francisco who migrated to Salinas but planned to return and open a bookstore, anti–German chauvinist hysteria as America entered the war, and a great deal more.

In between, re-telling the biblical story of Cain and Abel, we have Adam's teenage sons Cal and Aron—Cal the outcast who can do no right and Aron the good son who can do no wrong. And here is where writer Paul Osborn, the producers and the legendary director Elia Kazan came in and gambled on this section of Steinbeck's masterpiece. Their great insight was to incorporate the repressive cultural climate in America in the early 1950s and bring the first teenager onto the screen. Never before had there been an attempt to portray the conflicted nature of a male adolescent on the cusp of adulthood. And certainly the physicalized expression of love-hate toward a father and brother and the confused, aimless longing for a mother, nurturing love and sense of belonging had never been shown to a mainstream movie audience.

The tricky part was finding someone to embody all this. It mattered not how much leeway Osborn provided in his script, until Kazan decided that James Dean literally was Cal Trask (Steinbeck's surrogate Cain) with his farm-boy upbringing in rural Indiana, mercurial nature, feelings of desolation over his own long-lost mother and hatred of his errant father and all father figures to boot. And, perhaps above all, there was his training and gifts as a dancer who needed to express all his conflicted emotionality through his body. In effect, Osborn's compressed version of a section of Steinbeck's sprawling novel depended on Kazan's casting of Dean and giving him enough slack and goading him before a take and egging him on. In effect, that was how this central figure and seemingly complete tale came to life in 1955 as Dean hunkered down atop a slow-moving freight car on the way to see a brothel owner who may or may not be his long-lost mother; loped along, hands in his back pockets, eyes averting her wary gaze as he sheepishly followed her to town in Monterey; suddenly sprang to his feet and hurled large blocks of ice down a chute as he spied his brother Aron with Abra (the girl he too was smitten with).

Other moments include boyishly cajoling a servant girl to lead him to the madam's chambers; later on hurling his brother into those same quarters in a fit of rage; and most telling of all, shifting from childlike frivolity decorating for his father's surprise party to crumpling the packet of money he had earned, sobbing and pleading with his father to accept his birthday offering, and then spinning away out into the night, moving off like a slinking animal. Many could have filled in the slots allotted for a stern, self-righteous father, dutiful brother, tender and wistful Abra and the rest of the cast. But the success or failure of Osborn's adaptation relied on the casting of Cal.

In essence then, Osborn carved out a portion of a major literary work, centered it on the universal Cain and Abel story and, within its setting around World War I, gave it a contemporary spin. The overall result was a winning film focused on a teenager's rollercoaster quest that struck a chord with audiences everywhere.

Leaving the tack of grappling with parts and whole works of more or less accessible material, we can shift to the extremes: first the daunting literary challenge and then the clunky political thriller.

As for the literary challenge, what easily comes to mind is Michael Ondaatje's Brooker Prize-winning novel leading to the film of the same name, *The English Patient* (1996). The adaptation was made even more difficult by the fact that the author is a sworn enemy of anything linear. Events and locales bounce around in non-chronological order—North Africa before the war (World War II) and Italy at the end of the war, Cairo and various spots in and around the desert at various hours of the day and night—points of view shifting and, interspersed here and there, all kinds of arcane information about desert mapmaking, bomb defusing and other matters. To make matters worse, there are no quotation marks so that a reader has to work hard at recognizing who is speaking or replying or reminiscing, unless, perhaps, it's the omniscient narrator offering more arcane information:

> There were some tribes who held up their open palm against the beginnings of wind. Who believed that if this was done at the right moment they could deflect a storm into an adjacent sphere of the desert, towards another, less loved tribe. There were continual drownings, tribes suddenly made historical with sand across their gasp.
>
> Ask a mariner what is the oldest known sail and he will describe a trapezoidal one hung from the mast of a reed boat that can be seen in rock drawings in Nubia. Pre-dynastic. Harpoons are still found in the desert. These were water people. Even today caravans look like a river. Still, today it is

water who is the stranger here. Water is the exile, carried back in cans and flasks, the ghost between your hands and your mouth.

In the documentary *The Making of the English Patient*, Ondaatje admitted that he wound up with five years' worth of bits of paper and wasn't sure how in the world he could make it all fit. He then wrote "freely with no sure sense of what's happening or even what's going to happen."

As a broad framework, he pictured the world of the desert in the 1930s before the war broke out and there were any distinct boundary lines: an idyllic period when nations were working together, prior to the time they found themselves on opposite sides. Then he echoed this idea by bringing four people from four different corners of the world together in an abandoned villa. As a "child of movies," Ondaatje found himself filling his writing with cinematic imagery beginning with a man in a burning plane crashing into the desert—a fictionalized Hungarian count Almasy (the name of an explorer who actually charted some regions of the desert) as a dying burn victim who takes on the guise of an Englishman (the "English patient"). This was a character, however, whose mind-set Ondaatje never came to terms with.

After reading the book, the English writer-director Anthony Minghella also saw it all in filmic terms. He called the independent producer Saul Zaentz, who specialized in literary adaptations, and told him he'd found a book he wanted to make into a film. Minghella was certain there was a picture there but didn't know how to do it. After finishing the book, Zaentz too felt there was a picture there and had no idea how it would all come together. Nevertheless, asking himself, "How many adventures are left, how many chances to go to the desert and make a film that you know is going to be good?" Zaentz agreed to take the project on.

Soon after, Minghella decided to abandon the book, invent scenes and re-imagine a scenario. Write his way back into the characters and what seemed to have happened to them and compress it in the way a film requires, focusing on what Minghella felt was the heart of the book: a record of Almasy's visual journey and doomed love affair of the recent past, along with the healing of the four disparate characters Ondaatje brought together in the villa. Having them step out of the war for a time to make a temporary nest and a tentative circle of friendship until they were ready to step back into ongoing reality or, in Almasy's case, leave this world after piecing together the strands of his story.

In Minghella's script, the principal characters, apart from Almasy, were the nurse Hana who is emotionally damaged; Kip, the East–Indian sapper who, due to his short life-expectancy defusing bombs, has avoided all attachments; and the maimed thief Caravaggio with his drug habit and haunted war memories. Minghella then focused on the ill-fated romance between Almasy and the married English lady Katherine of the recent past and, as a parallel, the evolving temporary love affair between Hana and Kip of the present.

In addition, Minghella incorporated Caravaggio's present physical condition and Almasy's unwitting complicity a short time back, and the plight of Katherine's cuckolded husband whose act of revenge resulted in Katherine's demise despite Almasy's tortured attempt to come to her rescue. Minghella also incorporated sand storms, dances at the exclusive club in Cairo, wartime intrigue and other highly visual and intimate events.

All this turned into a story a movie audience could follow. Not only that, as director he gave his leads what they needed to create full and complex characters and, as screenwriter, provided them with distinctive dialogue, a way they each would talk and respond as their relationships evolved. From *The Making of the English Patient*, here is the actor Raph Fiennes as Almasy commenting on his character as written by Minghella:

"He is adept at putting on this uniform as a lover of the desert with things reduced to their most primitive. He is also a predator. I have this image of a bird of prey, what you see are not his real feathers. He wants to get back to the desert, to get out, get away (from his façade as a 'good old boy' and membership in the exclusive club in Cairo). But his journey takes him from being a loner, someone who doesn't extend himself emotionally. Because of the presence of Katherine, a married woman with whom he has become involved, he has to reveal and expose another side of himself."

From the same documentary, actress Kristin Scott Thomas discusses her response to her role before she began to plumb its contradictions: "She's an English woman, very well-connected, well-educated and married to a man who comes to the desert. She thus has her world turned upside down, much to her anger."

How all these reverberations and inter-weavings came together, no one can say. For the record, after its release in 1996, the film was nominated for twelve Academy Awards, winning nine, including Best Picture.

For our final example, we can now turn to that other kind of impossible task. This one was called *Executive Power*, a first novel by a young Washington lawyer who sold the worldwide book and movie rights for $5 million. The writer hired to transform the book for the screen was none other than William Goldman. Early on we saw how Goldman's rough outline and draft about the misadventures of a detective, his two children who wanted to follow in his footsteps and a kidnapping or two was turned inside out by a few of his colleagues. For want of a better term, this Hollywood practice of revamping someone else's plotline is called spitballing—literally tossing ideas around with little or no regard for the writer's intentions. At its best, spitballing produces schemes that make a shaky scenario work for a mainstream audience. At its worse, it produces a patchwork of bits and pieces that are stitched and shoehorned together.

At any rate, as a writer for hire Goldman's task was to take the novel *Executive Power* and turn it into a tight, self-generating thriller with elements. In Hollywood terminology, elements are any set of components that are highly marketable including star-driven leading roles and a storyline and dialogue by a known writer with a certain cachet. The studio which owned the rights to the book chose Goldman not only because of his standing in the industry, but because three of his previous thrillers enjoyed a modicum of commercial success: *No Way to Treat a Lady* (1968), *Marathon Man* (1976) and *Magic* (1978). Goldman accepted because he found something worth spitballing in the novel: a dramatic opening and a set of circumstances.

To wit: at night, a thief breaks into a deserted mansion in Washington, D.C., belonging to an influential billionaire. Making his way to the master bedroom, he points a remote at a mirror that swivels around to reveal an oversized vault. While bagging a cache of bonds, jewelry and cash, the thief is interrupted by sounds of an approaching drunken couple. Hiding in the vault, he discovers that its door is actually a two-way mirror and the tussling couple are the nubile wife of the billionaire and a man who is clearly not her elderly husband.

But the action doesn't continue. The author switches to the next chapter where, during that same night, we learn that a young Washington attorney is engaged to a beautiful heiress. Though he handles the heiress's family interests, he is still smitten by his former fiancée who just happens to be a state's attorney and the daughter of a man with whom he (the attorney) was very close and, unbeknownst to him, the very thief who is hiding in the vault.

In the third chapter, the narrative switches back to the bedroom; the nubile billionaire's wife finds herself trying to fend of her now violent partner and slashes him with a letter opener. As the man screams for help, a chief of staff and two Secret Service men race in and the older Secret Serviceman shoots the philandering wife. In the ensuing moments, the reader discovers that the naked man staring numbly at the bloody knife in the dead wife's hand is the president of the United States. While his aides plan a cover-up and rearrange the room, etc., the Secret Service duo realize that the letter opener is missing, chase the fleeing thief who somehow manages to make it back to his car and speeds away. Everyone involved in the cover-up is now faced with the fact that the letter opener is covered with the fingerprints of the president and the murder victim and the escaping thief is an eyewitness.

At this point, it becomes obvious to Goldman that there are too many characters: nine all told so far counting the thief's daughter. As if this wasn't enough, along the way the author added a detective trying to solve the conundrum, the detective's female assistant, the billionaire and the wronged husband's lawyer, a bystander who took photos of the thief's narrow escape, and a hit man hired to do away with the thief. Not only are there too many characters to keep track of, the thief, the best character and top candidate for a starring role is eliminated halfway through the book on orders from the president.

Goldman's first draft, settling for ten good roles instead of a lead an audience could root for, was barely serviceable. The only real advancement was a new title: *Absolute Power* (1997).

A second draft had the detective in the lead role, now furnished with twin teenage daughters (and yes, the daughters, as in the previous rough outline Goldman was toying with, are determined to follow in Dad's footsteps). This draft was sent to Clint Eastwood in the hope that he would accept the starring part. Eastwood, however, was only interested in playing the thief and insisted that the thief stay on to bring down the president.

Back at his home base in New York, scrapping once again the notion of a story driven by a detective and his intrepid kids, Goldman was at a loss. After six months, too overly familiar with the material to come up with a fresh take, Goldman ran his dilemma by his longtime friend Tony Gilroy, who, as it happens, was the son of the Pulitzer Prize-winning playwright and noted TV writer Frank Gilroy. With a fresh eye, with no allegiance to or even knowledge of the best-seller in question, Tony immediately came up with a tack denied by the original narrative: immediately after the robbery and his narrow escape, the thief goes to see his daughter, despite the fact that they're irrevocably estranged.

This idea freed-up Goldman's imagination. He now had a strained father-daughter relationship, plus the thief's need to elude the president's hired assassins, mixed with the desire to risk all to become close again with his daughter who, adding to the intensity, was a state attorney on the right side of the law.

And, happily, there was always Tony, bringing over more ideas like giving the thief a safe house. Tony also supplied the ending. The only person with the moral right to take revenge was the influential billionaire and wronged husband who, in an earlier version, was gunned down by the Secret Service but was now free to resolve the conflict.

Promptly agreeing to this new scenario, Eastwood went on to play the lead and the movie went into production and worldwide release. For audiences and all concerned, the plot mechanics delivered the standard clear setup and problem as a few characters fall prey to random or planned violence, the workmanlike scaffolding holds throughout with no ambiguity, and punishment is dispensed to those who deserved it.

If you recast Tony Gilroy as a writer who likes to step in, it becomes yet another option and an easy transition over to industrial entertainment.

11. Piecework at the Factory

On any given morning, across from the Writers Guild of America West at 3rd and Fairfax, you're apt to find a gaggle of screenwriters at the Farmers Market pavilion. Sipping coffee, munching on pastry and humoring themselves, there are likely to be writing partners who did well a few years back but are now looking for rewrite assignments punching up dialogue, tightening a through-line, clarifying relationships and the like. There also may be some who have vacillated between concocting ideas for TV sitcoms and feature films, others who have written dozens of spec scripts their agent is still trying to peddle, and a few who are in transition and don't know which way to turn.

But they're all well-informed about the business. They know about the recent test marketing of a horror flick and the teen critique that went something like this: "Not bad, but you've got to keep the cool bits closer together. Too many quiet spots between the scary stuff." They've read this week's "Who Sold What to Whom" section in *Script*, are up on the latest rumors and can tell you in detail about the pitches that have been sold, who won the bidding on a particular remake of a remake, and what writing team just devised yet another "gross-out slacker flick" and was given a green light based on an off-color premise. Like racetrack touts, they're apt to flip through the current issue of *Variety* and offer quips like, "There may be an audience for this thing if they figure out how to exploit it." "It only opened at 10 but it could do 30. If it doesn't, the word is out that heads are going to roll."

Now and then, they'll remind each other about the pitfalls of coverage—e.g., handing work over to an assistant script editor who will condense it to a logline and a dry, short descriptive paragraph, assign it a grade of excellent, good, fair or poor and pass it on to someone higher up the ladder. In this way the script will be marked according to routine guidelines and will never be read. A second theory has it that anything fresh will give the assistant nothing to do, no way to shine and prevent studio heads from taking a risk. By giving most scripts only passing grades, there's no danger a movie will be made based on an underling's say-so. In other words, according to the denizens of the coffee klatch on Fairfax, you should always position yourself to short-circuit coverage no matter how hard up you happen to be.

As a highlight of these sessions, someone will invariably make fun of making a pitch to a certain new studio exec:

"He's gonna ask, 'Is this guy in jeopardy?' And, 'Do they get together in the end?' So you deflect like you only half-heard him and say, 'It's sort of like some movie the studio just did that brought in money.' Or you jump in with, 'The lead is very intense. He's also a very bright, deep guy, also easygoing, got a great sense of humor and he's very real. But even better, the ending is happy but it's sad. And it can be done for so many million depending on who we get.'"

Often referring to themselves as "funny for money" (working mainly on comedies) or "hired guns" and "script doctors," a sense of irony comes with the territory. It's a necessity to slough off the ups and downs of life in the Hollywood trenches where CEOs may be suddenly replaced, a studio may go under or change hands, and a freelancer's lot is subject to the market's short attention span and shifting trends.

At this level, every veteran can recall by rote all the cautionary tales. Stories like the trials and tribulations of John Gregory Dunne and his wife, Joan Didion, while attached to a glossy star vehicle called *Up Close and Personal* (1996). A prime example of consensus Hollywood movie making, the pitfalls of story conferences, and dealings with studio execs who assume anyone can write. At this level, every vet can name the studio head who fired off this memo as an inspiration for a thriller: "When terrorists threaten to set off a nuclear weapon on the eve of a Presidential election, a top aide must find it."

As for *Up Close and Personal*, the springboard was a lurid biopic of the troubled newswoman Jessica Savitch. When the head of production praised Dunne and Didion for the best first draft he'd ever read, he meant it would take at least 26 more drafts to reach the desired goal: providing the studio with "what is going to happen that will make audiences walk out feeling uplifted, good about something and good about themselves."

In actuality, Jessica Savitch died in an auto accident, but in the studio's game plan that wasn't possible. Neither was any allusion to her abortions, drug abuse, two marriages—especially the one to a gynecologist who committed suicide—her own suicide attempts and her same-sex episodes. By the time the two hired guns were given the green light, Jessica Savitch, the middle-class Jewish girl from Pennsylvania, had become Tally Atwater from a little town in Nevada. Her husband, no longer a suicidal gynecologist, was a failed journalist who mentors his wife's budding career. Here are a sampling of the notes the Dunnes received as they submitted version after version:

"Keep it light. Keep the fun level up. Deliver the moment." "Better but not good enough. Don't let it go dreary. Lose or improve." "Too hostile. Modulate. Redo." "Punch up, bring down, rework, identify." "Make this scene more of an event. Clarify or change. More beats. Deliver the moment."

Scott Rudin, the movie's initial producer, advised the Dunnes that the picture was not about Jessica Savitch but a vehicle for two movie stars. Stars bring in the money. Content, cogency and cohesion are secondary. It doesn't matter about the plot holes as long as individual scenes "deliver the moment" and highlight whatever qualities the money-maker stars are noted for.

In the view of some old hands, the Dunnes were lucky they were allowed to stay together for the whole venture. In what is seen as a typical progression, the writer who initiates and sells a project idea is only expected to come up with a draft that is 40 percent or 50 percent up to par. He will get screen credit but has to make way for others hired by the producer and the director's input.

For example, not long ago the original writer pitched a comedy version of *Witness* (the crime drama-romance set chiefly in Amish country). The logline: In order to find a mother involved with an embezzlement racket, a tough, angry cop takes over a kindergarten class. After a 20-minute pitch, fielding questions about the beginning, middle and end, the "high concept" was approved by a star with limited acting ability, the producer notified the writer's agent and bought the project which then moved on to the next phase.

The star then chose a director who was able to keep things down to his limited acting ability and the writer was given 6 weeks to flesh things out and deliver a workable draft tailored to the star's one-dimensional popular image. Once the director decided that the first writer was "written out," he sought more perspective and other additions and corrections from a number of favorite freelancers.

One writer was brought in to give the narrative more action, another to focus on relationships (especially with the star and kindergarten kids), another to furnish the star with funny lines he could handle and sight gags, two more writers to supply more interesting situations, and another two to toss in more twists and turns. Of this group, two writing partners were called on to pull out unsympathetic characters and replace them with more pleasing personalities and decide how these new behavior patterns would affect each scene.

As this diverse material filtered in, the director cut and pasted, trying to keep the seams from showing, aiming for the illusion of a single unfolding story rather than the handiwork of seven workers on an assembly line and a capricious foreman. In the process, the director might approve one bit of rewriting while faxing other writers to try again. Each time an assemblage was given a temporary okay, it was tested in rehearsal and either vetted, adjusted on the spot by the director, or sent back for further cuts and pastes.

When asked about this approach, the director referred to the old studio system of the 1930s and '40s as writers under contract on the lot kept typing away, some adding snappy dialogue, some throwing in comic bits of business, some tightening the plotline, some beefing up a character and cutting down or eliminating another, and still others adding a little exposition here and there and fitting in bridges and transitions. For this director, in Hollywood nothing fundamentally had changed.

All told, as far as the veterans of the Farmers Market coffee klatch and most of their colleagues are concerned, L.A. is a company town and the product is a constant flow of marketable images that can be exported all over the world. A concept or a spec script is like a prospectus for a stock offering. The operative question is, What is the potential return on investment?

Apparently, the major preoccupation of initiators and fixers is keeping abreast of the market. The spate of horror films distributed far and wide may have run their course. While a few star-driven theme-park epics grossed $44 million during a first weekend in June, a number of irreverent, sophomoric comedies featuring little known TV actors may have grossed $30 million with a budget a tenth that of the tent-pole franchises. A closer look may also reveal that these R-rated comedies have become a staple, a reliable source of Hollywood profits and the under-known leads are ordinary looking guys who started out on the small screen as easily-identifiable types: the dolt with an unwarranted belief in his coolness; the put-upon loser, the ungainly goof who believes he has untapped athletic prowess, the bumbling everyman, etc.

Which, for some strategists, leads to a pipeline between TV and movies—e.g., a TV series that left some burning issue fans are dying to see resolved, not in more interrupted segments but in a complete feature film. Or a popular family show or cartoon that affords an opportunity for a full-scale adventure. Or a recycling of old favorites with fresh faces, trendy situations and dialogue while tossing in as much visual and auditory effects as possible; and then morphing into a sequel or brought back to people's living rooms depending on how it all plays out.

As for TV writing per se, for creators and staff writers, though a show may be shot on a studio lot, the development process is much more pressurized. The material has to be vetted, performed and broadcast within weeks rather than months and years. Just like the kindergarten movie, although there are exceptions, individual creativity is often sacrificed as some 20 writers contribute to a storyline, and dialogue is constantly tweaked. In the meantime, show runners and head writers are busy plotting the rest of the season's episodes, plot points, character arcs and the elimination and addition of characters to keep it all humming if the show appears to have a foreseeable future. The workload continues in the same vein or drastically changes in search of ways to boost ratings and avoid cancellation.

For the freelancer seeking to branch out or break in, the aim is to come up with fresh ideas during pitch meetings, either for a new episode of a particular series or for the kind of shows the producer is handling during a certain time slot. Given the insatiable demand for entertainment, programs vary from clever to mindless depending on your point of view:

"As unlucky lottery winner Dawn Budge, Rosie needs cosmetic help after an altercation with a bald eagle while paragliding." "The fact that Watros' fall pilot wasn't picked up left a spot open on her dance card. She will be playing Hurley's dearly departed sweetheart for multiple episodes during Desmond's flashbacks. There are still some very cool parts of her story left to tell." "*Dexter* feeds viewers' insatiable appetite for the macabre. The hero is a serial killer, albeit one who targets only bad guys. By day, he's a crime-scene analyst for the Miami police. But his life is spinning out of control and his killer timing is off. He's a little rusty after killing his brother. He feigns normalcy for his sister, girlfriend, and coworkers, but his mask begins to slip when his watery burying ground is discovered and an FBI 'rock star' is brought in to expose Miami's latest serial-killer sensation." "When a woman is murdered in Aaron's L.A. mansion, the team's investigation reveals a number of secrets and scandals." "This season, vampires have day jobs as detectives, reporters time-travel to get their stories straight, cheerleaders walk through fire, and people of all kinds talk to dead people, sometimes quite chattily. In addition, a piemaker-turned-detective also can raise the dead but only long enough to ask them whodunit."

As a variation on the last example, a character called Slacker Sam learns on his 21st birthday that his parents sold his soul to the devil before he was born and he is now an indentured servant to Hell. At any given time, in TV comedies as well as in dramas, vampires or the devil's henchmen may be infiltrating every conceivable profession. The rationale? As one television analyst put it, "When the world seems besieged by perils of our own creation, prime-time viewers seek a scapegoat like supernatural forces that are beyond our ken and not our fault."

Scouting around, a freelance script writer is apt to find more trendy clues that, like zombies, rise up or disappear in an era of short attention spans and aggressive jockeying for market shares:

"Tonight Joy revokes her husband's boudoir privileges after he insults her, and the naughty newlyweds are back with more domestic dystopia, sex-jinks and upscale shopping sprees, while Robin returns with a sexy souvenir: an Argentinean massage therapist." "A bashful computer and video-game whiz becomes a walking human database of government secrets when they're unwittingly downloaded into his brain. Suddenly he's the target of assassins and double agents and requires babysitting by two super-spies: lovely Sarah and brutish Casey." "Tonight, marine-biology major Amy finds that she's the only gal in a house full of messy guys, including one she'd like to know better."

For those playing the wild card that a spot on a TV writing team could be a ticket to future screen credits, there are more drawbacks, not to mention the prospect of a life sentence in and out of a TV ghetto. As indicated, the required research includes watching hours and hours of DVDs, learning each show's tone and style of humor (if it's a comedy), rhythm and pace of dialogue and typical stage business, plus the plots, character arcs and relationships the series has explored. Then it's a matter of getting hold of future plotlines to get a sense of where the storylines are headed within each format. All the while continuing to build up a large video and DVD library and concocting that fresh pitch at the most opportune moment as your agent slips you through the door.

On the plus side (if you're so inclined), those who devised the plight of Slacker Sam have managed to work both sides of the street—the Slacker series for TV and films replete with puerile brat humor, running roughshod over sexual taboos and invading what used to be called privacy. This kind of voyeuristic, irreverent humor often involves mishaps and embarrassments of an anatomical nature peppered with crude language and innuendos. The prevailing theory is that the more flagrant the behavior, the more true to life—what people actually do and say when caught in compromising situations. What follows in its wake is, supposedly, greater recognition on the part of viewers and accompanying guffaws, yowls and belly laughs.

What's more, it isn't just the young male demographic clamoring for this kind of entertainment. Marketers have found an equal distribution of males and females and both teens and their parents laughing and applauding just as heartily. For writers who feel at home here, the question becomes how to add to this brand of mayhem and how to hatch situations and bits of business that are even more outrageous.

Another clue is the home-burned DVDs of mating rituals of 20-year-olds cropping up on MySpace and YouTube disclosing intimate relationships that go astray. They're another source of information to add to the personal library, mine and offer to the networks in return for a seat around the table.

The Internet is also a platform for other programs beyond the static conversations and behavior of young mating rituals. Vuguru, Michael Eisner's (the former Disney chief) production company has offered questionable titles like *Prom Queen* and *Prom Queen: Summer Heat,* and who knows what else will appear as a spur for spin-offs or opportunity to find work.

Some, like the easygoing character in the musical *A Chorus Line* may say to themselves, "I can do that!"

At the same time, some veteran fixers may have misgivings, not only about the uncertain pipeline between television and film but about the direction both industries may be heading. They accept the fact that the chief function of the business is to stay in business. However, though they may consider themselves funny for money and hired guns, a number of them may also prefer to wait and see. The rationale: nothing in Hollywood is so rare as a new idea. A premise from yesteryear judged today as very done could attract old fans who are now listed as producers. As cycles change, the time may come around, just as it has with recycled old TV shows and comic heroes.

Veteran fixers may also recall work on a much different level and look for a chance to employ their old skills—not as initiators or repairmen, nor among those willing to go along no matter how loopy or inane the task— but as team players sharing the same sensibility and appreciating one another's work.

Seeking a Higher Ground

Harkening back to the advent of the talkies, some writers still insist there is a marked difference between a New York or East Coast sensibility and Hollywood, and even a difference in outlook between members of the Writers Guild of America East with its offices in Manhattan and the WGA West on La Brea. According to tradition, the silents perfected slapstick and low comedy but Hollywood required witty dialogue as soon as the talkies took over. The solution was to invite the playwrights and authors who congregated around Broadway and Greenwich Village to hop aboard a train and offer their services to the new medium. With all the shuttling back and forth and the number of writers from the East who have become Angelinos, this notion no longer holds water. Network shows emanating from New York are geared to putting out product and countless movies shot in and around Manhattan are green-lit with mainstream audiences and net proceeds in mind. Still and all, there are members of the WGAE who cringe when told that instructors in film schools in L.A. tell their students to draw a line between each page when writing comedy to make certain there is a funny bit of business or a funny one-liner above and below the mark.

During a conversation in New York at the WGA East with Larry

Gelbart and that other icon of stage and screen, Neil Simon, both men quoted the legendary Broadway producer George Abbott's golden rule: "You don't try to be funny. You play comedy as though it's serious dramatic material." They also pointed to Oscar Wilde's comic masterpiece *The Importance of Being Earnest* where witty characters talk about their lives and relationships, and experience a slew of misunderstandings, but there are no gratuitous pratfalls and not a joke to be had.

Gelbart and Simon went on to mention that in the golden age of live television and the Sid Caesar shows, "Sid would kill you during a writers' session if you came up with a joke-joke." Everything was based on the character within the given circumstances. The consensus was that first and foremost you needed a dramatic story. In Simon's *Brighton Beach Memoirs* (1986) the only one who seemed funny was young Eugene. The family went about their business and dealt with all sorts of problems. Eugene was antic and complained and mused like an antic kid from Brooklyn circa 1937 who fancied becoming a writer would complain and muse. There was no comic business within a contrived situation, no random one-liners or embarrassing mishaps solely for their own sake. In fact, Simon would often cut situations that received too many laughs, even though they were in character, because he wanted theatergoers and moviegoers alike to listen. In effect, through his characters he was saying, "I'm going to tell you something that I've never told anyone in my life." Like the moment in *Brighton Beach Memoirs* when Eugene confesses his feelings about his nubile cousin Nora who, in tandem with his aunt, has just taken up residence in his overcrowded home during the Depression.

To Simon and Gelbart this approach appeals to "the youngest instinct we have. We want to hear a story and something very personal." For both writers the main task is to come to terms with what the story is really about. This may entail fastening onto a vibrant memory or someone else's rich experience and then deepening it. And, whether in collaboration or on your own, letting the characters take you to the resolution.

In the 1950s on *Caesar's Hour* and *Your Show of Shows*, in collaboration with fellow writers like Mel Brooks and Carl Reiner, Simon and Gelbart would submit ideas for the good of each sketch.

In one session, from a Neil Simon idea anchored by Caesar's known drinking problem, a sketch was developed revolving around an avowed teetotaler played by Caesar. At his boss's insistence, after much protesting, the teetotaler reluctantly joins in a toast in honor of his wife's birthday and the couple's anniversary. Insisting that he will only have one, Caesar cautiously licks the drink like a cautious cat at a saucer of milk. Presently, he's seen at work, sneaking booze from an inkwell, flower vase, hollow leg of his desk and his typewriter roller until he becomes so inebriated, his boss has to fire him. Comedy, exaggerated but, at the same time, supported by closely observed behavior. Less farcical than a short TV sketch but within the same character-driven framework girded by closely observed behavior and a known set of circumstances, Simon wrote a screenplay based on Elaine May's adaptation of Bruce Jay Friedman's short story *A Change of Plan*. In this scenario (now called *The Heartbreak Kid*, 1972), Lenny, a young man, encounters a beautiful blond WASP from the Heartland while on his honeymoon in Miami Beach and subsequently tries to jilt Lila, his bride. Lenny's sexual anxiety was a syndrome endemic to repressed Jewish males brought up in the New York area, pressured to marry within their closed circle. For moviegoers well versed in the rituals along the New York to Miami Beach trail, the ensuing events were comical and rang true.

Some 35 years later, under the same title but in the hands of five studio writers who've been given screen credit, the plot is exploited, the venue relocated, and the relationships and action brought down to the lowest denominator. Here is an excerpt of a review of the 2007 recycled version of *The Heartbreak Kid* by A.O. Scott, film critic for the *New York Times*:

> [The writers'] squeamish, childish fascination with bodily ickiness, when crossed with the iffy sexual politics of the original, yields a comic vision remarkable for its hysterical misogyny. It is not just that their hero, a San Francisco sporting-goods salesman named Eddie, has some issues with women. These—narcissism, fear of commitment, a longing for the greener grass on the other side of the fence—are standard among romantic-comedy bachelors. The problem is that, unlike Ms. May and Mr. Simon, [these writers] have no interest in examining Eddie's psychology or his soul.
>
> Maybe that's because, back in 1972, when Eddie was named Lenny ... he actually had one. As impersonated by Ben Stiller, Eddie has only a collection of familiar grating behaviors....
>
> Rated R ... it has lots of profanity and several displays of extravagant—and, under the circumstances, inexplicable—female sexual enthusiasm.

Eddie, as played by Ben Stiller, is one of the marketable ordinary guys shuttled from television to movies. Gross behavior in the guise of realism is, again, the rationale behind the product.

And now back to the WGAE. In the top echelon of their own list of the greatest screenplays you will find *Annie Hall* (1977) by Woody Allen and Marshall Brickman, and *Tootsie* (1982) by Larry Gelbart and Murray Schisgal, with strong contributions by Elaine May and others, scripts that fall within the guidelines of, for want of a better name, New York rules.

During more recent times, those unwilling to compromise or who are seeking collaborative work outside the assembly line have had to rely on more limited markets. Producers like Sydney Pollack (the director of *Tootsie*, a trained actor at New York's Neighborhood Playhouse who has appeared in many films), who were once tightly bound to the studios, have reoriented their careers around less commercial fare in order to be free of current business models. Similarly, Fox Searchlight and its allied producers have generated modest projects, some that feature damaged characters who find themselves in alien territory.

Small teams of writers and writer-directors have concentrated on bittersweet tales like *The Darjeeling Limited* (2007) in which a trio of semi-estranged brothers join up to refresh their brotherhood after the death of their father. Moving from whimsy to melancholy and frustration, the brothers try to come to terms with their father's legacy and go on a trip to India in search of a mother who abandoned them to become a nun. This fixation on dysfunctional families (not unlike *Little Miss Sunshine*) that perplex its members may register as comic folly. But the object is not laughter at any price.

In another Fox Searchlight film, *The Savages* (2007), a daughter and son hurry to an off-center retirement community in Arizona and back to the East Coast in service of a mentally deteriorating father. The point being, there is a vast difference between the revelation of character and feeling as opposed to cranking out comic plots with little interest in finding out who these people really are, in searching for what is resonant and true instead of what is embarrassing in everyday life.

Which, in practical terms, still leaves writers on this level with the same dilemma: how to hire themselves out? Admittedly, it's far easier to meet at the coffee klatch on 3rd and Fairfax and break down the latest formulas in comedy, horror, action thrill rides and all the rest of it. While producers retool or modify old models to meet market trends, freelancers can do likewise with their old specialties, or retrain themselves to fit in. Or gripe and joke about it for the time being.

But no matter what direction a writer chooses to take, there is always the need to come to terms, to literally put the cards on the table and start to work.

12. The Screenwriter at Work: Guidelines and Gauges

All things considered, the first stage of composition relies on lessons learned and tools of the trade picked up along the way. In this way, you can determine where you're going and why, how you're going to get there and keep refining the storyline until you're ready to commit to a written draft. You don't have to do it this way, but through experience many screenwriters have discovered that it saves time to basically know exactly what you're doing.

The Seed and the Essentials

More often than not, the process begins with a promising notion which leads to a gathering of material which, in turn, spurs the writer on. Recalling the heartland's Ali Selim, he first became engrossed in a short story, let the story merge with his own immigrant legacy and research on a bygone era, refined it all and retold it through a certain set of images and scenes of yesteryear.

Michael Arndt started with a climactic image (a chubby pre-teen by the name of Olive competing with Barbie-like contestants) and then came up with Olive's dysfunctional family and the incidents that led up to their arrival at the contest and the final debacle.

When struck by a theme like Butch Cassidy and Sundance's second coming as South American bandits, William Goldman collected a number of facts and legends to draw on and then laid his plans.

To be more specific and complete, we can look at the creative progression of James C. Strouse's *Grace Is Gone* (2007). The seed was a concern over a disconnect between his brother and two nieces on a car trip in the Midwest. The issue was never disclosed. Strouse dearly wanted to resolve whatever was troubling them but was in no position to intervene.

As it happens, the war in Iraq was also on Strouse's mind and the toll it was taking on the families of loved ones at home. This concern, coupled with the still-troubling memory of the tension between his brother and his two daughters, eventually evolved into the notion of a father who failed his physical and was left with his two daughters while his wife served overseas in a combat zone. What if something happened to the wife? thought Strouse. How could he break the news to the girls (thus incorporating the strained silence in the real-life car trip but with stakes that were infinitely higher as the father tries to keep the devastating news from his children as best he can)?

After a time, the circumstances began to accumulate: Stanley Phillips' unassuming job as a manager in a home-supply store; a military officer and chaplain ringing Stanley's doorbell to deliver the crushing news; a younger liberal brother John who has no idea what is going on and likes to goad his patriotic older sibling; passing scenes of American highways and byways by day and night. Adding on, there is Heidi, the 12-year-old's insomnia over concern for her mother, her problem of falling asleep in class coupled with growing pains on the verge of puberty, a scene inside a shopping mall as Stanley tries to appease and please Heidi and her young sister, scenes revealing Stanley's guilt over flunking his physical due to his poor eyesight and his semi-ineptitude in understanding and dealing with his children.

The problem of skipping school and taking time off from his job leads to a trip to a theme park in sunny Florida as Stanley attempts to work out his impossible dilemma—keeping up a façade, breaking down alone at some point, trying to create some kind of joyous experience for his girls while holding off the inevitable great sorrow as long as he can.

In marked contrast to Strouse's tender, simple aim, Beatrice Christian came across a story by Raymond Carver, the American minimalist, and let the ramifications spin out in all directions. Carver's self-contained tale concerns a fisherman who discovered a body and kept the news to himself. In Christian's imagination, the setting shifts from small-town America to present-day *Jindabyne* (2006)—a fly-fishing resort in the middle of the Snowy Mountains in Christian's native southeastern Australia.

In former times, Jindabyne was an old settlement (now underwater) which, to Christian, gave the place a great deal of resonance with its shadows of submerged life hovering under the surface of daily experience. To this she added the body of a murdered young woman from a nearby Aboriginal community. As the building blocks progressed, characters and events began to take shape. Stewart, the husband of Claire, a transplanted American, makes the gruesome discovery of the body while fishing in the mountains with some male friends. Though shaken, Stewart and the others keep fishing, tethering the corpse to a log near the shore and letting a day and night pass before alerting the police.

As if this wasn't enough, not only did Ms. Christian graft on a local scandal that follows the news of the fishermen's behavior, but she also imbued Claire with a deep concern over the obligations of the living toward the dead. This then pitted Claire against the other white husbands and wives (who want to move on) and her husband, Stewart, who vacillates between guilt and confusion. And, as if all this wasn't enough, Christian adds other elements to the mix like the cross-customs, rituals and outrage on the part of the Aboriginal community and incomprehension between the two populations. Then there is a murderer (known only to the viewers), a hermit-like local electrician; Claire's marriage shadowed by her earlier breakdown and desertion after the birth of her son Tom; the unwelcome presence of Stewart's meddling mother; and a spooky preoccupation with death and drowning on the part of a secondary character's granddaughter. Added in also are aspects of local day-to-day life contrasted with the vastness of the outlying region and visual allusions to the natural world's active spiritual presence.

Arguably, Christian threw in much too much material relative to her inspirational source (Carver's short tale), but the film was made and her process serves as another kind of preliminary work.

In contrast as yet another option, there are times when a single, tightly charged seed is more than enough. Sifting through a novel by Michael Ledwidge, screenwriter Kelly Masterson found all of this: drug-dealing thugs in the Bronx, an embattled NYPD officer and his long-lost uncle (an IRA gunman and parolee from San Quentin), "a media-and-politics stoked murder rap" and racially tinged court trial, a shootout in the Pennsylvania woods with crazed white supremacists, a nervy Mafia widow and getaway driver, a celebrity diamond heist with military assault weapons in the heart of Rockefeller Center which inadvertently involved the Secret Service and the vice presidency, and enough fast-paced violence and chase sequences to fill a typical Hollywood actioner.

Casting almost all of this aside, Masterson came up with a catalyst. Retaining the title for the Sydney Lumet film *Before the Devil Knows You're Dead* (2007) (based on the Irish drinking toast, "May you get to heaven an hour before the Devil knows you're dead"), plus a remark about a win-win proposition, Masterson keyed on the conceit that you could commit an armed robbery in such a way that no one would get hurt and everybody would win. He then devised a setup, a set of characters and circumstances, and a self-contained cautionary tale about the vagaries of fate.

In Masterson's scenario, Andy, an older brother and Manhattan accountant, finds himself in need of a large sum of money and convinces his gullible younger brother, Hank, who has alimony problems, to hold up the family jewelry store in peaceful suburban Westchester at the most opportune time. In Andy's mind, surely neither he nor his brother would be a suspect; the nearsighted attendant could easily be locked in the back room cowering before a hooded Hank brandishing what she mistakenly believes is a real gun. Hank would know the exact location of the valuables, and the insurance would cover any loss for mom and pop. Masterson's chief problem was how to keep viewers engrossed and informed without giving too much away as this ticking time bomb and fiasco goes off.

With Strouse, the problem was how to begin at the last possible point and deepen Stanley's relationship with his girls while allowing for a private breakdown and recovery. How to setup a valid springboard for Stanley's spontaneous plan, setting off a variety of highs and lows that would avoid any semblance of a predictable road trip.

Clearly, Ms. Christian's structuring problem was more complex. How to juggle all her multi-stranded material? What would be a good starting point? Perhaps with the enigmatic electrician in his truck, bearing down on the unsuspecting young woman as she tools down a barren highway, singing a folk song. But then, how much time do you spend on Claire's marital problems, introducing the secondary town characters and their relationships and unhappy lives before you get to the fishing trip, the horrendous discovery, what it took to finally make the decision to call in the police, and the subsequent aftermath? Not to mention the murky subplots, rituals and the huge gap between the Aussies and Aboriginal spiritual world. How do you incorporate all this into a workable progression viewers can follow?

How do you devise a workable progression of any set of bits and pieces no matter how straightforward or complex?

The Storyboard and the Card System

The number of visual elements Ms. Christian had accumulated, coupled with the changing character arcs and relationships, required the use of a storyboard to put all her bits and pieces in some sort of order. In general, a storyboard is much like a graphic outline for a comic strip in that it consists of a series of rough sketches, flitting from panel to panel which, taken together, form a rough storyline. Later on, during preproduction, her director, Ray Lawrence, papered the length and breadth of a hall with colored images and descriptive headings and subheadings, working purely intuitively, never knowing exactly what he would find on location. He was also careful not to impose anything on the actors and allowed them to respond moment to moment, hopeful that he could capture a percentage of what Christian had in mind. In essence, even with a storyboard the structuring process was still loose and open-ended. Still and all, considering all the visuals and multi-layered material involved, it's safe to say that without a storyboard there would have been no way to lay out a coherent scheme.

For his part, taking into account his clear, simple trajectory, Strouse organized an intimate see-saw of occurrences to accomplish his aim and give Stanley opportunities to rediscover his two children while keeping his heart-breaking news as long as he could.

In this way, along the route from Minnesota to a theme park in the Sun-shine State, Stanley would be able to learn more about his daughters, who were naturally much closer to their mother. Heidi, his bright and sensitive 12-year-old, would have ample opportunity to express her moodiness, the cause and ramifications of her insomnia, and her growing unease and con-fusion over her father's behavior. Strouse also provided a stopover at a mall so that Stanley could grant the girls' wish to get their ears pierced and choose new dresses, leading to an episode when Dawn, the youngest, gets lost and crawls inside an oversized toy house. She then induces her father to get on his knees and join her along with sister Heidi and embrace within the safety of this home away from home—the incident acting as a forerunner to the "Enchanted Land" that awaits all three in sunny Florida. Then an episode of joy, then the inevitable disclosure. All in keeping with the tender, unhur-ried tone, all in sequence, all within the parameters of Stanley's fatherly mis-sion.

In a much tighter, more intricate vein, Masterson's structural ploy got him to the pivotal event in short order (a botched robbery). Instead of mov-ing forward like Christian and Strouse—all in due time—Masterson decided to back up using flashbacks that followed each of the main characters (over-confident Andy, hapless younger brother Hank, and their mother and father) up to the point of the heist. By then, Masterson assumed audiences would catch on to the fact that it was the mother who was critically wounded dur-ing the fiasco (taking the place of the nearsighted clerk who had to baby-sit). By then, audiences would realize that, though badly wounded, the mother had managed to shoot the perpetrator—a foolhardy small-time hood who had taken the place of frightened Hank and insisted on using a real gun. Now, presumably all set with this information, including the fact that Andy was embezzling money from his firm in Manhattan, Masterson decided viewers would be free to move past the crime and watch the domino effect take over as each move on the brothers' part raised the stakes. Everything, in turn, would get worse until the surprising but inevitable climax when Andy loses all control, gets shot in the interim, and his inconsolable, revengeful father finally puts the pieces together and removes his son's life support system in the hospital room.

What makes the intricacy of Masterson's preliminary scheme all the more remarkable is how he also charted Andy's growing desperation and added a scene with his father after the mother's funeral, an encounter they should have had long before, one where Andy finally confesses that he always tried to impress his father and get his approval, and the father confesses that he was too preoccupied and should have done a better job. All this, while Masterson made sure his plants and foreshadowing would keep paying off.

For instance, in one of the flashbacks before the robbery, Masterson placed Andy in a cage-like room in New York's diamond district making a deal with an old man he remembers from the old days when his father was a diamond merchant. Andy leaves the man his card and tells him to call him the moment he has his share of the take. After the senseless death of his wife and having received no satisfaction from the police, while pursuing the matter on his own, Masterson has the father call on the same old man for a lead. The old man, expressing his longstanding resentment of the father's self-righteousness and disdain, hands him Andy's calling card and says, "The world is an evil place. Some people make money from it and some people are destroyed by it." It's a message, carefully placed at just the right time in just the right order.

Summing up, in this way of working, once a seed becomes compelling, you begin stockpiling a world with ample material to choose from. Then you establish a tone and put it all in some kind of order. Back to Goldman's *Butch Cassidy*, taking a cue from Butch's affability, a plethora of fact and fiction and a keen sense of the waning years of the wide open West, Butch continues to commit lively robberies with his pal Sundance, makes his getaway in a hole-in-the-wall canyon and all the while no one gets hurt. Then the duo take off for South America when the going gets rough and play bandit all over again until Butch and Sundance pass into legend.

In random, modern times, substituting a cold, calculating, dysfunctional Andy in a compressed urban setting, Masterson makes certain every criminal move has a ripple effect and everybody gets hurt. Andy's plan to manipulate mindless Hank and take the loot and run off to South America with a wife who is secretly cheating on him with Hank gave Masterson a totally different tone and set of options than Goldman's orchestration of comedic, romantic and western elements from yesteryear.

The same process applies to projects like Ms. Christian's *Jindabyne* with its juxtaposition of crime, family strife and psychological factors, strained relationships, social and inter-cultural issues, underlying mythic forces and rituals. How to handle it all became so problematic, storyboarding was the only answer. Strouse had far less to juggle as did Selim, but Selim had to do far more research. In relation to Strouse, Arndt had a road trip leading up to the spur for his composition (Olive and the silly beauty contest) instead of the other way around, a greater range of characters but hardly anything as meaningful at stake.

At any rate, when making rough sketches and jottings and tacking them up on a bulletin board or taping them across a wall won't do, one device seasoned writers use is a pack of index cards—3 × 5 or 4 × 6—labeled and shuffled until they lay out in some workable order.

Typically, each scene card is marked with a slugline (EXT. HOLE IN THE WALL ENTRANCE—MIDDAY). Cards can also alert the writer about the progress of each major character along their course, the length and rhythm of the shot flow and the variety of locales. In this way you can also note when characters have overstayed their welcome or need to be brought back, which supporting players are helping or obstructing (which makes them vital), which minor characters can be eliminated or morphed into one or two single roles.

In using cards in this way, some writers underline each character's name in a different colored pen to keep track. Cards can be numbered and color-coded—e.g., white for plot movement, green for pointers and foreshadowing, light blue for character development, red for pivotal scenes or moments when plants pay off and the stakes grow higher. Yellow can be used to indicate possible visual effects, or a montage of shots indicating a sense of place or span of time and some kind of linkage. Other colors can mark interludes or points when the tension subsides for a while before building up again.

Some writers choose to work with only a partial deck (so to speak) when the aim is to churn out a timely message. This seems to have been the case when Matthew Michael Carnahan contrived *Lions for Lambs* (2007), the one prompted by a moment when he found himself skipping past the TV news looking for a Southern Cal football game. This just after occasions when he and his friends panned U.S. foreign policy, ingratiating journalists and crafty politicians. It crossed his mind that he and those like him did a lot of talking but contributed nothing. First conceived as a play, in Carnahan's story-line, Todd Hayes (Carnahan's stand-in) is kept seated in a history professor's office for an hour while being chided for his flip complacency, bad attendance record, lack of initiative, and other matters re: current affairs and the generation gap.

As the notion transformed into a movie scenario, two other set pieces were added: one in an engaging Republican senator's office, the other on a darkened, snow-blown mountaintop in Afghanistan. Each segue to the senator's office was as visually inert as the cutaways to the professor's domain.

But somehow that didn't seem to matter. The senator attempts to sell his idea of a military initiative to a timorous lady newscaster and one-time supporter. Again Carnahan sketches in a generation gap (she is 20 years older), the same timeline (she's given an hour for this exclusive), and an act of verbal persuasion. The only difference being that this time the power belongs to the younger person who has a background in military intelligence and the seated newscaster can only resort to making notes, a few twitches, blinks, shrugs and head bobs, comments and quiet misgivings.

The third cutaway and centerpiece shifts to the results of the senator's initiative as Todd's two marginalized classmates, one Latino and one African American, fall out of a helicopter under enemy fire. Badly injured, they both land within close proximity and, except for occasionally firing their weapons and two intermittent supportive air strikes, they too are unable to move as a superior enemy force closes in.

This schematic hinges simply on whether the senator, with his eye on the White House, gets a call as to the fate of his Afghan misadventure. The cutaways to Todd's meeting with his professor simply hinge on whether Todd will change his attitude, agree to start attending class again and become proactive. All the while, there is the fate of the two stranded buddies hanging in the balance.

Using a full deck (so to speak), Carnahan could have brought this scenario more fully to life, focused on character development and raised the stakes. He could have found a way to keep Todd out of the professor's office, disrupt his easy lifestyle and flip banter and set him in motion. Keying on the light blue cards, there would have to be more to Todd than meets the eye, a range of colors and actions in conflict with other characters with an equally varied palette so that something could be risked leading to ramifications. The yellow cards would involve the camera as the scenes now have to open up. The green cards (pointers and foreshadowing) could indicate events and matters unknown to Todd himself leading to some compelling event. And the red cards (pivotal moments) detailing when, for no apparent reason, a character does something like turn onto a country road at the first flicker of dawn, leave his car and shamble up a slope toward three grazing horses (*Michael Clayton*, 2007) and remain there in quiet communion. This saves his life and turns the whole story in another direction as his car is blown up below through a remote-control device and he becomes a relentless pursuer instead of a complacent "bag man and janitor."

But again, it all goes back to the seed, followed by the gathering of material and the overall aim. The more complex, the more parts to the engine, the more knowledge of the working parts required to build it and make it run.

Beats, Scenes and Sequences

In screenwriting terms, the basic unit is a beat—a single action, pause or expressive moment. Each scene is composed of a number of these beats which complicate, intensify, advance the action or quiet things down and spill over. A sequence is made up of a number of scenes and associated beats that combine to serve a major purpose, like the opening wedding reception in *The Godfather* (1972). Hot-headed elder son Sonny confronts photographers and breaks one of their flash-bulb cameras by the vintage parked limousines; suited men arrive on the periphery who appear to be from a law enforcement agency; a scene takes place inside the sprawling estate as the Godfather holds court in his darkened chambers, stroking a cat, meting out favors and justice on this, his daughter's wedding day. There is a sing-a-long of a popular Italian ditty in the expansive sunlit patio; a beat with a stocky, tipsy, middle-aged man making a joke about the canapés he's been sampling, calling them "a can of peas"; a soldier in uniform, quiet and articulate, sits across from a genteel, well-dressed young woman, politely discussing the nature of his family and heritage; a popular singing star comes on the scene to great applause and dedicates a number to the bride; and then a montage of swirling dancers in fancy-dress period garb. All of this serves as exposition, set-up and provocative mystery.

In index cards terms, a great deal of yellow and white.

When breaking a project down into a conventional 3-act structure, one or two sequences can form a first act, a half dozen can make up a second act, a final act can consist of a long heightened, dovetailing sequence with many intercuts, followed by a few short scenes that tie up the loose ends. As ever and always, it all depends. Breaking it all into three conventional acts may not do at all, and a series of scenes of varied lengths that bleed into one long sequence may seem to be more effective. Or an aftermath of many smaller scenes, and a short sequence highlighted by a few memorable moments. In fact it may turn out that a few memorable moments are what the work is truly about, and madcap or heightened sequences would be totally inappropriate. It's all a matter of orchestrating and finding the right rhythm, highs and lows and the kind of momentum best suited for the tone and nature of the particular outing.

Less cards to deal, but each one, hopefully, a gem.

An example of a memorable moment can be found in screenwriter Joan Tewkesbury's love of the dramatic pause: that tension between words, where words are superfluous and time is suspended. In this case, the setting is a seedy motel room in Jackson, Mississippi, during the Depression. The girlfriend of Bowie, the bank robber, sits at a dressing table and asks if Bowie loves her. After a long silence, she asks again. The dual reflection in the mirror catches what each is afraid to say: her desperation for a reassuring answer; his anxiety in the shadows as he glances off, perhaps awaiting imminent capture, perhaps wishing he wasn't so poor or had a chance to undo his crime, perhaps simply avoiding her. Because of the camera's ability to penetrate and capture the essence of a moment, the non-verbal indication was all that was needed and the reverberations speak for themselves.

Sometimes a writer can decide to avoid full scenes altogether, opting for a headlong, rougher style like the French New Wave of the mid–20th century, employing abrupt cuts to suggest unpredictable lived experience. The aim: moments that accumulate with an on-the-fly immediacy instead of the standard beginning, middle and end. A feeling that the camera is tagging along, wondering what it will find and what will happen next; the total opposite of a more stilted style where everything is controlled and contrived down to staged entrances and exits.

In any event, the use of beats, scenes and scenarios calls for a second pass, a more detailed set of cards and more shuffling and reshuffling. With this kind of fine tuning there's a hope and a sense that the construction is becoming richer than ever.

There's also a growing sense of involvement on the writer's part as the beats, scenes and scenarios begin to unfold, a greater feeling of an actual movie as the actor-characters move from point to point.

A prime example is a transfer from Strouse's concerns about his brother and nieces on the real-life car trip to the unfolding happenings during the construction process. At a certain stage in *Grace Is Gone*, Heidi, the oldest daughter, gets out of bed in a darkened motel room while her father and little sister Dawn are sound asleep. She looks around aimlessly, drifts outside, meets up with an older teenage boy who offers her a cigarette. Stanley wakens, realizes Heidi is gone, races down the hall looking high and low, finally spots her and the older teenager and shoos him off. Next, Strouse indicates a cut to Heidi and Stanley by a wall, as Stanley pulls out a pack of cigarettes and they dicker over whether to have one apiece or share. Heidi suggests they share, tries a puff, Stanley says, "Good one," takes a drag himself and goes into a coughing fit as Heidi runs off for water. As soon as Heidi is out of sight, Stanley takes a deep, consoling drag from the cigarette and then another.

Implicit in all this is a tie-in between the screenwriter's growing involvement and the probability of the same kind of caring on the part of the audience (provided it's all cast and directed properly). If so, the unspoken questions would go something like this: Is Heidi thinking about her mother again? Is she disoriented? What will she do? What will happen to her? She saw the teenage boy earlier at the indoor pool with an older woman, but who is he? What is he capable of? What is he doing out there on the sidewalk at this time of night? Will Heidi be safe and able to hold her own? Will Stanley catch up with her in time? Has mild-mannered Stanley been remiss, especially when you take into account Heidi's recent bouts of insomnia? Is he capable of warding off the loitering teenager without further complications? Under these trying conditions, will he scold Heidi or find some way to keep things on an even keel, find a way to satisfy Heidi's curiosity and discourage her from smoking without making an issue of it? And then, when she's not looking, calm himself and sustain his tack of postponing the inevitable?

And what about young Dawn, all alone in the motel room? What if she wakes up and finds her father and older sister gone?

Presumably, if the detailed work is going well, these kind of concerns will be built in. Heidi is changing, perhaps even more rapidly because of the circumstances she finds herself in. She must be wondering why her dad is doing this. Did he lose his job? Her mom would certainly be mad if she found out. What's going on here, and within herself, and how can she handle it all?

If the detailed work is not going well, the construction process will just be done for its own sake and the evolving emotional factor will be at a minimum on the part of the writer, the characters, influential readers, actors, directors and audiences. No one will be wondering what's going on and what will happen next.

No doubt it takes an ability to see from all these angles, including through the lens to make, let alone test and keep track of, evolving sets of color-coded cards. It's easy to get lost in all the details and forget it's just a preliminary blueprint. That's why there are those who would much rather rely on a simpler, more calculating first step and worry about the rest later.

The Log Line or Premise

In commercial terms, instead of a seed or compelling catalyst, it all boils down to a one-line story description called a high-concept or log line—e.g., "A streetwalker is paid 3,000 dollars to be a week's companion for a millionaire." Or, "The last man on earth discovers he's not alone." In commercial terms, a good log line is catchy, one that can translate into a big-budget star-driven movie that has great marketing potential. In creative terms, a one-sentence log line can also serve a purpose. It can tell you what all the cards or sketches add up to so far or even that they don't really add up at all.

Before the Devil Knows You're Dead can be distilled to, "An overextended accountant lures his younger brother into a larcenous scheme but when the seemingly perfect crime goes awry, the damage lands right at the family's doorstep."

Often a first attempt at a log line can seem too pat: "Two people meet, spend a day walking around New York and learn about each other." By being much more specific and doing a lot of observing, a more promising log line can emerge: "A former international sports star confronts his past and demonstrates how a loving family can assist his new friend Tammy in coming to grips with her feelings and confronting her future" (*Bella*, 2006).

There are also times when writing a log line can alert you to the fact that the whole project may be misguided. At the outset, it may have seemed like a pure indie take on life on the fringe but, early on, a log line can tell you something is amiss. Consider this clunky example:

"Sonny, a would-be country singer, leaves his dead-end job, abandons his wife and young baby to set off with his funky manager in a run-down pink Cadillac in hopes of doing well at a karaoke contest in Jackpot, Nevada, and landing a record contract."

Looking a little deeper would signal that even on the most marginal art house and college circuit, there is something off-putting about the whole enterprise. Especially after a glance at even a few specific scenes the writer may have in mind. Take Sonny's mailings of lottery tickets to his wife in lieu of child support. Or, a self-help cassette blaring advice as the Cadillac speeds along a bleak western landscape; Sonny's conversation with his father and mentally challenged brother over his dubious childhood; Sonny's liaison with an underaged girl (the daughter of a woman he picks up in a seedy bar), etc. The prospect of raising money and going through the process of production and marketing based on a tale about a mindless, deadbeat dad is certainly borderline at best (*Jackpot*, 2001).

A Motif as Linchpin

When a log line still seems too pat (off-putting scenarios like *Jackpot* aside), an underlying strain may boost a simple, preparatory effort.

Chances are, themes that come readily to mind just won't do. The story may not be about healing, or finding your way home, redemption, searching for a one true love no matter how long it takes, or the light at the end of the tunnel, or any other familiar strand. There's also a good chance that an old myth can't be grafted on either, especially if you're dealing with the real world. In all likelihood it has nothing to do with a hero going forth into strange territory, learning new rules, being tested, experiencing a death and rebirth, encountering and defeating a nefarious foe and returning with a boon that benefits the community. In all likelihood it isn't about reason winning out over irrational and random forces either, or a self-sacrificing heroine saving the day.

Once you've set up some kind of reality along with three-dimensional characters who have a stake in the outcome—even in as light a piece as *Little Miss Sunshine*—it all has to be played out on its own terms. Even if the occasion for this particular outing has a built-in movie appeal—a voyage to a foreign land, a sporting event, a feud, a trek into the wild, a search for a mole in the upper echelons of British Intelligence—this in itself may be familiar but it's missing some necessary thread that strikes a chord.

Arndt's *Little Miss Sunshine* rides on an underlying need for authenticity; Selim's *Sweet Land* and Goldman's *Butch Cassidy* revolve around a quest for renewal; Masterson's adaptation of a cautionary tale rests on the age-old price of hubris and folly. The haunting presence of a young woman who has recently died runs all through *Grace Is Gone* and *Jindabyne* and affects everything that happens. All five are new takes supported by a universal thread.

If you look hard enough, you may find two general strands running through a chain of possible events, like family and secrets, which, taken together, become a motif of family secrets. Since a motif provides you with a subject everyone can relate to, and a log line can reassure you that what you're up to is comparatively novel, the only thing left to do at this point is make sure there are some underlying engrossing questions.

For example, in the Danish film *After the Wedding* (2006), Susanne Bier created a dramatic situation, a motif that struck a chord (family secrets), and the kinds of implicit questions that keep an audience involved. In her scenario, Jacob Peterson, a manager of an orphanage in India, is sent back to Copenhagen when the orphanage is threatened by closure. A pivotal character in the form of a Danish businessman then offers him $4 million to keep the orphanage going. Only there is a catch. Peterson has to attend the businessman's daughter's wedding, stay in Denmark and run the trust from there.

The first in a succession of provocative secrets is the disclosure at the wedding that the businessman is not the bride's biological father; the next disclosure reveals that that honor belongs to Peterson. Other family secrets are prized out including details about Peterson's checkered past and the bride's mother. Peterson is caught between his role as a father figure at the orphanage and the pressure to take on a new role of father to the bride, plus another revelation that the businessman is dying and desperately needs Peterson to take his place, reside in Denmark permanently and take care of the family. To underscore all of this, Ms. Bier made certain there was a strong backstory of secrets that kept impinging on the present and future.

Of course, this takes us well beyond just a log line and motif, but it shows how running with a motif leads to a set of scenes and engrossing questions.

In another variation on the motif of secrets, Naomi Foner's *Running On Empty* (1988) has a plot that could be broken down into a log line about a tight-knit family of four (a father, mother and two sons) whose unfortunate secret kept them running, held them together and threatened the future of the older child. The secret? In the backstory, Arthur and Annie Pope blew up a napalm lab to protest the Vietnam War. As a result, they've been a fugitive family for the past 15 years. To make matters worse, a janitor who wasn't supposed to be in the building was blinded.

The engrossing question? How long can they keep this up? Parents are powerful people; children are dependent. But now that the eldest boy is seventeen, the piano lessons Annie, the mother (a once promising musician), gave him have brought his talents to the attention of a high school music teacher who is also the father of the girl he's falling in love with.

And now the premise, the motif and the engrossing question begins to steamroll. Though Arthur, the father, is the son of an ardent Bolshevik and keeps telling himself that he and Annie had to do something 15 years ago to gain the attention of the hawks in government and has to now keep the family unit intact, Annie realizes that her son deserves to accept a scholarship to Julliard and have a life of his own. Constantly changing identities and running from state to state is simply unfair. As painful as it may be, she must risk everything and go to her capitalist father—though she hasn't seen him all these years, though he was the sworn enemy of the cause, though he might even turn her and Arthur in.

More backstory, based on undisclosed information that impinges on the present and future.

At a point of no return, Annie goes to Manhattan and pleads with her father to look after her son. Family, plus secrets revealed under pressure as the eldest son confides in his girlfriend because he doesn't want to lose her and assume yet another false identity; and Annie confides to her father that she has missed him and her mother, has cried out to them in the middle of the night, has suffered tremendous feelings of guilt and is truly sorry.

Looking further, sometimes a general motif can be split so that, say, family matters take second place and then become more prominent. Turning back to Tony Gilroy's *Michael Clayton* (the one about the passive bag man who finally becomes active), not only is the title character a mystery to his estranged family (including a brother-in-law on the police force), he's a mystery to himself and what's really going on in his life: 45 years old and broke, a divorced father trying to stay close to his son, in debt to mobsters after going into partnership with his alcoholic brother who is still an enigma.

Moving on, as Gilroy's motif and premise begins to build, Clayton has been working for years for a prestigious Manhattan law firm that cleans up messes he doesn't understand until he finally learns that a $3 billion class action suit brought against one of the firm's clients, a large chemical company culpable of selling a toxic weed-killer. The whistleblower he's been dispatched to contain has been murdered and all along he's just been that selfsame bag man and "janitor." Amid all the dirty secrets and moral squalor of corporate power and what passes for what's left of his messed-up family connections, it's little wonder that he veers off the road to commune atop a hill with three horses and then, after his car blows up at the hands of some high-tech thugs, at last begins to come to terms with things. And perhaps most important of all, he has a scene with his bright 10-year-old son in an effort to keep the boy on the sensible path of decency.

Admittedly, this has gone well beyond a premise, motif and engrossing questions, but that is perhaps the whole point. It becomes what appears to be a tale worth telling.

Storytelling and a Treatment

At some juncture, regardless of how simple or complex the preparatory approach, a number of writers become storytellers and write it all down as if they were telling a tale to a captive audience around the campfire. Some, thinking in purely commercial terms, practice telling it over and over, envisioning themselves seated across from a studio executive after being given a 5-minute time limit, just like the pitchmen in *The Player*.

Pitchmen aside, in one method the story is retold in a traditional form. At the outset there is the life, the establishment of the kind of world we're in. This sets up the logic and the rules of the game. At the same time, within this world, there is a sense of something in the air, a kind of volatile balance that's about to be disturbed and set everything in motion. This is definitely not just another day. This is the day that Butch discovers a new, formidable bank vault; the day that mom brings home her suicidal brother and little Olive is on pins and needles to hear whether or not she's been accepted as a contestant in the Miss Sunshine competition: and cock-sure Andy, the embezzler, is about to learn there is going to be an internal audit.

This is also the day Stanley will hear the tragic news about his wife, and the day the Popes' eldest son will discover a suspicious car lurking in the neighborhood which will send the family on the run again, but this time to a state and a school district close enough to Manhattan that will change everything and everyone. It's also the day that Michael Clayton will be sent to baby-sit the firm's chief litigator who has gone off his medication and is ranting about a day of reckoning; and the day that Jacob Peterson has to fly to Denmark or else, and on and on it goes. When the disruption hits, it leaves in its wake an imbalance seeking balance. But any effort to right matters will meet resistance leading to complications. A new, uncharacteristic set of tactics under the circumstances (active or deflecting) will only cause other unknowns. As a result, whatever balance or truce is finally achieved will in no way resemble the old way of being. Significant changes have taken place and nothing will ever be the same.

In commercial terms, no matter what storytelling form is used, it's called a treatment. It runs from 5 to 20 pages and is written in the active voice, present tense, and includes only what an audience will hear and see on the screen. Key exchanges of dialogue can be added as a selling point if the story is geared to attract certain box-office names. In commercial terms, along with a log line, the purpose of a treatment is to convince a producer, executive, first reader or story editor at a studio that there is a marketable movie experience in the offing. Generally speaking, a treatment can be composed at any time but, as a marketing tool, it usually comes into play after all is said and done.

Other Patterns, Other Plans

As indicated, the procedures noted have been used in part or in various combinations. Recalling Goldman's treatment about an estranged detective and his intrepid offspring who wanted to follow in his footsteps (with a few kidnappings thrown in), a few colleagues who'll peruse a quick treatment and tell you the direction you could or should have taken is another option.

For writer-salesmen who stay strictly within the framework of a genre or current sub-genre, a premise is more like a catchy advertising phrase: "The truth can always be adjusted," "One spark of faith is all it takes to revive a magical toy store," "In open country you can find most anything."

Or they'll start with a catchy what if. "What if a popular political satirist ran for president and won?" From there they can segue to a log line, transcribe it to a standard 3-act outline (see the appendix) and transcribe that into a treatment. On a more creative note, one prominent screenwriter can't begin unless a question really scares him or he finds some great human dilemma that's worth trying to answer whether he succeeds or not. And with each of his characters the question always arises: What's the worst thing that can happen to him? More often than not, these concerns lead him into a weave of three or four storylines.

There are writers who tend to be philosophical and know exactly where they are going and why but need to go through a great deal of trial and error in order to discover who their characters are and how they're going to get to where they're going.

Back to strictly commercial considerations, some adjust their method trying to keep one step ahead of the market, a pattern that might consist of a setup and then a hook that literally hooks into the story and sends it spinning off in another direction, followed by a calibrated set of twists and turns at different intervals, leading to a climactic sequence and a surprise ending. Often the format goes like this:

> The main plot involves a protagonist who goes through a forced series of crises, plot twists and major reversals. To enhance the main action, a subplot is introduced after the initial turning point which serves as a counterpoint to the main plot. It may seem totally unrelated but somewhere along the line a connection is made. The subplot can develop its own separate plot line, hint at secrets or be used to drop clues that will develop and/or pay off later as more serious crises increase the pressure on the protagonist, all of which brings us to the major crisis and resolution.

One award-winning screenwriter simply refers to his bent for over-surprising in an effort to keep producers reading and viewers watching. In a somewhat similar vein, some crank out blueprints that turn on hook after hook, climax after climax and are well suited for franchise theme-park rides, low-grade suspense tales and fantasy escapades and the like. As another selling tool, still others map out a storyline tailored for a particular star or co-stars with other characters serving solely as functionaries.

Moreover (as noted earlier in the development of the Amish story), there are partners who brainstorm and compliment each other's strengths and weaknesses, one perhaps in charge of the plotline and the other handling character development. Screenwriters have also been known to sketch a loose-knit storyboard centering on shot flow and action, centering on memorable visuals like locusts endangering a wheat harvest at the turn of the 20th century in Russia. Indie writers, working on a shoestring, have made do with just an idea, like two carefree friends wandering off in the desert just for the fun of it and losing track of both the road and their car. What happens next is open-ended.

In the final analysis, with over 12,000 professional screenwriters on the rolls, there may be too many first-step approaches to even begin to calculate.

On the total opposite end of the spectrum, there are one-size-fits-all programs for those who have no approach, want to try their hand but feel they need a prompter. One that comes to mind is a software product called

Dramatica Pro which bears a close resemblance to a Create-Your-Own-Adventure-Story guide. Using popular models like *Star Wars*, a generic writing partner cues subscribers to answer a series of simple questions like, "What's your story called? Who are the main characters? Do your characters' efforts achieve overall success like killing the shark in *Jaws*, or failure like not opening the dinosaur theme park in *Jurassic Park*?"

Of course, anyone serious about the craft realizes that screenplays are based on thoughtful, informed and highly individualized groundwork. And that once a plan is in place, you press on and create the final product.

13. Scripting, Polishing and Other Nuts and Bolts

We began with the first sequence from Lehman's *North by Northwest*. An opening scene from Goldman's *Butch Cassidy and the Sundance Kid* appeared in the following chapter and other polished excerpts cropped up as we went along. In that light, you could say that segueing from the card shuffling, etc., and putting it down into script form marks the true beginning. Then the multiple revisions with breaks in between to let the work gestate before the script is in good enough shape to be shared.

The first draft may contain beats that are too choppy, dialogue that's stilted, montages that are more like jump cuts, and scenes that get bogged down. Some writers go at it slowly, one scene at a time, moving through the action before tackling other matters like character development. Some go at it hurriedly, trusting to instinct before concentrating on any given aspect. In any case, the aim is to finally get the story down on the page keeping the ultimate end in mind: a professional-looking script ready for submission.

To avoid any formatting concerns that might get in the way, writers have turned to software like Final Draft, which does the work for you. This program has a feature that formats to industry standards as you write. It also remembers and automatically fills in character names, scene headings, transitions, and locations. The claim is that all you have to do is "use your creative energy to focus on the content and let the program take care of the style."

As a tried-and-true alternative, writers have opted to maintain total control by learning the proper format from others, or by example from their favorite published scripts, or by downloading screenplay style sheets on the Internet and creating their own programs.

In all cases, Courier 12-point type or Times New Roman is standard, and italics, bold or different sized fonts are avoided. Each 8½ × 11-inch page of script generally equals a minute of screen time. Scenes are not broken into camera shots but are treated as master scenes. The more freely-paragraphed—

written in the present tense, active voice, double-spaced between concise stage directions—the closer to a final draft each go-round will be and the more easily revised.

Seeing It Through

For the aspiring screenwriter there is, of course, no tried-and-true, no successful copies of his final drafts and shooting scripts to draw from. At best, if everything is in place, there is a sense of readiness and the prospect of trial and error and encouragement down the line.

During the first run-through, it might be best to create a rough draft all the way through from start to finish. And to keep in mind that it will take more run-throughs, revisions and fine tuning on its way to some kind of hoped-for but never fully realized perfection. This sure and steady approach is the direct opposite of churning out a commercial product, gambling that it will still be hot as it makes the rounds of agents, producers and production companies. Depending on how many layers of meaning you're trying to juggle, it will take a comparatively longer period of time to shape, distill and mature. In working this way with that selfsame sense of purpose and ultimate reward sometime in the future, there may be no better model than the steps Michael Arndt took in shaping his Academy Award-winning script for *Little Miss Sunshine.*

Misrepresented as "a rookie screenwriter" who just happened to "hit a classic comedy home run his first time up," the path he took is all the more meaningful in that he could have easily lowered his sights. He could have aimed for yet another road comedy. He certainly could have simplified his task and settled for far fewer revisions, which included making marked adjustments to his characters and changing locales from Maryland to Boca Raton and switching from Albuquerque to Redondo Beach. He also could have blocked out any mainstream concerns and lost himself in a personal, indie exploration. But he was one of those who know exactly where they're going and why but need to go through the mill in order to discover how they're going to get there. A writer who would rather keep scripting until he finds a throughline that's both accessible and unique, focused and controlled, yet fully human and spontaneously alive.

How this style of composition works and how it all came about becomes clearer when you spring forward and compare an early version of *Little Miss Sunshine* with a finished shooting script. And when, at an appropriate interval, you pull back to appreciate how Arndt arrived at this project in the first place.

The following rough opening of what became a final set of 23 scenes was entitled "The Hoovers Plus One":

FADE IN:
VIDEO PIXEL
Five young women stand side by side, waiting to be judged—breathless, hopeful. A name is announced. Four hearts break.
The camera zooms across the smiles of the losers to find a winner. She bursts into tears, hugs the nearest runner up.
Begin CREDITS.
MUSIC—quiet and melancholy—plays over all the opening scenes, leading to the Title card.
The Contest Winner cries and hugs the Runners-up as she has the tiara pinned on her head. Then—carrying her bouquet—she strolls down the runway, waving and blowing kisses.
INT. BASEMENT REC ROOM—DAY
A six-year-old girl sits watching the show intently. This is OLIVE. She is big for her age and slightly plump. She has frizzy hair and wears black-rimmed glasses. She studies the show very earnestly.
Then, using a remote, she FREEZES the image.
Absently, she holds up one hand and mimics the waving style of Miss America. She REWINDS the tape and starts all over.
Again, Miss America hears her name announced, and once again breaks down in tears—overwhelmed and triumphant.
                    RICHARD (VOICE OVER)
         There's two kinds of people in this world—Winners ... and Losers.
INT. CLASSROOM—DAY
RICHARD (45) stands at the front of a generic community college classroom—cinderblock walls, industrial carpeting.
He wears pleated khaki shorts, a golf shirt, sneakers. He moves with the stocky, stiff-legged gait of a former athlete. His peppy, upbeat demeanor just barely masks a seething sense of insecurity and frustration. MUSIC continues underneath.
                    RICHARD
         If there's one thing you take away from the nine weeks we've spent,
         it should be this: Winners and Losers. What's the difference?
With a remote, RICHARD clicks through a Power Point presentation, projected on the wall behind him.
The slides mimic Darwin's "Evolution of Man" chart, except that they show a lumpy, hunched-over, sad-sack "Loser" evolve into a smiling, triumphant, arms-over-his-head "Winner."
                    RICHARD (CONT'D)
         Winners see their dreams come true. Winners see what they want
         and they go out and get it. They don't hesitate. They don't make
         excuses. And they don't give up. Losers don't get what they want.

After 20 students clap half-heartedly in a classroom that could seat 200, the scene shifts to Sheryl, in her 40s, wearing office attire and a name tag, smoking and talking on a cell phone in her car. In a short bit of dialogue she tells Richard she doesn't know how long it will be and that "*he* doesn't have anywhere else to go," claims she's not smoking, announces she's at the hospital and that she'll pick up a bucket of chicken.

The scene then shifts to a hospital corridor where Sheryl goes from room to room checking numbers. She finds the room she's looking for and nearly collides with a doctor who, in the space of four clipped lines of dialogue, informs Sheryl to keep her brother away from sharp objects and depressants. Switching immediately to the interior of her brother's hospital room, there is a shot of a wheelchair parked against a wall. The script informs us that it's Sheryl's brother, Frank, who is also middle-aged and whose wrists are wrapped in bandages. There is an exchange of three quick lines and a hug as Sheryl tells her totally withdrawn brother that she's glad he's still here and he replies that that only makes one of them. All told, it takes only about 30 seconds and two shots in adjacent locales to establish that there is something quirky going on. Attempted suicide certainly isn't comical but, given Arndt's tone and point of view, it seems to be a part of Sheryl's dysfunctional world. Almost as if it's just another day but a little bit worse.

For the next few seconds, we're in a bathroom in the suburbs as an 80-year-old man (GRANPA) secretly snorts a few lines of cocaine. Instantly, the scene changes to the interior of an adjoining bedroom as a teenager with a Mohawk haircut presses a barbell under a huge portrait of Friedrich Nietzsche, does sit-ups, push-ups, goes to a long roll of computer paper blatantly marked "Enlistment" filled with a seemingly endless amount of squares and fills in one of the squares with a magic marker.

The next beat finds Sheryl silently driving Frank home from the hospital. She sneaks a glance at Frank, asks if he wants to talk, Frank keeps staring at the road in front, finally says, "No," she nods and keeps driving. A FADE TO BLACK is indicated. Then, TITLE: "Little Miss Sunshine," end of music, INT. KITCHEN—DAY, an empty kitchen, Sheryl and Frank enter through the front door carrying several bags and suitcases.

It takes 4½ pages to reach the point where, supposedly, the audience has been prepped, the tone and rhythm set so that the characters can carry on with the situation they find themselves in. Here, Arndt clearly established a visual rhythm and flow: at least 50 camera shots and 12 locations. The focus on the disparity between winners and losers in America is also clearly hammered home along with a preoccupation with quick tips to success.

Judging from the final shooting script, changes had to be made. It's much more fitting to have the opening shot on Olive and her oversize rose-colored frames (not black-rimmed) with the video images of the ecstatic new Miss America reflected in her glasses. The reason? In contrast, the final moments will show Olive and her family leaving the superficial, reflecting images of America's celebrity culture in favor of the open road which is tangible and real. Along these same lines, the music should be unobtrusively soft and upbeat (not "quiet and melancholy").

There is also a missing sense of place which will be remedied by the announcement that the video Miss America hails from Louisiana, a state not far from the Sun Belt where optimistic Olive (who will become at least 9 or 10 to carry out her mission) lives. The winner strolling down the runway blowing kisses is unnecessary; Olive's special nature and imaginary response to her own crowning will come into focus instead.

The Darwin slide is more overkill, and making Richard a cliché middle-aged stocky, frustrated ex-athlete gives one of the leading actor-characters nowhere to go. In fact, he and his wife, Sheryl, and brother Frank all need to be younger, in their mid to late 30s: Richard and Sheryl, part of the current mainstream, open to possibilities, counterbalancing Frank who is philosophical and suicidal—all three giving adults in the audience something to contemplate or empathize with.

By the same token, though it's fairly common for teenagers to hate their parents and want to start a new life, Dwayne should not be just another cliché overtly aggressive alienated teen pumping iron with an outlandish hair-do, but someone much less predictable.

Again, the particular sense of place needed to be firmly established. Not the original references to Maryland and Florida (the Sunshine State) but a southwest landscape in the background outside the open window of Sheryl's old car (indicating the season and the reason Olive is out of school), with the car radio in the background announcing the dry conditions in Albuquerque and the sense of distance from "the promised land" (Southern California) but still within reach via a beat-up VW bus. Moreover, a retro, slightly run-down ranch-style tract home will need to be indicated as Sheryl and Frank enter, because the lifestyle has to accommodate a crossroad of hope and despair, reality and a comic irony—a tone and a point of view that hold the whole journey together.

The shots of cocaine-snorting Grandpa and a long-suffering Dwayne (which should precede what Frank is stepping into under Sheryl's wing) indicate another of Arndt's motifs: families often consist of disparate people who have little in common except for the fact that they are thrown together. At the outset (in future drafts) Grandpa will surreptitiously lock his door, sneak his paraphernalia out of his fanny pack, lean back and sigh, and Dwayne will surreptitiously make his little markings sans any telltale huge sheet of squares and "enlistment" sign as he serves his time, taking the path of least resistance until the way is clear to make his ultimate escape.

This kind of tweaking and attention to detail becomes necessary when, in addition to his love of exploring and "winging it" through scripting, you consider Arndt's background and overall objectives.

Personal Background and Sensibility Coming into Play

He was a graduate of New York University's acclaimed film school, and focused on the films of Preston Sturges, Billy Wilder and Woody Allen who, as it happens, started out as comedy screenwriters. Arndt was also well-acquainted with the works of noted foreign filmmakers, major playwrights and literary figures like Proust.

Balancing all this with an eye toward a career in the industry, the scene shifts to L.A. where he spent ten years toiling in the fields as a script reader for producer Deborah Schindler, then perusing the scripts that came through Hollywood's prestigious CCA (Creative Artists Agency), then becoming a freelance reader in his own right, and joining Francis Ford Coppola's Zoetrope Virtual Studio where he received feedback from fellow screenwriters re: the script in question.

As a result of this Hollywood stint, he discovered that the usual character goals in the majority of spec scripts—like getting the pretty girl or a large sum of money—were boring and commonplace. Agencies, producers and movie audiences alike wanted to meet characters who were trying to do something different. Audiences, in particular, also needed a strong sense of recognition and something to empathize with, like the fact that dreams usually clash with people's lot in life. He also found it boring and flat when each page was peppered with gags and funny lines while, at the same time, writers were intent on just keeping things moving. Moreover, he had discovered early on that humor grows organically out of the situation and it matters not if the storyline is labeled a comedy with dramatic touches or a drama with comic touches. You raise the stakes so that the audience has something to invest in and has no idea what will happen next. Characters in real jeopardy, expressing a range of emotions, taking audiences to unknown places lurking around the corner.

As to the opening beats, he decided that you have to make sure you've established the life and introduced the distinct way each character has of looking at the world under the given circumstances, trying to make sense of it all, before the main line of action starts and things start popping.

Then, when things do take off, for Arndt the philosophical stakes are the most important part of the story not the external ones. In this case, finding the courage to do what you love and measure your life by your own standards are much more significant than winning or losing competitions or meeting popular expectations.

In his overall plan, the philosophical stakes in *Little Miss Sunshine* would reach a specific climactic moment: Olive's decision to go on whether she won or not with the extraordinary routine Grandpa had secretly taught her; this in blatant contrast to the routines of her peers—underage, sequined flesh-pots writhing to the frenzied applause of their parents and sponsors.

Also fueling this work were aspects from his own life. There were talks with his twin brother, David, a depressed academic who teaches Proust, who was transformed into the character Frank. In those exchanges, such things as the incompatibility of family members came to light. Another experience centered on a VW family bus from Arndt's childhood, with its stuck horn and faulty transmission. It also came in handy as part of something famil-iar undergirding something surprising. It fit in perfectly with this atypical road story, with its see saw between hope and despair—the pull of the prom-ise just around the next bend if you can get past the breakdowns.

But how to get this dysfunctional set of six onto the bus in the first place? Which brings us back to the point where we left off.

At the start of Scene Two, when Frank enters the ranch house and is added to the Hoover clan, all kinds of questions arise. Not the least of which is, what will happen to Olive's pageant dreams in a household that now includes: a suicidal uncle; a passive-aggressive older brother who has taken a vow of silence until he can enlist in the Air Force Academy, literally fly off and become a test pilot; an irascible druggie of a grandfather; and a father hell-bent on marketing a 9-step self-help program to ease the family's finan-cial problems? And can harried Sheryl continue to hold the fragile ties that bind with the added inclusion of her problematic brother, relying mainly on buckets of takeout chicken and nurturing concern?

New Issues, More Cuts and the Throughline

As we delve a bit further, we could say that many of the additions and corrections stem from Arndt's attempt to have it both ways. Consistently, there is something familiar and reassuring about what the story is about and how this offbeat family handles its issues. There is also a familiar story pro-gression. At the same time, there is the unknown, a kind of balancing act between total control and a sense that every beat has a life of its own.

As for the familiar progression or throughline, if you study any of the drafts, there is a strong indication of the kind of traditional 3-act narrative mentioned previously. At some point within the first 30 minutes, there is an inciting incident that sets everything in motion.

Act Two centers on approximately 40 minutes of proliferating obstacles and turning points leading to a crisis that raises the stakes exponentially.

Act Three, now in full swing with self-generating momentum, takes up about 17 of the last 20 minutes, leading to the brink and the surprising but inevitable climax. In the final 3 minutes or so, things are wrapped up. Shades of dozens of films in search of greener pastures. And Frank Capra classics like *It's a Wonderful Life* (1946) as leading characters go through an ordeal leading to a break with the old false dreams and an embrace of more lasting and meaningful bonds which often were there all the time.

So much for the carrying power of the familiar throughline.

On the other hand, once actor-characters are fully shaped and the yardstick of plausibility rules, no one is going to just sit still and go along for the ride. With the 6 characters in question, there are that many more relationships and that many more possible responses. Sex-obsessed, foulmouthed Grandpa (Richard's father) is going to say and do things that can't be controlled while harboring great love and affection for his granddaughter at the same time. Frank's suicidal despondency over a failed love affair with a fellow male academic will bring him into direct conflict with brother-in-law Richard's overbearing self-help teachings. Now toss in Dwayne's need to jot down his alienated responses on a pad of paper like "I hate everyone," Olive's innocent responses and Sheryl's constant attempts to keep everything from unraveling as she maintains her role of the one truly wearing the pants in the family.

Having his work cut out for him, Arndt had at least three main considerations: how to keep things progressing while giving his distinctive characters their due and while providing just enough exposition without getting bogged down.

To illustrate.

As Sheryl and Frank enter the house, Frank can't be manipulated as indicated in the early draft. It's not logical for him to passively follow Sheryl, meekly "sitting on the cot in his nephew's bedroom" with Dwayne present, "glancing at a Muppet sleeping bag with the Cookie Monster eating a cookie." In fact, the Muppet sleeping bag has no place in Dwayne's room. In all probability, Frank would hang back in the hallway, half in reality, half staring off into open space.

Then, after finally persuading Frank to enter and promise to keep the door open as a precaution, Dwayne would naturally slip past them and this weird situation, thereby allowing the quick-fix dinner preparations to proceed: Dwayne compliantly retrieving the bucket of fried chicken in the car (which sets up this particular world), Sheryl making a salad after calling down to Olive in the family room, discounting the fact that Olive is rehearsing God-knows-what with Grandpa, simply saying, "Okay, dinner in 10 minutes." Thus, in relatively no time, the routine of what passes for family time is reset.

The next problem comes as erstwhile breadwinner Richard enters. Is all the exposition in the early draft necessary? Can't the phone call re Stan Grossman (Richard's quasi-agent handling the sale of Richard's 9-step program) be cut? And a long voice-over on the answering machine from somebody named Jeff detailing how Olive was a runner-up in the regionals but has now won a place because...? What about a cutaway to Frank and Dwayne, with Frank asking about Dwayne's mute behavior in deference to Friedrich Nietzsche, something Frank in his present state would never do? And do we need to know that Cindy is Sheryl's sister and a pageant mom, that Olive's parents and brother have never seen any of Olive's routines, that Grandpa has been kicked out of the old folks home because of his incorrigible behavior and that he moved in and decided to help Olive out with a new routine because he is the only one who has time to pay any attention to her? As it turns out, all of the above can be cut. There is no need to have everything explained. It can be implied and, if and when necessary, quickly indicated. For instance, on the trip, Richard can yell back at his father when he gets out of hand and remind him why he was kicked out of the old age home.

Another problem. Though Arndt's knowledge of Italian art-house cinema tells him that families reveal a great deal around the dinner table, do we need 11 pages to establish the new dynamic with the addition of Frank? Do we need discussions with Grandpa about what he and Olive are up to (thus ruining the whole surprising final sequence), and Richard's diatribe about pursuing your dream through his invaluable 9 steps, and Frank's lengthy, totally implausible confession about his aborted gay love life and why he tried to kill himself as innocent Olive tries to take it all in? All that's necessary is a 3-minute exchange laced with Grandpa complaining about the same old "goddamn bucket of chicken" and a terse remark from Richard when Olive asks Frank what happened to his wrists. In the silence, Richard need only remark, "Uncle Frank gave up on himself."

Then the phone call from Aunt Cindy and Olive's screams of joy—the inciting incident. The point where everything hinges on audiences investing their hopes and fears in Olive's plight. If the actress playing the part doesn't deliver, if the audience doesn't buy this moment and care, there is no story. No reason to go on. In short, Arndt is gambling everything on this phone call and Olive's response.

And now we come to that big conundrum: how to get the whole clan on the bus? In the early draft it was all deflected with 6 sluglines over 6 pages. Eventually, Arndt had to solve this dilemma head-on, with the parents in this together, arguing, along with Dwayne's written protests, Olive's hope-against-hope, Frank's disassociation, Grandpa's go-with-the-flow attitude, culminating with Richard's flawed response. Looking Olive in the eye, Richard tells Olive she can't go unless she goes all-out to win, thus setting up the emotional stakes and driving the story forward.

By this stage as the revisions became more and more polished, a dialectic came into sharp focus: Richard's vertical thrust diametrically in conflict with Grandpa's horizontal way of being in the world—competition and status vs. doing whatever makes you happy.

At the same time, Arndt's view that tragedy and absurdity dovetail into comedy took over. Having pushed his cocaine habit and lascivious lifestyle to the limit (and, in a sense, played out his role), Grandpa passes away at a pivotal point. Call it the crisis at the end of Act One.

Running into insufferable red tape at the hospital and spilling over into that selfsame thin line between absurdity and tragedy, Richard, with his over-the-top fixation declares, "I'll be damned if I'm not going to make it to that contest." Joining in the fray against the autocratic, red-tape-ridden hospital system, united against a common foe, the family bands together for the first time and slides Grandpa's mummified form out the first-story window. Outside of the law now, they will cart Grandpa across state lines into California in the back of the van, a vehicle that now has to be given a running push to get it going. In effect, Arndt's comedy-drama has now ratcheted up into uncharted territory as the van travels on and everyone is fully engaged in what can be called Act Two.

Ever changing as far as circumstances and relationships go, a little beat is inserted that previously was earmarked as a voiceover. Everyone is subdued. Richard is behind the wheel driving, inconsolable. Sheryl is beside him, speechless, patting his arm. Olive is seated behind them next to her uncle Frank. Olive tries to ask her dad what is going to happen to Grandpa but Richard is unable to answer. She asks her uncle Frank if there's a heaven but he doesn't know for sure. She tells her uncle she believes there is one. Frank then asks Olive if she thinks he'll get in. Without hesitation, she reassures him. With fourteen short lines and in the space of about 26 seconds, Grandpa, Olive and Frank are taken care of and Olive and her uncle are closer than ever before.

In this same fashion, the scenes continue to unfold, one interesting obstacle after another, difficult and then not so difficult, serious and sometimes sweet, always filled with the familiar tinged with the unexpected. When the car horn sticks, the van is pulled over by a state policeman. When, as the trip proceeds, Dwayne discovers that he's color blind and can't hope to become a pilot (Arndt's Uncle Larry failed his test for the same reason), Dwayne becomes hysterical and Richard has to pull over in the middle of nowhere. Now we have yet another family crisis.

As these pilgrims finally make it to Redondo Beach, (as outlined) the momentum kicks into high gear for Act Three. They are late for the contest and can't find an exit ramp. Then the contest's registrar won't let Olive enter due to the rules governing tardiness. When Olive does finally manage to perform her Grandpa's routine, the scenario lurches into pandemonium as the family members stand and clap, the registrar tries everything in her power to abort Olive's stripper act, Richard comes to his daughter's aid and attacks the M.C., and the entire enterprise comes crashing down.

Character Arcs, Actability, and Supporting Themes

By examining earlier and later drafts, you can also trace another way the work evolved. You can isolate each ensemble member's role and, in many cases, see how it touches on the main theme. You can also appreciate how many passes it took to accomplish this, perhaps even to the point of working on each set of changes, beat by beat, scene by scene. And then, by watching the DVD, realize how the gifted cast members took the material and added to it, building on all the work that went into bringing it to this level.

Take Grandpa's role. To be a 3-dimensional human being who is not just irascible and quirky, there has to be something endearing about him. Not only to embody a lifestyle in direct conflict with his son, Richard, but to gain his granddaughter's trust and love. Openings in the script gave the actor (Academy Award winner Alan Arkin) room to improvise—blow his nose at the dinner table whenever he felt like it, etc.—and ad-lib to overcome Olive's misgivings on the eve of the competition by just indicating that Grandpa consoles Olive and leaving the words up to both actors:

> OLIVE
> I don't want to be a loser.
> GRANDPA
> You're not a loser. Where did you get the idea you're a loser?
> OLIVE
> Because Daddy hates losers.
> GRANPA
> Whoa, back up a minute. You know what a loser is? A real loser is somebody who is so afraid of not winning, they don't even try.
> Now you're trying, right?

OLIVE nods.
Then you're not a loser. We're gonna have fun tomorrow, right?
          OLIVE
Yeah.

          GRANDPA
We can tell 'em all to go to hell. (long pause) Goodnight, sweetheart.
I love you.

The young actress playing Olive is herself free to put on headphones, listening to her iPod while riding in the VW van so that she can't hear Grandpa's obscene observations, then console Dwayne when he freaks out after discovering that he's color blind without saying a word. As far as her character arc is concerned, her outlook has to change from embracing the childish illusion of winning the contest to thoughtfully deciding on her own to go on, though she has little chance of winning, and dedicate her performance to her deceased grandpa.

Richard undoubtedly has the furthest to go, from A to Z. Borrowing from Tony Kushner's provocative question, What does it take for a person to change, Arndt took Kushner's answer to heart: you have to be torn apart and then reassemble yourself. (Kushner is the award-winning playwright and winner of the Pulitzer Prize for *Angels in America* and a screenwriter and Academy Award nominee.) With Kushner's insight in mind, Arndt takes Richard from a nice guy who is trying to convince himself of the marked division between winners and losers, to enduring back-to-back setbacks (the failure of his 9-step program and his father's death), to his blind determination to live vicariously through his daughter's triumph, to the point when his true feelings erupt and he throws all caution to the wind, forfeiting the credo he thought he once believed in and literally losing it on the stage of the competition.

The actress playing Sheryl, in tandem with her acting partner who plays Richard, is free to add gestures and other non-verbal signs in confrontations over Olive's fate, what to do about the red tape over the disposition of Grandpa's body, and all manner of ups and downs as she continues her struggles until the final emotional release on the selfsame contest stage.

The young actor playing Dwayne has one of the hardest tasks, silent but fully engaged for ¾ of the action, and then (as Arndt borrows again from Italian art house cinema) going into a frenzy as he flees from the van over the news that he's color blind and vents his rage at his family, only to finally calm down and share disenchanted philosophies with his uncle Frank, and then do his anti-establishment dance, joining in with Olive's routine and the rest of the brood, causing joyous havoc.

As for the actor playing Frank, his part calls for him to slowly come back to life, his responses limited to low-key clipped sentences and wayward looks at first. At some middle point, he is given free rein to run here and there with his bandaged wrists flapping at his side, and, at the climax, employ his unique dance-patterns. As for his ultimate moment of closure, borrowing from Proust he enacts a parody of misery while bonding for the first time with his nephew, ironically embracing the philosophy that there is no escape, no way out; unhappiness is the universal force that makes you who you are.

At the Crossroads, Taking Stock

There finally comes that risky point, even for someone with Arndt's background, when you can't go any further and have to share your work. When you've gone as far as you can go, hoping that someone whose opinion counts will feel the script has potential and is good enough for further development. And hoping against hope that further development will be entrusted to you alone as the original author.

Fortunately for Arndt, both hopes were realized due to the enthusiasm of two contacts: a pair of first-time feature film directors—husband and wife team Jonathan Dayton and Valerie Faris. Their previous experience centered on innovative projects in a variety of mediums including making music videos, co-founding a commercial production company and directing commercials, and producing some TV episodes and one or two films.

During a somewhat tortuous production and financing history—involving what became known as Big Beach Films, Third Gear Productions, Deep River and Bona Fide Production companies—Arndt was asked to make a number of additions and revisions. However, the directors did indeed insist on retaining Arndt and maintaining his singular voice and vision.

During this (for want of a better word) development stage, Arndt was asked to add a scene where Richard takes off in a borrowed motorbike from a motel room, in sheer desperation to confront Stan Grossman (his alleged agent) only to be turned down and hit a brick wall. In effect, the scene underscored how far Richard will go grasping for success.

Another scene, and one Arndt had to wrestle with, was the encounter with the trooper during the stuck-horn incident. Finally realizing that the answer is always in the script somewhere, and not to be found by grafting something on or tossing in some gratuitous jokes, Arndt remembered Grandpa's lewd magazines in the back of the van, now lying next to his wrapped body. The magazines served to captivate the lustful trooper who, instead of examining the contents at the rear of the van right in front of his nose, thumbed through the pages, made suggestive noises and glances and let the family travel on.

Among other changes that eventually were honed down to the final 23 scenes was the ending. It simply wasn't working. After more trial and error, Arndt decided that the simplest and shortest exit was best. He had the now-happy family push the van with Richard at the helm until it slipped into gear. One by one they all hopped in and wended their way home on the real road to fulfillment.

The final reward was an extended round of applause after the screening at the Sundance Film Festival, followed by negotiations among representatives of major Hollywood studios with Fox Searchlight (a division of 20th Century-Fox) winning the bidding war for U.S. and worldwide distribution, and the subsequent nominations and Academy Awards, Independent Spirit Award for Best Feature and too many more to mention.

On balance, the evolution of *Little Miss Sunshine* is still only one scripting experience on the part of a single writer with a singular background and sensibility. By chance and by design, Arndt was in the right place at the right time with the right property. The commonality here is the fact that every screenwriter faces the same crossroads: after trying by chance and design to shape a viable property, how to go on to the next level? As Arndt learned during his stint as a Hollywood script reader, a majority of scripts fail because they're underdeveloped. Instead of a fully imagined world and a finely calibrated interplay of visuals, character, action, language and theme ready for consideration, he found much that was predictable, shopworn and unexplored.

One reason may be that writers with limited backgrounds and networking opportunities frequently rely on standard evaluation checklists that read something like this:

"Eliminate plot holes, excess camera or actor directions. Make sure the main character and opponent are in constant conflict. If, on second thought, your main character seems boring, give him or her some interesting trait or skill or family. Check to see if the dialogue is too strong and is masking a dramatically weak scene. Does each character have his/her own voice? Can you still eliminate or combine characters? If the script is too long, check and see if you've repeated information or have too many subplots. If the script is too short, your story may be underdeveloped and may need a subplot."

The guides that supply these general pointers offer other standardized tips like getting feedback from trusted friends to see how they feel about the story's strengths and weaknesses. Afterwards, gather some people to read the parts and see how it sounds and whether or not it seems to hold up.

Unfortunately, trusted friends aren't seasoned script readers. Aside from the fact that screenplays are difficult to read, it takes an old hand to talk about matters like visual threads and narrative momentum. It's even more difficult to gather people for a reading who can get into character, interact with others, and offer constructive criticism about such things as apt dialogue, motivation, growing or faltering relationships, missing moments, and space to improvise or take the time for a wordless moment or telling silence.

Some guides also suggest leafing through a copy of the *Writer's Market* and mailing your work to producers and agents open to submission. Many times, however, by the time the current issue is printed, the information is no longer accurate. Besides, at best, this tack is still just a shot in the dark and may be as dubious as standard tips and sure-fire methods.

To make it all even more problematic, to paraphrase William Goldman's famous dictum, at any given point, no one in the industry knows anything. In other words, it's always necessary to be as well-informed as possible, to take into account how things really work and make certain you've truly got the whole picture.

III—THE INTERVIEWS: THE VOICES OF EXPERIENCE

The Top Flight Agent

Lucy Stille is a principal at the Paradigm Agency in Beverly Hills, representing writing and directing talents such as John Sayles and Peter Bogdanovich, and teaches script development at the University of Southern California's School of Cinematic Arts. She is one of eight chosen top literary agents on the panel of the Words Into Pictures Forums organized by the Writers Guild Foundation and listed in the front ranks of *The Power 100 Women* in Hollywood.

For openers, it would probably be best to start off with your background.

I went to Harvard and thought I was going to be an academic but discovered that I'd like to be with people more than I'd like to be in the library. I became a high school teacher and ran the drama program and wound up working in summer stock. At the end of the summer, the producers offered to help me get a job in theater in New York. So I moved and got a job working for Olympia Dukakis' repertory theater in Montclair, New Jersey. I went on to work for Playwrights Horizons, which was committed to producing new plays by American playwrights. We would not take on a play unless the playwright was willing to come and work with us throughout the rehearsal period. We believed that a play was a working, breathing thing and that a playwright needed to hear it performed in order to fine tune it. It was a very exciting time in the off-Broadway theater with successful transfer of *A Chorus Line* and the launching of Theater Row on West 42nd Street. Eventually I got to the point where I was spending more and more time at Exxon and Mobil, writing fundraising proposals and organizing theater parties, and less and less time in the theater. Having experienced the hurly burly of the business side of the arts at Playwrights but still being interested in storytelling, I decided to explore book publishing and became a literary agent at Sanford J. Greenburger. I happily worked there until I fell in love with a journalist who lived in Los Angeles. I moved to be with him and, as there is no publishing to speak of in Los Angeles, figured out that the best way to work with writers was to get into the film and television business. In three weeks I got a job working for a small little boutique agency called Bloom, Levy, Shorr. A year later he said, 'You brought in all these new interesting writers. I'm going to put your name on the door.' Since there was no Bloom and there was no Levy, only Fred Shorr, we changed the name of the agency to Shorr, Stille. A couple of years later, Fred decided to retire. By then I had a husband, a baby and an agency and I went looking for partners. That search ultimately led me to Paradigm, a new company that came together as a merger of four existing agencies. Since then, Paradigm has grown organically and dramatically, but still allows me to focus on what I care about, which is story.

So, in terms of how you made your mark in the industry...

While there were agents at ICM (International Creative Management) and William Morris, etc., who were terrific salespeople, I was willing to roll up my shirtsleeves and actually work on screenplays with writers. When I started out, a lot of scripts that I was given were from young executives at the studios and were not scripts that were ready to go to market. They were scripts that showed promise. I would call the young writer up and say, "So and so gave me your script and I think there's a lot that's terrific about it. Would you come talk to me?" They would come to my office and without promising them anything, I would try to get them to "fix" the script. I might say, "The first two acts are really good. But I don't think you know how to end it. What are your thoughts? What themes are you interested in?" They'd go back and do some more work. I'd then go back and call the executive at Warner Brothers and say, "Remember John Smith and the script you gave me? We worked on it, and I think you should take another look." The executive would usually agree to reread it, and most typically would say, "It's still too dark, it's still too small, but you're right. You got John Smith to do some really good work and I'd be very interested in what John Smith writes next." Some of these writers would become clients, but all of them were very grateful to have somebody who would actually close the door for forty-five minutes and talk to them about their work.

I've noticed that some of the seasoned writers I've talked to have taken their work directly to influential stars. Does that represent any kind of shift?

The problem is that we've seen a major contraction in the studio marketplace in the last fifteen years. When I started in this business, Disney had three divisions: Touchstone, Hollywood Pictures, and Buena Vista. Each of those divisions was supposed to make twenty movies a year. There is now one division and they make fifteen movies a year. When you and I started out, there was Columbia Pictures and there was Tri Star Pictures. And they were each making twenty movies. Now it's Sony Pictures and they're making fifteen. Fewer pictures means less development, i.e., less work for writers. With the corporatization of the film business, the studios are making fewer movies at bigger budgets. That means that the competition to be one of those movies is greater. That has meant that the more elements, the more goodies you can bring to your script, the more interested the studio is. So that while you can still give a studio a naked script—a producer and a script go into the studio and if they like the script enough, they buy it. That still happens. But a lot of people are hedging their bets by trying to bring a director or an actor and an actress to the project. So if the studio then sees that the material is validated by the creative community, they feel like they're one step closer to production.

In that case what happens to the talented newcomer with, let's say, two polished spec scripts under her arms? How does she get through under these circumstances?

If a script is good enough, it gets through. There is no agent in the business who won't give you an example of a newcomer who wrote a great script which opened doors for that writer. We represent a young woman who was working as a paralegal named Melissa Stack who wrote a script, *I Want to Blank Your Sister*. It was a high concept comedy. We sold the script to Paramount and she now has three or four assignments off of one screenplay. That still happens. The script was sold with no attachments. It had a producer, no actors, no director, nothing. It was high concept, and funny, and the studio knew how to make it.

So, if you had to pinpoint the key to all the scripts you take in...

The key to all these scripts is voice. The studios are going to make *Romeo and Juliet* in space, in the Barrio, in the fifteenth century, because the basic story works. The trick for the studio is, what's the fresh voice, the fresh approach that's going to make *Romeo and Juliet* work for the coming year? What we look for in new clients is an original voice. A sense of humor, a way at looking at the action world, a poignancy in the drama that's going to make the story jump off the page. If they have that, but the stories they are telling are too art house, too quirky and esoteric, we can work with them to come up with a story that puts them closer to the mainstream. If they don't have that unique point of view in their writing, no amount of plot will make their script great. You are always going to have movies about boy meets girl, boy loses girl, boy gets girl. They probably painted it on the cave in the caveman age and they're going to make it in 2050. But who's the boy, who's the girl, what's the story, what keeps them apart, what brings them together? That's what's going to make it a fresh movie. Part of good agenting is helping those writers develop those stories that match their voice.

Then what is your take on the indie world and the smaller intimate story?

The movie world is divided now. There is a studio world that is interested in what we call a four-quadrant movie, which from the marketing points of view gets young adult males, young adult females, mature males and mature females. *Pirates of the Caribbean* is a four-quadrant movie. The studios are interested in those movies. The independent movies, the Fox Searchlight movies, the Focus movie, the Paramount Vantage movie, the movies that are made for probably under $25 million, can take a much more niche approach to films. But their budgets are much smaller as a result. So the difference is, if you're going to make *In the Bedroom*, you know you're not going to get the 15-to-25-year-old audience. That's not who's coming to that movie. You're going to get mature men and women who want to go to a sophisticated review-driven film on a Friday or Saturday night. So if you make that movie at a price and you get enough of that mature audience, you can make money.

However, what if you create an indie like *Little Miss Sunshine*, which eventually takes off for practically everybody?

But look at all the little independent movies that have not taken off. *Lars and the Real Girl*, which is a terrific movie and a feel-good movie, like *Little Miss Sunshine*, has not performed. And nobody can tell you why. But the point is, we are in a business now where there is a big studio movie and there is an independent movie, and with the dawning of the digital age it may change even more. In today's marketplace, for example, no studio would make *Driving Miss Daisy, Kramer vs. Kramer* or *Ordinary People*. Those films are too intimate for today's studio marketplace even though we know that when they were made they were all Oscar-nominated and critically acclaimed films. Those kinds of films are now independent films to be made for a price. The question is the price point for making those stories and how those stories are going to get to their audience. There may come a time when you and I will pay $25 to go see a movie on the big screen in a movie theater. And we may pay a different price to download a film that's a more intimate film and less expensive film on a large-screen television set at home with three couples on a Saturday night. All of this is changing. That's what the future is about. Movies are going to be sent digitally wherever they need to go. There isn't going to be a can of film anymore. Ten years from now if somebody goes out and makes *Blair Witch Project*, it will be something that's downloaded on the Internet.

Which, in turn, I assume, affects little production companies.

They do the best they can. The days when there were lots of big studio deals are gone. Producers have to go to new places to get capital. More and more people are raising funds to make movies, finding equity investors to bank on them and bank on their company. We have studios, we have mini-majors and we have equity investors out there. There is a lot of private capital out there in the marketplace. The founder of eBay started a company. The FedEx people have a company—there are little pots of money all over the place. The studios love people who walk in with money because they're trying to hedge their risk. Village Road Show is a company housed at Warner Brothers. If Warner Brothers has a big expensive movie, they go to Village Road Show and say, "Do you want in on this movie? Do you want to help defray the cost? You can take 60 percent of the movie and have foreign (distribution)." Village Road Show evaluates the project and has capital so that Warner Brothers' risk is minimized. Warner Brothers is a publicly held company, part of Viacom, it's traded on the stock market and it's got to show profit or it's vulnerable. That's the new corporate studio world we're in.

All of this notwithstanding, can people still write a screenplay they believe in without overly concerning themselves with its commercial potential and still get an agent?

Of course. It happens all the time. Every university has a film program, not to mention the numerous top-flight film schools, so lots of people are writing screenplays these days. Those people are finding their way to managers and agents all the time. I read two new writers over the recent holiday. One of them has never written a screenplay. The other comes out of U.C.L.A. Maybe this is her third screenplay but the first she's prepared to show anybody. But it is harder. I don't take people who send me a letter or send me an e-mail. I'd drown. Somebody I know has to call me and say, "I read this screenplay, I think it's pretty good, you should take a look at it." And because I know that they know what they're doing, even if ultimately I may not agree with them, I may not have their taste—at least I know that somebody with a professional eye has read it before I'm going to read it. But plenty of the writers they refer are brand new babies. And if we like the script, if we respond to the voice and respond to the writing, we may say to them, "You're a terrific writer but the kinds of stories you're writing are problematic for the following reasons. And can we figure out a story that interests you that might speak to a broader audience?" I just got a script from a guy that's set in the world of academia. It's too cerebral, and not visual enough. So the question is, do I say to this guy, "You have a nice voice, but pick a world that's more universal, that more people can relate to? Don't make it so talky." Can I teach this writer that writing a screenplay, unlike a novel, which can have an interior voice, requires that thoughts and ideas be externalized? You have to see how so-and-so's anger is manifested in a visual way. What are the visual clues? How do you think and write visually? It's a different set of skills than writing prose. Can he write a story that will have broad appeal? Even small films need to reach out to hundreds and thousands of people to be successful. And big films are reaching out to millions of people. So if you write a movie about a relationship between a father and son, that's pretty universal. All of us have had fathers.

And if we could just touch on a lighter vein.

Young comedy people are putting things on the Internet. Zwick-Herskovitz, two of the most successful television creators in the business, have created a new show for the Web. (*Quarterlife*, chronicling the angst-ridden lives of creative twentysomething pals, self-financed on MySpace with 36 8- to 15-minute installments or Webisodes.) On the Web they can own what they make and they can experiment in ways that just aren't feasible anymore at the networks. If NBC, CBS or ABC want to pick it up off of that, they can. But once you're making a show for CBS Productions, to be distributed on CBS, CBS is holding all the cards. That does not usually encourage the most creative solutions. So more and more people are choosing to create something on the Internet. They retain the creative controls and if the project finds its place in a mainstream marketplace, that's great. What the Internet is providing is a place for the kind of risk taking that has become too expensive at the studio or network level. With the cost of making films these days, you can't afford to experiment. And the studios would rather put more resources into a $100 million movie than they would into a $20 million movie.

So back to you or someone like you, a writer just starting a career and the submission process.

I only read scripts that come from referrals, but there are agents, and particularly managers, who may agree to read off an e-mail or letter. Though the marketplace is tighter and more constricted, people can still get through.

Talent will out. I teach script development at USC in the Peter Stark program. There are invariably students of mine who say, "Would you read this screenplay for me?" Even if I don't take it on, they can network through all the people they meet in the program. And there are lots of programs. Playwrights sometimes make fabulous screenwriters since they are trained to write for character and dialogue. I am always happy to read a play. But it's important to remember that a screenplay is a learned form. It's not a natural form like prose. It is, in essence, a blueprint for a director to work with. Scenes can't ramble or digress. They have to tell us something about the character or advance the plot. And they have to tell a story cinematically. It kills me to say this, but when the studios read spec screenplays, they care less often about the dialogue than they do about the story.

Coverage and the Script Reader

The young lady who consented to this interview wanted her name and the name of her Hollywood production company to remain anonymous. She cited potential legal issues and the possibility that she is privy to information about the current development of specific projects that's meant to be kept in-house. At the same time, she thought it might be helpful to let aspiring screenwriters know what they were up against as far as the mini commercial market was concerned, both specifically and in general.

Could you cite a few movies your company has made?

We've made *Ghost Rider*, *Bratz*, *Baby Geniuses* and other commercial projects. For instance, *Ghost Rider* was based on a comic book and starred Nicholas Cage. He rides a motorcycle and makes a contract with the devil. And there's a whole complicated sub-plot about becoming on fire and that kind of thing. *Bratz* is a very popular children's story. There's some controversy over *Bratz* because, though the movie is all live action, it's based on the little fashion dolls for girls that are dressed really trashy. Overall, my understanding is that we do the bigger movies in conjunction with a major studio and in partnership with the company that makes the Spider-Man and Marvel Comics adaptations. *Ghost Rider* is a Marvel comic. But even though they're produced and distributed in partnership, my company is in charge of the actual physical production—hiring the actors, the director, finding the location, shooting the movie—all of it.

How do you obtain the scripts?

Through agencies, but only agents that we work with, which are the better ones. Unless the CEO knows the writer and the writer is a personal friend. A lot of times the scripts are part of a deal that's already put together. Other times, maybe there's a well-known director that's interested in the script and wants to work with us. Then it's, "Such and such director wants this to be his next project. Or such and such director wants to adapt this book into a screenplay." Or it may start at the script level with a book the company wants to adapt.

But if it's simply a script, how and why does it get passed down to you?

Because even though the amount of scripts is reduced significantly through the approval of top agents, the executives don't have the time to read them. They can't possibly get through all the material fast enough, so they pass it down to me. That is, the CEO passes it to his assistant and he passes it to me.

Because of your background and because they feel you know what you're doing?

Yes. When, after college, I moved to L.A. I made it my job to learn about screenwriting. Over the past few years I made friends with writers and dated a screenwriter for 3 years who taught me the basics. Act 1, Act 2, Act 3—whatever. And I read a book called *Myth and the Movies*. All together, I learned about the elements that make up a good story. That every story has to have a main character so that you can see the story through one point of view that can carry you all the way and not scatter the story through too many characters.

In terms of the demographic, the age range and sensibilities of your target audience.

Mainly. There are other ways and maybe other characters that you love to love, but that's what I focus on. Even with multiple stories, each story has its main character. It holds the script together. If you don't have that, it falls apart. I've read scripts where there's no main character. And all the characters are underdeveloped. There's one character who you think is the main character and starts to develop a little bit, but then forget about it and start to follow a different character. You have a trip from beginning to end but it's not the same person. You never get to know any character well. It's like all over the place. I grant you, it is one of those things where you can play around with it. I've read books where the main character dies, and I thought it was cool. But if you don't have an understanding of what the basics should be, then you can't mess around with it. It's like an artist not understanding composition. There are great paintings that don't follow the rules, but the artist knows he's breaking the rules. If they know what they're doing they can do it well. If they don't, it's just a bad painting.

So is it safe to say that your company is drawn to a certain type of material that doesn't break those standard rules?

Yes. Basically comic books, action movies and comedies—that kind of thing.

And when you give coverage, how do you go about it? What aspects do you key on in order to give your boss, the assistant CEO, a good assessment?

At the top I write the title and all the relative information so he and the other execs can get a relative idea before they consider it further. I write down the genre, whether it's a family movie, a children's movie or sci-fi, fantasy, thriller or crime drama. I write down the number of pages and the location, where it takes place and the time period. Then I write down a log line if it's a good script, like "A down-and-out guy comes across a magical object that brings him power but then he has problems with his family"—whatever. But if it's a bad script, it's hard to write a log line. Like, "A down-and-out guy finds a magical object, then meets a girl, then comes across a wooded area and then goes off in all kinds of directions." The better the script, the easier it is to summarize. A log line should include a short description of the character, object and goal. It's not the whole movie but it gives you the hook. A lot of time when the log line is bad, I'm given a log line that tells me what the script should be but it actually really isn't. Like, "A down-and-out guy finds a magical object that turns his life around but then he realizes that, in the end, it's all not so great." But in the script, the guy can't find the magical object until page 60. It's badly structured. He should have found the object on page 5. So obviously the writer didn't know what he was doing and it goes downhill from there.

Even though the material was supposedly vetted by a top agent?

Even so. But to go on, after the log line I write, I make a chart that will say, from 1 to 5, how I rate the script. Like about the quality of the writing, because some times I'm not asked to rate the script itself because we may be wanting to adapt a novel and are looking for a writer to do it. Then there's the quality of the script, because a lot of times the script may be well written but you don't like the premise. The writer can be completely competent, but we don't want to see a movie about a bank robbery. It's well written but I don't think an audience would like it. I wouldn't particularly want to go see this movie in a theater. But I would couch it in terms of, I don't think there's much in this movie that's appealing to an audience. There's no twist in the end, no government conspiracy; it's about drug dealers when today we're interested in terrorists.

So it has to strike some contemporary theme.

Yes. If the material is dated, or if I saw a trailer for this movie about a bank robbery, I probably wouldn't want to go see it unless there was something else about it that was interesting. Like the *Oceans 11* and *13,* movies which are about a bank robbery but really about the cool guys who are doing the bank robbery. So that's the thing you're looking for even though it's well written. Then I go to specifics, like dialogue, structure, plot, character. Everything may happen when it's supposed to happen and who it should happen to if it's a good story, but then it could be horribly written. But that's not critical because it's easy to rewrite dialogue. You just hire a different writer if the basic story is in place. On the other hand, if the dialogue is great and the writing is great but the premise is boring, then there's a big problem. If it's boy meets girl, is it something we haven't seen before? On an Internet dating site? What's the different angle, different twist about modern life? Are they mutants?

Maybe the guy wants a relationship but the girl doesn't want it. Maybe the story has great action scenes. If it's based on a comic book, it already has a great fan base and has that going for it, but that's not enough.

And because you are the right age and, in a sense, are a highly knowledgeable representative of your target demographic, you are aware of the kind of hook or other element a story needs.

But also we make kids' movies, so that's easy to judge anyway, and movies for teenage guys, which I admit I like, in addition to the ones based on comic books and sci-fi. But yes, I am working for a company that makes the kinds of movies that I like to go and watch genre-wise. If I was working for a company that made Oscar-nominated dramas, then my coverage probably wouldn't match. I'll see them eventually, but I'd much rather go see an action movie, a thriller or a comedy. I want to be entertained.

Can we touch on your taste in comedy?

It can't be too juvenile. It all really has to do with a sense of humor. Like the one with the young couple trying to have sex when she's pregnant. I've never seen that on the screen before. It wasn't X rated or offensive. It was funny, and uncomfortable for both of them, and crossed the line of where comedy has gone in the past. It was so real and so human. Writers have a hard time being funny, but if you can be genuinely funny, that's a big plus. I've read a lot of scripts that are supposed to be funny, but there's not a joke in the whole thing. Like the ones that are supposed to be romantic comedies but nothing at all funny happens and nothing that is said is funny either. But whatever the genre, you can always tell in the first 10 pages because writers are pretty consistent. It won't all of a sudden pick up on page 11 and be funny or interesting or exciting the rest of the way.

Do you ever get a script that's not just the work of one writer who may have missed the boat but one that's been worked on by more than one person, and that's why it's been accepted?

Yes, but when that happens, it will seem like the writing is competent because the person who re-wrote it is competent. But something is basically missing. Like the main character starts out with no identity but you should have been privy to who the main character is at the beginning. But you can tell that's not how it was originally. The exposition comes along later. The plot points pick up at the wrong time.

Back to the usual single writer. Are there any common flaws that tell you right off the bat that this isn't going to work for you?

In the action scripts, there's frequently no character development, no plot development with everything in the right place and the right time. All these fights scenes, but who's fighting and why? The main thing I look for is a good sense of story. Everything else can be rewritten. I'm amazed that after going through an agent and passed to me how bad the scripts generally are. The logical inconsistencies, the loose ends that aren't tied up. I mean, the process of getting through our company is pretty difficult to start with.

But when it does it get through to you and your coverage is returned to the execs?

They can just glance at it and tell it's not the kind of movie they want to make, or see that the rating is low. Or, like I said, they were already attached to the project to begin with and this either confirms their hopes or tells them how the script needs to be changed. If that's the case, I tell them what I would do if I were the producer. Things like, even though there's no main character, it could be fixed if you combine several characters. These are the notes, if I were the producer, I would give to the writer or writers. And that's also the kind of thing I pass on.

The Hollywood Producer

Mace Neufeld's awards include the Hollywood Film Festival Award for Outstanding Achievement in Producing (2000), the ShoWest Award as Producer of the Year (1993) and a star on the Walk of Fame (2003). He has produced a seemingly countless number of major motion pictures including *The Hunt for Red October* (1990), *Patriot Games* (1992), *Clear and Present Danger* (1994), *Lost in Space* (1998), *Sahara* (2005), and *The Human Factor* and *The Equalizer* (2009). His offices are located in Beverly Hills.

As I understand it, you were with Warner Brothers and, later on, under contract at Paramount.

Then I went over to Sony for four years and now I'm on my own.

Would you mind if we went back in time and used *The Frisco Kid* as a starting point?

Sure. It was original material from a spec script by Michael Elias and Frank Shaw called *No Knife*. I read the script and thought it was terrific. I gave it to Mike Nichols, who said he was interested in it at the time. I got John Calley, who was then running Warner Brothers, to read the script and he liked it. And there was an agent at the William Morris Agency, Bob Shapiro, who then came over and got a development deal at Warners. A month later he called and said, "You've lost a partner, but you have a picture," because he was then elevated to president of production.

Was there something about the premise that attracted you—a tale about a Polish rabbi going through an ordeal, trying to make his way across the untamed West to his new post in San Francisco?

It could be almost any stranger to the United States at that time. It pushed universal buttons and I thought it was very funny. It all came together rather quickly because I sent the script to Gene Wilder's agent and Gene wanted to play the rabbi. We had a director at the time, Dick Richard, who Warners said to put on the film. But we had, as they say, creative differences and then Gene Wilder suggested Robert Aldrich, who shared the same lawyer with Wilder.

I'm assuming that Gene Wilder's input was a major factor.

Yes it was. He wanted to play the rabbi as authentically as possible. At that time Gene was a big star. By a series of circumstances that don't have anything directly to do with writing, we got Harrison Ford to play the bank-robbing cowboy. Parenthetically, Aldrich had sent the script to John Wayne and John Wayne loved the script. Aldrich and I had a really good meeting with him. He actually read aloud to us from the script. We went driving back about ten feet off the ground because here we had Gene Wilder and John Wayne, an American icon. Gene Wilder even agreed to take second billing saying, "Any day I would do that." Then, as happens in the movie business, we called Frank Wells, who was then chairing Warner Brothers and basically making their deals, and said we have John Wayne and you should talk to his agent. About two hours later his agent called to say the deal was off because, he said, "I don't want to insult John Wayne. Frank Wells said to defer $250,000 and John's price is $750,000. Period. That's what he gets." So we had John and we lost John. It would have been Wayne's last film. And then Henry Winkler suggested we look at this film about a Vietnam War vet with this young actor Harrison Ford.

In addition to the casting of the bank-robbing cowboy and Gene Wilder's insistence on authenticity, did anything else affect the original concept? Did Gene Wilder create any additions?

Gene Wilder added the opening where you see him ice skating in Poland. It was kind of an unlikely thing for him to be doing but he takes a fall on the ice and is called into the board of rabbis. They then tell him that he's going to America. So the opening of the picture was suggested by Gene, and Elias and Shaw just wrote that in. The script stayed basically the same though, not too many changes except for the title and the opening sequence. I did put two of my rabbis on the film as technical consultants. They coached Wilder in the praying and the chanting. As a nice touch, one of the prop people gave my rabbi one of Al Jolson's original prayer shawls from *The Jazz Singer* (the first talkie). In its initial run, admittedly, the movie didn't do very much, Warners didn't know how to market it. But it's since become a cult film.

After that you seem to have segued into material taken from action-adventure novels. Is there any reason for this big change?

No. I got a copy of *The Hunt for Red October* from one of the development people who worked for me who went down to the Dallas Book Fair and picked up this book from a small booth that was run by the Naval Institute Press. It was their first work of fiction because they did mostly subjects of marine engineering and Navy things. I read the book and ran around to various studios and kept getting turned down. In the process I had optioned the book and the book became a favorite of Ronald Reagan and everybody in Washington, D.C., was reading it. At the time I optioned the book, Tom

Clancy was still selling insurance. He had not become a fulltime writer. It eventually wound up at Paramount as a last stop. The reason this book kept getting turned down was because it didn't synopsize well. Studio executives read coverage; they don't read books. It just happened that Ned Tanen, who was then running Paramount and was an old friend of mine, was leaving California for a flight to London. I said, "I've got a great book that'll make a fantastic movie." He said, "Well we turned that down." I said, "Yes, but did you ever read it?" He said he'd read the coverage. I said, "If you don't have anything to read on the plane I'll send the book over by hand. Call me when you land in Heathrow and if you don't think this is a movie, you never have to take my phone calls again." He then called me and said it was terrific but it was going to be very expensive. And I said, "No it isn't," and ad libbed and didn't have a budget or a script and said, "It's going to cost $18 million." And he said, "You'll have to get the Navy cooperation as part of the contract" and I said, "I'll get it." I eventually did and there were several scripts done on it. Finally Larry Ferguson did a script that was not as much like the book as I thought it should be but Paramount loved it. Don Stewart had actually written the first draft and gave us a blueprint for the movie and then other writers came in. One interesting story was that we had initially cast Klaus Maria Brandauer who kept stalling on signing his contract up to three weeks before the start of principal photography. Then he told me he had to have ten days off in the middle of the schedule because he owed a friend of his a cut on a film he had directed and it had to be ready for the Cannes Film Festival. And here we were with Alec Baldwin as Jack Ryan and no Captain Ramius. I called around and finally got Marty Baum at CAA and asked him about Sean Connery. Marty said Sean had a throat problem but just got a clean bill of health and may be interested. We faxed Sean the script and he called back the following day. He said, "It's détente and perestroika now and it doesn't make any sense." I told him that the rollup at the beginning of the movie says it's before perestroika, that the following thing happened and both governments denied it. He didn't get that. I told him it was on the first page and faxed it to him. He called back and said, "It now makes sense but I need some really big speeches. I don't seem to have any big speeches." I said we'd get a writer to do that for him. He wanted to know who I'd get and, at that moment while I was on the phone, John Milius poked his head into my office because John and I were working on *Flight of the Intruder* together. So I said, "Well, what about John Milius?" Sean said he loved John; he did a picture with him and wanted to know if I could get him. I said, "Just a minute" and put John Milius on the phone and right after that Sean said, "Okay, if John's on it, I'll do it." Milius came on to write a couple of big speeches for Sean but didn't do enough writing to get the screen credit, but he was one of the main factors in that film being made. The studio was all excited because Sean had just made *Indiana Jones [and the Last Crusade]* appearing as Harrison's father and, as they say, the rest is history. The film went right through the roof.

You've mentioned Don Stewart. Does he frequently do first drafts for you?

Well Don Stewart did *Missing* and had gotten the Academy Award for it. He had a great facility for taking a long book and giving you an outline of how it could be a movie. So we also went to Don on each of the next two Clancy projects. Don wrote the first drafts. And on *Patriot Games*, which was the second film because Paramount optioned both *Patriot Games* and *Clear and Present Danger*—I thought we should do *Patriot Games* next because it was more about Ryan and his family rather than pure action—there were several drafts written because Alec Baldwin left the film and Harrison Ford came on to play the Ryan part. Serendipitous for me but not so serendipitous for Alec Baldwin who went off to Broadway to play in *Streetcar Named Desire*. So here's the writing story on that one. We were up in Washington, D.C., up in Harrison's hotel room discussing the scene with James Earl Jones watching a live satellite feed on the attack of a terrorist camp. Harrison said that the scene didn't really work. There's just too much talk. He said it was such a horrifying event seeing it live, "What I can do is, you can play it on my face and let me play what I'm seeing and cut out all the chatter, cut out any dialogue between me and James Earl Jones. And let just one of the TV controllers say, 'That's a kill.' And then cut to my face and let me do the rest." So all the dialogue Don had written was cut out. We played it that way and, of course, it's one of the most effective scenes in the film. Harrison was one of the few actors who had the confidence to externalize without speaking what he was internalizing.

If I may interrupt for a minute. How did you go from this kind of material to *Beverly Hills Cop III*?

Sherry Lansing came over as head of Paramount, wanted to do it but the budget was over $90 million and they couldn't spend that kind of money. My partner at the time and I did know these kind of films and Sherry asked if we could take over as producers and bring it in at a substantially lower figure. It was developed under the producer Joel Silver and came in under a very high budget because they were trying to rush it for a certain release date. So I asked Sherry if we were producing a movie or a release date. So they postponed the release date. What happened was that John Landis was the director and I didn't think much of the screenplay. So I made some notes and went to see John at his offices at Universal and sat down and began to talk about some changes. But John Landis had final cut on the film and was very happy with the script. I, in the interim, had started production on *Flight of the Intruder* in Hawaii, so my partner basically did the housekeeping on the film. So this was done as a favor for Sherry Lansing. I don't take any responsibility for that film.

Moving back to projects you want to take on, when and how do you come in contact with a new writer?

That happens all the time. We get spec screenplays. When I was at Paramount, for instance, I bought a spec screenplay by a writer named George Nolfi called *Pathfinder*. We spent years trying to get that made and he did many drafts. For various reasons Paramount did not go forward with them. It was a mano-a-mano story between an American serviceman in a group called the Pathfinders who had highly developed senses and the ability to visualize things. The maps, for instance, in three dimensions. He's captured after being sent into a country to spot targets. In Desert Storm when those smart bombs went in to hit targets they were spotted by Pathfinders who were sent in without any help. He spends a year with another French intelligence officer and they escape together. It turns out that the French officer is really with the Serbian military and was in jail to find out everything he could from our leading Pathfinder. It's a very exciting script and Nolfi went on to write a lot of screenplays including the *Oceans* movies and a Matt Damon *Bourne* movie. His price has gone from $80 thousand to several million.

So, even if you believe in a project, there's no telling what will come of it. Or, in William Goldman's famous take on Hollywood, "No one knows anything."

Well, Bill Goldman is probably talking about motion picture executives. Actually, there's a good writing story. *The General's Daughter*, which I produced from a Nelson De Mille book. We had several screenplays and couldn't seem to attract the right actor to play the lead. And it was suggested that Bill Goldman had a three-week window in which he was looking for a rewrite assignment. Of course Goldman was one of my idols, had read the screenplay and the De Mille book and said, "I think I know how to rewrite this and would do A B C & D. But since I only have a three-week window, I may not be able to deliver you a first draft and a polish." But he did. His name went on the title page and actors all immediately responded when they saw the name Bill Goldman. And John Travolta signed on as a result of that. So Goldman got no screen credit because the Writers Guild determines that in a kind of arbitrary way. But if it weren't for Bill Goldman, *The General's*

Daughter might have never been made. But let's get back to *Clear and Present Danger.*

The third in your Tom Clancy series.

Yes. This became a very unusual situation. In the middle of shooting *Patriot Games*, Harrison Ford called me into his trailer and said, "You know, we're having so much fun we ought to make the next one right away." So we took essentially the same crew and Don Stewart, who had written a screenplay. It went through the usual revisions because you always get notes from the studio, etcetera, etcetera. We're finally at the first script reading with the director and I always bring all the drafts with me in my briefcase. Steve Zaillian had come on to do some rewriting and we brought John Milius in to write just one action scene. I had the experience of having three Academy nominees all sitting in the same room discussing the sequence when the Suburbans are being attacked. They were friends of mine and great admirers of Harrison Ford. So they kind of collaborated on that scene. But for the next to the last scene in the film where Jack Ryan confronts the president of the United States and the president says, "Don't bark at me like a junkyard dog," that scene had been written differently. We were around the table reading it and Harrison said, "This is just not working for me. This is the climactic scene and it's just not working. We've got to rewrite this." I said, "Just wait a minute, guys." There was a totally different scene that Don Stewart had written in the first draft. I pulled it out and I gave it to Harrison and the other actor playing the president. And Harrison said, "Wow, this one really cooks. It's a great scene. How did we miss it?" I said it was because there were so many revisions and it was taken out. So I always bring all the drafts to readings. I also try to get the writer, if he's available, to come and be on the set in case something doesn't work and we have to rewrite it.

The initial writer?

Well, in this case, Don Stewart was on the set while we were shooting it. Steve Zaillian was on the phone with us but not available to come onto the set. Because inevitably on any film, once you get the scene on its feet, it may not work the way you want it to. And many times the actors, who I trust implicitly because they've got the most to lose, come up with their own scene. There's an example of a scene between Willem Dafoe and Harrison Ford and they came to me and said that they've been reading it over and trying it out and it just doesn't work. And Harrison said, "Why don't you give us about half and hour and maybe we can come up with something." They went back into Harrison's trailer and about a half hour later they came out and said, "How do you like this?" And they started to play a scene that they had written. Don Stewart was standing there and we said that it sounded great. Don put it down on paper—it was a scene that was going to happen two days later—and that's how that scene was born. It's a process. It involves the actors, the writers, the director and the producer. When you're shooting, it's very expensive. When something isn't working or you're rehearsing the next day's scene, it's very costly to shoot a scene that you know is going to wind up on the cutting room floor. We're always open to suggestions. If we like them, we'll incorporate them; if we don't we won't. It leaves an open door between the cast and the production people. It's a collaboration.

The Independent Producer

Tony Bill has played over 60 roles in feature films and on television, directed over 30 films and television episodes, and produced 14 films and TV movies. He won an Academy Award for producing *The Sting* (1973) and was awarded the Children's Jury Award and Certificate of Merit for producing the television version of *Oliver Twist*. His production office is located in Santa Monica, California.

I'm assuming you're not especially caught up in the Hollywood scene or invested in mainstream fare like outrageous comedies, action films, adaptations of comic books, sci-fi fantasies and the like.

Those aren't my cup of tea. I have an unusual attitude toward the movie business and an unusual connection with it in terms of screenplays and the world of scripts. Of the movies I've produced or directed, about 90 percent are original screenplays by first-time screenwriters who never wrote a script before or never had a movie made before. So my specialty, if you will—I didn't set out this way, but looking back on it, my MO is to make movies by someone new. I like to work with new writers, new actors, new directors, new cameramen, whatever it is. And, by the same token, most of the scripts are first-time scripts.

How do you find the writers?

Well, that's my point. I don't know how other people find them, through agents and parties and things like that. My style is more serendipity. I come across scripts or they come to me in the most unlikely manner. Which makes it very frustrating because there's no method to that. So I'm as likely to find a script in a little town in Connecticut as I am in the middle of L.A. where I live. I can speak as an observer as to how the rest of the world works but, for the most part, the movies I've gotten made came from first efforts from Terry Malick, like *Deadhead Miles* (1972) , David Ward, Paul Schrader, who wrote *Taxi Driver* (1976), and others.

Just for example, how did you come across *Deadhead Miles*?

I met Terry in L.A. and commissioned him to write a screenplay. I just had a feeling about him. For me, in a way, being outside of L.A. or in L.A. doesn't matter very much. For example, I met a guy in Connecticut who is an aspiring screenwriter who I've been in touch with. I met a guy who's a fireman who had a screenplay. The phenomenon of thinking you can write a script and sometimes correctly so, isn't confined geographically to Los Angeles. Just so you know, my corner of the world of screenplays is actually dedicated to first-time screenwriters of original material. Also, I for one have never switched screenwriters on a movie. I don't have the attitude that somebody can do better and I'm not sure they can. And I don't have the temperament to fire somebody and hire different writers to work on a project. Or even the skill, so to speak, of knowing who can possibly do better. So it's a style, my personal style.

Does that also apply to you as a director and Blake Evans' script for *Flyboys*. Wasn't that also a first script?

Actually, that was brought to me by the producer, Dean Devlin. And it was a first script ever written. However, it was clear that it needed a lot of work and in this case we had to bring in other experienced writers because we were under the gun and just a few weeks away from shooting and we needed some stuff done. *Flyboys* is the product of two people's decisions— the producer and me. There was nobody else calling the shots.

Even so, taking into account the production pressures and the fact that the script needed a lot of work, was there something about this first script that prompted you and Dean Devlin to go ahead with the project? Something about World War I and the Lafayette Escadrille Squadron?

You always have to convince yourself that it's a good time to make a movie. Because it's so hard to get a movie made and by the time you get it made ... *Flyboys* was a product of almost 7 years of waiting and trying to get it made. It depends on who you are. Some people have the skill to say, "I want to make this movie because I think it's going to make a lot of money. I have my finger on the marketplace and I can prove it's going to make money." But some people make movies because they want to see them and that's why I make movies. Not because I have any second or sixth sense whether it's going to be successful or not. You make what you want to make. To use *Flyboys* as an instance, here's a movie nobody had made in 80 years. An American movie about World War I aviation. It was a genre that had been forgotten yet World War I aviation is an exciting, extreme form of flying. So you say to yourself, yeah, I think this will be good and people might like it. You have no idea if you're right or not. And I already knew how visual it would be. You have to understand, I've been a pilot for 50 years, so to me it was preaching to the choir to say that this was an interesting subject. I usually do quiet, intimate films. *Flyboys* is an exception to the rule for me. I've never made an action movie. Never made a movie that costs more than $10 million. I've been the small, personal movie guy all my life. But then *Flyboys* came along and broke the mold. But that's fine, that's great. It's fun to do something new.

So if it's usually intimate but could be on a larger scale, that still leaves a lot of leeway.

It's like looking for a wife. How do you look for a wife? Do you say I want to find somebody tall, short, redhead? There are certain qualifications you tell yourself maybe you want to find, but when you find them, they probably break the rules. And hopefully they surprise you. Something comes along and sweeps you off your feet when you least expect it.

Given that a first-time writer has something that might, by some coincidence, sweep you off your feet, what criteria would they use and how in the world is he or she going to find you?

They tend to find me a little more easily than other people because I accept scripts that aren't agented. You've probably come across this syndrome that if you're a writer without an agent, your chances of getting a script to a producer are slim to none. A few of us out there, and I don't know who the others are, will accept a script that's not agented. But I look to be surprised about a new project whatever the subject is. Hopefully it's something I never thought of doing. Hopefully it uncovers, or reveals or takes me to a place I never expected to go. Which is what I expect the movie to do to the audience. But there are certain things I can predict that I'm not going to be excited by. Like a ghost movie. And I'm not a vampire guy. I'm not a spaceship guy. Gross-out comedies I'm not the right guy for. I don't have rules, but I do have predictable tastes. People do know things, and people do know themselves and I know myself well enough to know what I'm probably not going to like which, unfortunately, are 90 percent of the scripts that I get.

But there's that one, one in a hundred, which is a very high average. I would love it if it was one in a hundred.

Looking at it another way, is there anything that tells you right off the bat that this material isn't up to standard regardless of the subject?

I can tell you easily. You can open a novel, you can page through a magazine, you can tell if you're in good hands. Have you ever taken a magazine off a rack and come across a paragraph and thought, God, I have to go back and read this? This is so interesting. Any page will do. To me, a page of a script is like a drop of water from the ocean. The drop of water from the ocean contains all the elements the ocean contains. It has all the salts and minerals. And any page of a script contains the freshness, quality or style or economy that the whole script will contain. I start reading on page 1 and by page 2 or 3 I know if I'm in good hands. And, frankly, I've never been wrong. I've never found out by page 30 that what seemed to be beautifully written isn't. Or what seemed to be shabbily written isn't. And that somewhere in-between gets me to the end of the script. If what's on the page doesn't get me to the end of it, that's really the only test—if it makes me turn the page. If you're not hooked, then it's not your cup of tea. It's that simple.

Which leaves a gap between "beautifully written" and "expertly followed the formula" of, say, a how-to-write-a-screenplay book.

All those books are crap except perhaps two or three of them. Formulas don't work. They're distracting and the mark of an amateur. Look, we live in a how-to world. How to be happy, how to be your own best friend. How to live forever, how to lose weight. If you want to make money, publish a how-to book. You don't have to be right, you just have to provide a formula. Everybody wants the easy way out. They all want to know how to do it. There are the people who write the how-to books, which is like the old cynical, There are those who do and those who teach. But they're not the same people. There's no how-to book writer who's written a script that's been produced. There is acquired wisdom and there is experience and there is such a thing as knowledge. But it doesn't boil down to a formula or a how-to book. Often it's inexpressible. Often it's a matter of mileage. In my case, it's just a matter of personal taste. And I think in most people's cases that's true. But if you're the head of a studio, you can't indulge in personal taste. You have to prove that what you're doing is going to make money. That's the job, to seem to know something and act like you do. In my case, it's my resume. In my case it's the movies I've produced and directed. Within that range, there are some that represent my taste more than others. There are times when you do something that comes to you and you say, I wouldn't have picked this, but it's kind of fun, kind of a good idea.

But the first original screenplay you were drawn to with no reservations, the one that started it all for you, was Terry Malick's script, is that correct?

Which I commissioned. I had an idea to do a movie about big-rig truck driving and that's the script I commissioned Terry to write. I told John Calley, the head of a major studio, that I wanted to become a producer and the first movie I want to do is that one. There's a whole library of country and western music about trucks. It's a kind of subculture. This was before the CB phenomenon when truckers would talk to each other over the CB while rolling down the highway. But there's a whole world of singers and music about those earlier days and that subject. So that kind of turned me on to the idea of guys that are alone driving big trucks. And there's a mythology around it, a whole romance of the road that surrounds it. And I knew this young guy, this peer of mine named Terry Malick, who wanted to write movies and I thought he'd do a good job. And he came up with *Deadhead Miles* about a lone truck driver in a kind of a magical story. I loved it. I didn't love the way the movie turned out, but that's another story. The director stepped all over it and decided to rewrite it. The producer and director have to be in sync and as a first-time producer I learned the two biggest mistakes a producer can make. That's hiring the wrong director and then not firing him. But after that, all the rest of them worked out. Maybe not big hits, but they were honorable movies that turned out well.

And where did the script for *The Sting* come from?

David, a guy from UCLA, wrote a script called *Steelyard Blues* and I thought this kid was talented but it was a tough movie to get made. I asked him what he wanted to do next, and he gave me a 3 or 4 minute description. He said he wanted to write a movie about a con man in the 1930s and I said, "Great, let's do it. I want to see this movie."

Again, with no thought about its potential success.

You can't let the so-to-speak common wisdom intrude upon you or you'd never get anything made. *Rocky* was a phenomena that went against all the rules of the day. Nobody wanted to make a boxing movie. Nobody wanted to make a movie starring Sylvester Stallone who'd never been in a movie of note before. The only key that I know of to success is rejection. If something's been rejected over and over and over again, it's a pretty good sign it might be interesting. But it also might be crappy, one or the other. So, back to *The Sting* and the idea of the 1930s con man whose friend gets conned out of all his money and sets out to con the guy who conned him. I loved that idea. I got a couple of people to help me pay David to write the script.

Two years later he finished the script before Paul Newman or Robert Red-ford or the director George Hill or Universal ever saw it.

Did you offer any notes? Do you ever, and if so, are they major notes?

They could be. Every script has changes. Some are major, some are minor. But it's not like a studio who's paying somebody for the right to change it the way they want it. And there are a lot of theys there, maybe a dozen people. I, and I now include my wife, develop it without the input of the dozen other people. So it's not written by committee. When I go out with it [looking for backing and distribution] the question is not, "Would you like to develop this script?" It's, "Would you like to make this movie, yes or no?" That's the ideal. If it's a huge hit, I'll benefit from it greatly. If it's an embarrassment, I'll suffer from it greatly. It's hard to get up and dust yourself off. But so far, I've dodged that bullet.

Shifting just for a moment to TV. Where do those writers come from, the show-runners and the staff writers, etc.? Is there anything significantly different in a first writer's quest to work with others you can touch on?

There's a range of styles and situations. For the most part, most shows have multiple writers because shows have to have 24 episodes written every year, which is more than any one writer can handle. Writers write a spec script, their agent sends them over to meet people, they're a friend of a friend, all different ways. If you look at the history, many of them knew each other in college. They've been old friends of people. That's very smart because you know their strengths and their talents and you say, "Come work with me." You get a job as a writer and you know a starving writer from college and you call him up. You tell him that we've got an opening here for a writer, come on. This happens a lot. It's not some kind of formalized method by which TV writers get work. It's kind of an accident of relationships.

And the same applies to partnerships on feature films, like Ray Gideon and Bruce Evans who met in acting class.

Absolutely. And those two are wonderful writers. It's a mystery. It goes back to my wife theory. You don't say, I'm going to get a wife. You just say, I wish I had one and somewhere along the way you find one. There may even be a bulletin board somewhere with a note posted, "I'm looking for a writing partner" and that's how it's done. Or you say to someone in the business, "Who do you know who wants to write a script?"

To come to some conclusion, can we say that somewhere in the back of your mind, above and beyond strictly commercial considerations, is your taste and the ideal movie-going public?

Who wants to be enthralled and entertained. But not by anything formulaic, which is the sign of a bad everything. It's bad design and it's boring. It's breaking the formula that's exciting and interesting.

And to reach you and eventually reach that audience...

The material has got to be unlike any movie I've seen before. It's got to be fresh, original and well-written—good writing. Like someone once said about pornography, I can't tell you what it is, but I know it when I see it. Good writing is good writing. And everybody, not just me, will consider your work if you're clever enough to get it to them. A closed door doesn't mean it's all over. It just means you have to find a better way. I have always found it exciting to discover people rather than go with the sure thing.

The Film Festival Director

Steve Lawson has been executive director of the noted Williamstown Film Festival (Williamstown, Massachusetts) since the year 2000 where he has screened a countless number of independent films. Aside from being a member of the Writers Guild, his background includes the directorship of the Manhattan Theatre Club's *Writers in Performance* series, the creation of a play based on the letters of Tennessee Williams that went on to play at Hartford Stage, the Kennedy Center and Ireland's Galway Arts Festival, and a stint as the Williamstown Theatre Festival's first literary manager. He has taught at Yale and partnered with Alec Baldwin as artistic director of City Center's *Voices!* series. His television credits include the Christopher Award, nominations for an Emmy and a Humanitas Prize, the television adaptation of Broadway's *The Elephant Man*, a biopic of Edith Wharton, a stint as story editor on the television series *St. Elsewhere*, and an Emmy for the documentary *Broadway's Dreamers: The Legacy of the Group Theatre*. He is also an experienced actor and holds an M.F.A. in criticism from Yale School of Drama.

If you could reminisce a bit about your background so that readers could get some idea of what you bring to the selection process.

Actually I started out as an actor. Then I got depressed because I saw a lot of actor friends who should have been working but were not working in New York. I saw a lot of gifted people not getting a break. I can't do that. A friend of mine who did get work told me that he didn't have more talent than his colleagues, just more stamina. That's what it takes. You have to inure yourself to disappointment, unfairness and heartbreak. I gradually saw that I couldn't act in a vacuum, but I could write in a vacuum. You can't act without an audience of some kind. Writing you can do alone. I segued into journalism and wrote for a number of magazines. And out of that came my big writing break. I wrote a piece on the Broadway production of *The Elephant Man* for *Horizon* magazine based on an interview I had with the leading actors at Sardis. Right afterwards I had a residency at the MacDowell Colony where I was going to write the great American something or other. I then got this call from the head of Lincoln Center who wanted me to write *The Elephant Man* for television. He loved the article and thought I had a feel for the play. And that was my big break on television. They could have gone to any number of screenwriters and I wasn't even in the Writers Guild. After handing in the first draft I was told that you really don't have to put in camera angles. I had put in, "We zoom in on his tortured face." And that got me into the Writers Guild and led to many other things.

Like a feature film for television.

I had worked on the medical series *St. Elsewhere* and as story editor had written several scripts. Hallmark called me and asked if I wanted to write an adaptation of *The Room Upstairs*, which was based on a British novel. It's about a woman who runs a sort of boardinghouse for students. And she also has a gift with troubled kids and some betray her trust. She has cut herself off emotionally from any guy. Along comes someone who rents the room upstairs. A cellist actually, and they fall in love. It's not soppy. It's kind of prickly and interesting. Stockard Channing played the woman, Sam Waterston was the cellist and Linda Hunt played the psychiatrist. It was a remarkable cast, was shot in Vancouver and I got to go on my first location shoot.

And now we can flash forward from you as screenwriter to the one judging the work of indie writers and writer-directors. How many submissions do you usually get?

About 900, 300 feature films and I pick 11, and 33 shorts out of 600. I watch some of all of them and our local board members watch the rest and give me a very detailed evaluation. I mean, I watch so much mediocrity. You know, the trouble with a lot of indie movies these days, it's become so physically easy to make a movie. Especially with the digital revolution. It's like, hire your friends, get your mother to cater and aim and shoot. I'm serious, that's what a lot of the stuff I get at the Film Festival seems to be. I watch

7 awful shorts in a row sometimes. You won't believe this. Three years ago I had 5 shorts on the same subject about a plumber who thought he was Christ. Each one worse than the last. Maybe it was a conspiracy. Did these people know each other? No, they were sent in from all over the country. Maybe they had the same nightmare, I don't know. But you don't know when something good is going to come along. And that justifies everything.

If you had to spell out a criteria, a standard a film had to reach in order to be selected here, what would it be? In other words, how do you pick them and why do you pick them?

Having been an actor, having been a writer, those are always paramount to me. Because I was an actor, that's the first thing. If something is badly acted, it's painful. And quite often it is. Because they did hire their friends. They were cheap or they were free. I've auditioned a lot of people for the Theatre Festival and it's ruthless. And that's true now for watching submissions for the Film Festival. You can tell within 10 seconds whether or not you want to watch something. So acting is terribly important. As for writing, most bad movies are alike in more or less the same way. There's not much of an idea. It doesn't seem like a person made it. A committee made it. Or a group. I like a film if it doesn't seem as if it's been made by a committee, which most do. That's what the studios are after. They're not after originality unless it comes with a big gross. Then it's okay. Samuel Goldwyn once famously remarked, "Art and box office, fabulous. Box office and no art, good. Art and no box office, forget it." Or maybe it was the germ of a clever idea that does not necessarily make a film. In this country, we tend to confuse the idea with the achievement. Just because you tackle a serious subject does not mean you've made a serious work of art. That's the fallacy. You have to have the idea and some kind of vision of how to carry it through. Those are the films I admire most. You have the feeling that one person had the idea and knew how to do it. You get the feeling that there's one sensibility behind it. There's an intention. You're trying to say something and you have some kind of technical gifts or means to express what you're trying to put across. And the people who want to work with him or her, it's because they admire that vision. So many films you see are cranked out and anonymous. The Hollywood franchise movies that are cranked out for 19-year-old boys. But the reason many good indie films have trouble is because they don't fall into the pigeonhole. They're more complicated. Most people go to films basically for popcorn and fun. But I don't have anything against fun. I'd rather go to a wonderful comedy than a bad serious movie.

What is the background of the indie writers and writer-directors whose work you've chosen who didn't just gather their friends, aim and shoot? Who may have had an interesting idea or vision and the ability to carry it through?

A lot of them were actors and writers. Some went to film school, some didn't. It's a total mix. Basically they all wanted to make films. But even then you don't know whether or not you've really got something. I don't think you ever know until people see it. *Sex, Lies and Videotape* broke the mold. It cost $35 thousand to make and it made millions. It seemed like it was a pornographic beginning, but it didn't go in that direction; it went into the relationships of the two friends who break up over these two women. Soderbergh had an idea and he wasn't going to follow the mold. He just wanted to explore these four people. A lot of it was improvised during shooting. Which, again, was unusual. No time to do that on a big studio movie and no time to rehearse. For the four actors, who were unknown then—one was a model, one was a stage actor—it was unlike anything they'd ever done. And they certainly had no idea it would become an event at Sundance. I was knocked out by it. It was unlike other films. You have to have the goods and hope that someone appreciates it and tells you you have the goods.

And the goods for you have to include the performances.

Stanley Kaufman, one of my favorite critics, may have said it best. I think he was talking about Glenda Jackson. He said, "When she enters a room, the room then exists." You get the feeling that you're coming into a life in process. This existence is happening and we're privileged to watch it for 2 hours. And it's a fascinating existence. And you say that of any great actor: Meryl Streep or any other name you want to conjure up.

Can we talk about a feature film you've picked that wasn't associated with Sundance? Say, Brad Silberling's *10 Items or Less* with Morgan Freeman in the leading role. That's also a narrative that doesn't follow any standardized structure. How did that all come about?

Ten Items just sounded interesting and I got to meet Brad because he's married to the actress Amy Brenneman, who was at the theater last summer. Brad brought me the screenplay, which was having its world premier in Toronto. I read it. It's one of the two times in all these years where I have booked a film without seeing it. The other was *Roger Dodger* starring Campbell Scott. I just knew instinctively *10 Items* was worth doing. There was something about the script and I also knew who was in it. I admire Morgan Freeman enormously who, as a character in this script, was having a flat period in his career and was trying to get back into things with a good indie film. He's going out to observe life in East L.A., but his chauffeur gets lost and he hooks up with this unlikely friend, the checkout girl. And over a long day, she gets him back to Brentwood. It was the adventures over a long day and the way they challenge each other's perceptions. I thought it was just a good quirky little movie and an interesting meandering. It's not a story film, it's not a plot film. You're asked to be immersed in a sort of a world. I knew it was all going somewhere and I just wanted to stay with them. To see these actors play them. And the ancillary angle would be that we would be the first festival after Toronto and we would be the American premiere. Which is nice.

Can we say then that you've chosen first-class material featuring notable actors, as well as less ambitious projects because of—

Damn good taste. You know what you like and you go after it. We've had a lot of major performers like Morgan Freeman, Meryl, Gwyneth Paltrow and John Cusack who have appeared in these films. Cusack, as it happens, was also a producer on *Grace Is Gone*, which was part of his participation when they wanted him to play the lead. The producer credit went with it. And, of course, that didn't hurt in selling the film having someone like John associated with it. But I don't go after films just because they have well-known people in the cast. I just happen to like the films these people happen to be in and the fact that they were not made within the studio system. They're not commercial products; they were independently financed.

So a writer or writer-director might submit a work to you, or you might go after it after Sundance as in the case of *Grace Is Gone*. Films go to Sundance first because...

Because that's where your film sells. It's a great forum for film because most people who matter in indie film in this country go to Sundance. Buyers are there, distributors are there. Festival directors are there, other filmmakers are there. So it's a great chance to network with other people. So I go to Sundance, I also go to Tribeca in New York, and we have hundreds of films submitted to us every year. I make my wish list. I go to people directly. In the case of *Grace Is Gone*, the writer and director and producer had been here before with another feature called *Lonesome Jim*. Jim Strouse wrote that and because he and his producer wife had had a good time here, I knew I had at least a step up because they were happy to come back. *Grace Is Gone* was a big hit at Sundance; it won two major awards. It won the Audience Award and it won the Waldo Salt Award which is given for screenwriting. And it's a remarkable film. It avoids all the clichés. It could have been so hammy or melodramatic. Never. And that's why I wanted it very badly.

In the case of entries that have less cachet going for them. Would you sketch in a storyline or two that were good enough to still be on an A level?

Or at least a B+. I mean, some of them are not really bad; you can give them a B. But a B is not enough. It's never easy to put into words. It's more of a visceral feeling. There was one I chose about a Maine lobster fishermen and how this guy's territory is being poached and he accidentally causes the death of a son of one of his rivals. He goes to prison and when he comes out, everything is changed. His wife has left and he has to deal with a whole other way that he's now regarded. There was another film I booked called *Primer.* As you know, the best ideas come out of the blue. This one came out of left field and was made for $6 thousand, almost nothing. It was sort of a time-machine film about these white-collar guys who invent a machine that moves you a few moments in either direction. There's a scene where these two guys are talking about the consequences of this invention and they see themselves five minutes from now. They want to use this for the benefit of mankind, but inevitably it's corrupting. You know—"I can see what the stock market is going to do." This film explored some things that were almost impossible to show. Because it wasn't using effects or fancy time traveling.

To wrap this up, for the filmmaker whose work gets chosen here, the pool expands.

Because the more you do, the more you do. And, what's more, after you get feedback here from our audiences, it's an educational experience for the artists. You can still make changes and move on. And if you do a short and it's well-received, it's a calling card to make a feature. Like *West Bank Story*, a takeoff on *West Side Story*, about two rival falafel stands. The Kosher King and the Humus Hut are next to each other and they hate each other and try to ruin each other's business. And, of course, an Israeli border guard falls in love with the Palestinian cashier. It's not only a funny take, it also makes fun of the whole musical genre. "I will come to your balcony tonight and sing this overly dramatic song." It's only 20 minutes long and it eventually won the Academy Award. Ari called me afterwards and said, "This will help me get my feature made."

At the same time, to keep the indie world going, you're providing a service for your audiences.

Because they're hungry for something different. To be exposed to something they don't know, a take on life or on a particular subject. Expanding their horizons. It's done freshly. The writing, acting and shooting takes it into another dimension with a certain quality. Most movies you feel you've seen before under different titles. It's the same old story. They're just basically interchanging actors. A good film makes its own rules. It violates the prescribed laws. It surprises you. That's what I want, to be surprised. Cocteau said very famously, "Astound me." Surprise me. I want to be surprised. I want to have a new look on life because of what I've just seen.

The Actor for All Seasons

Campbell Scott's film appearances, which number well over 70, range from the title role of *Hamlet* (2000) to leads in *The Secret Lives of Dentists* (2002), *Roger Dodger* (2002), David Mamet's *The Spanish Prisoner* (1997), the role of Thomas Jefferson in *Liberty! The American Revolution* (1997) and Robert Benchley in *Mrs. Parker and the Vicious Circle* (1994), to work with Emma Thompson in *Dead Again* (1991), to a benign stint in *Phoebe in Wonderland* (2008). His awards include the NBR Award for Best Actor for *Roger Dodger* and six nominations for Best Male Lead and Best Actor (Chlotrudis Award, DVD Premiere Award, Video Premiere Award, Genie, Independent Spirit Award) for various other roles. In addition, he won the Boston Society of Film Critics Award for Best New Filmmaker for *Big Night* (1996) and was nominated for the Grand Special Prize at the Deauville Film Festival, The Golden Precolumbian Circle, The Sundance Grand Jury Prize and the Independent Spirit Award in the same category for this same film.

No doubt you can shed some light on the whole process. What if we started with your role in *Dead Again*, working with actress Emma Thompson and that script? Then compare that experience with, say, director Robert Altman's loose attitude toward scripts and way of working, and just take off from there?

With *Dead Again* we pretty much did what was exactly on the page. But everybody's different, right? They all make their movies in a different way. Altman thought of a script as a blueprint. I worked with Craig Lucas a number of times, who is essentially a playwright. He's no blueprint guy. It's all there, very economical, very well thought about. There's not a lot of ad lib with Craig Lucas. Just like in screenwriting, there are no formulas as far as I'm concerned.

But we can at least say that, at any rate, as an actor, the words in the script do something for you.

Of course. But, as an actor, I'm always gauging what I'm playing against. In that, it's very specific. The fact that in trying to convince Emma Thompson (who is suffering from amnesia) I'm her boyfriend, I'm not telling the truth. I'm doing something else. As the character, I was paid to do that, so I was just making some money. The thrill for my character was that he was involved in a false act. Which was fun and he was crazy. You see, I think more like a writer-director when I'm acting. I always look at the whole thing. It's about rhythms. It's all music to me. It's about getting beats right, getting rhythms right. And doing the unexpected. Being mysterious. All that stuff. In *Dead Again* I was just trying to be as kind and sweet as possible until the Kenneth Branagh character found me out. When I act, I'm always looking for different things to happen in each take based on what's written there. If the writing is great, you're always trying to do one of two things. You're trying to exactly capture the complexity of what's there because it's that well written. Or you're trying to go off the track in some way. Do what's written but find something that no one would have thought of. 'Cause it's all resolved in the editing room anyways, let's face it.

What if it's not well written?

If I take the job, I have to make it engaging for myself before it's engaging for you. I've got to come up with something. Like I said, I have to find something to play against. The cliché is, if it's a happy scene you play it seriously. There are all kinds of little nuances involved. You have to go with your instinct plus you're also guided by whoever is directing you. In the case of *Dead Again,* Scott, the screenwriter, was on the set and we all knew that movie was a big con game. I've done a couple of those and those are different than reality playing right out in front of you.

Which takes us to David Mamet's *Spanish Prisoner*.

Another con game. But this time I wasn't the con guy, I was being conned. David likes to think in that way. What he's interested in is, "What is superficial? What is on the surface? The rest of it will take care of itself." That's one way of looking at things. His movies definitely have a style that's unlike other movies. That script was very, very concise. He's very particular being an ex-playwright and still a playwright. He's very particular about getting all the words correct. He's not an ad-libber like Altman, who is the opposite. Bob is interested in you, the actor. Alan Rudolph, a writer and another director like Bob Altman, is the total opposite of David. He loves the actors and he can't really decide what the scene is about until you show him what it's about based on what you're doing and what you're throwing out. That's a lot more rewarding as an actor because you feel like you're more a part of it. Just different styles.

What if it's very specific on the page and a known figure? Is it still an either-or—lots of room to explore or more tightly controlled—depending on the specificity of the script and who's calling the shots?

If I'm playing Robert Benchley in Alan Rudolph's *Mrs. Parker and the Vicious Circle*, I'm playing someone I can actually look at and watch. A lot of the dialogue was stuff that had already been said by these very smart, witty people. You show up, you have the clothes on and you're in the room and you've been with all the actors talking about who you're playing and what it must have been like. But it's all false. Nobody really knows what the people were like, which is always what's dangerous about it. I've played real people a couple of times. I've played a Kennedy. They're always scarier because you're not going to be them. With Benchley, who was truly funny and a wonderful comic, actually I looked very much like him when he was younger. Then he started drinking and got kind of roly-poly. Those are more dangerous jobs, especially if you like the person. So you've got to come up with an essence of some kind. As far as what's on the page, that's just your starting point. We had all kinds of old film clips. But yes, it depends so much. Like they say, film is a collaborative art. You better get along with that, you know, or you're going to be pretty lonely. What I mean is, when you make a movie like that, you have all this material, a certain amount of research, you have your feelings and your instinct and then you have your talents, whatever they are. They can be short or long. Then you have the guy who's guiding everything, the crew, the day and the rain.

So, project after project and over time...

I think what you learn, hopefully as you get smarter and older, is to get it together. To learn like you learn anything. To—like any great athlete will tell you—relax more as opposed to trying to make a point. The worst scripts are the ones that keep, as you say, keep making points every 10 seconds. None of us want to see points and we don't recognize the points when they come up to us in our lives. We don't recognize the messages. These are cumulative things. We go to our child's graduation, we don't understand how we feel. Maybe six months later we can figure it out, what it means to us and them and all these things. At the time, when it's actually happening? No, we don't know. That's what makes it so interesting. So it often comes down to like we said, Shakespeare was the best, right? Who asks the questions the best? There are plenty of scripts that answer all kinds of questions. They're shallow. Those are the easy formula scripts. Not only in structure but in what they say. And when we see these movies, they begin, we immediately know who the villain is, who the protagonist is, we know what's going to happen. We like a certain kind of food and go and eat that for a while. It's like taking a little ride or something. To make a differentiation between the kinds of movies you're making is an important thing and in the kinds of scripts you're looking at. Nowadays when I get a script I always ask other things. Who's making it? What's the budget? How long do they have to make it? Who wrote it? All those things are important. You get a feeling like, "Oh, this is a commodity script. Or is this actually something we're going to explore?" You go into it knowing one thing or the other as opposed to being resentful of either one. Hopefully that helps you in how you translate it. I've been on the kinds of things I would call mortgage paying jobs and not resent them. Your colleagues are always still your colleagues. You try to mix it up and still find good things to do. And surprise yourself. And go from there.

Have you run across a script you just absolutely couldn't do anything with?

No. I would have never taken the job in the first place. Even if I'm broke and desperate and it's a silly TV movie, I have found something in it. Whether it's the character or what the character does or somebody who's involved or whatever I can count on.

But obviously it's much more rewarding for you to work on a Craig Lucas script.

He wrote *Longtime Companion*, which I acted in. He adapted Jane Smiley's novella which became *The Secret Lives of Dentists*. He wrote from his own play and directed *The Dying Gaul*, so I've done three of his scripts. I love his writing because, as I say, it's very concise. There's very little on the page, yet you know there's a lot of thought behind it. There is nothing arbitrary. They're very delicate scenes. David Mamet is a wordsmith, which is nice and fun music to play. Craig is that but he's always working on another layer. Craig can kind of put you in a real scene. It's all fake, as we all know. But no one is looking for what's real but what's true. That's what Craig is good at. His scenes are severely accurate about behavior and little changes in the dynamics of a room between two people and what they do. And he's very deliberate about that. He's a pleasure, obviously, and I keep going back. But very different than everybody else. The difference between working with one of Craig's scripts and Alan Rudolph's is a huge difference. You just have to know before you go or figure it out as you go.

So, based on the material, you know going in whether it's a commodity or a creative springboard. If it's a springboard, you're fairly certain it will provide you and your fellow actors, plus the director and everyone else concerned, with a unique challenge and you take it from there. If we shift

to the times when you yourself are wearing the hat of the director or producer and/or writer, what additional or similar things are you aware of?

In the material, I look for mystery. I look to be surprised. I really look for the un-understandable. I mean I look for something that feels true but isn't explained. 'Cause that's what life is. Life feels true but no one is explaining it. The best thing to work on is something that reflects that as much as possible. Shakespeare did it. He was shockingly, psychologically accurate and at the same time he had these huge themes that you could never conquer. Everybody talks about Hamlet. I've played it a couple of times. That's the perfect example of a long script in which there is not one answer. Nothing but questions. But they've never been stated like that before, either perfectly, beautifully or provocatively. And that's why people keep working on it. I always compare all this, everything we're talking about, either to athletics or nature. Because they're activities or phenomena that we engage in but can never quite describe. But we keep going back. A great piece of writing is like a mountain. You can scale it a million different ways, give up halfway up, or can only make it to the top when you're older and can understand it better. Or you can make it to the top when you're young and don't understand a damn thing about it. And the experience of that mountain will change, even if it's beloved, because you change. That's what great writing is. Scripts are the hardest because they are really the first step. The old cliché is true. You make three movies: the one you write, the one you shoot and the one you edit. Every time I make a movie I learn the same lessons over again. Now when I write it's all about what to remove. You do so much of that in the second and third phase. You're always in a place where you say, "I don't need this. Why did I think I needed it? Get rid of it." That's a huge lesson that you learn over and over again. I did *Hamlet* and we were taking stuff out.

Even though that writer was the best.

Which made us very intimidated about removing stuff. But once we started, it was fantastic and liberating and amazing. The way things started to juxtapose against each other was great.

And when you yourself write a movie script?

It could start anywhere. It could start with an idea, a character, a line. I never finish anything. I have to make the movie to finish it. I wrote a 10-page outline trying to get a movie made over my fascination with reality television. It's more manipulative than fiction, but I don't care as long as it's engaging. It was about two guys, a producer and director who pitch a reality show which is doomed from its inception. They're doing it just for the money. They enter the mountains with all these contestants and the show bottoms out. So it's really about what happens to people from different companies in the mountains when they thought they were going to battle each other in teams—white collar and blue collar—on company-themed contests. But because it's not well thought out, they find they don't have anything to do and it turns into chaos.

Totally un–Craig Lucas. More like an Alan Rudolph or Bob Altman blueprint.

Here's a good way of explaining it. The movies I've directed or co-directed before this were all very well scripted. I wanted to do something that I couldn't control. I wanted to do something that was improvised. I really wanted it to be a lump of something that we chipped away at. Because I'm usually very definitive when I'm working at something. It was a way of challenging myself. Because it was a quick script with a hand-held camera, it lent itself to that kind of movement. It had 50 speaking parts; it was crazy. It became more about the experience of making it than what we were making. Forty-five hours of material and I haven't even started editing. This is more than anything a movie that will be written in the editing room.

But back to the ideal relationship between scripting and acting. In that great movie you produced and directed, *Big Night*, there was so much really fine actors could bring to this '50s New York story. Like Isabella Rossellini's character. What is her backstory? Why is she still married to this shady restaurateur with his flashy restaurant and low-grade food who is trying to con the master chef from a rival restaurant that's hanging on by a shoestring? What does the restaurateur feel about himself underneath it all as he works this scam? How, in turn, does the chef juggle his own feelings and desire to succeed in partnership with his brother, the part played by Stanley Tucci, while sensing the irrepressible pull of Italy calling him back?

I agree. I think it was one of the best scripts I ever read. It allowed for all those things. You knew if you had good actors playing these parts, it could become something special. But that script took seven years to write. That was Stanley, an actor, and his cousin, a writer. And it started off as a ridiculous farce. And it just got more and more real as they worked on it on and off. By the time it got to the script I read, it was no longer a farce. It was a really deep, interesting, thoughtful script. But that's just good writing. I don't know how you describe that or explain it. In many ways it's unexplainable. But you know good actors are going to be attracted to it because it's not what we see most of the time. Opening the script is usually damage control. How can I make something out of this? When you open something and you're actually turning pages, half the work is done. How often does it happen? Why? Because it's hard to write a good script. One of the keys is, new information only. That has become almost a mantra with me. It can become many different kinds: emotional information, story information, character information. Just don't ever repeat it. We're too worried about people understanding and getting it.

But if it's there and it's good, ultimately...

If you've done your job, movies ultimately become about the people watching it. It has nothing to do with you or your script. It just has to do with them. As I got older, that's what I realized. Why am I trying so hard to make my point? My point is never going to be made anyway. It's not my movie anymore. It's about them and their lives. Don't ask me questions. Answer them. I don't know anymore. I had a whole other thing in mind when I made this. Now the movie is about you. In *Big Night*, ultimately someone will tell you a story about their family or their brother. Or the guys who had the good hardware store and the guy down the street who had the flashy store. They'll say, "Oh, I get that." It has nothing to do with me or those two guys and their problems with their little restaurant. That's what's good about it. There's no message, no formula. A formula is the antithesis of writing something good. It doesn't mean you're not informed by architecture or try to express yourself in informed ways. And what you and I mean by formula is an easy way to describe what to do. It takes me back to athletics. It doesn't mean you don't train and watch other athletes. To get inspiration, to learn how they do it. You go up against others and challenge yourself in that way. It doesn't mean you don't take a rest from it all sometimes. It doesn't mean you don't read about it. But in the end, when the gun goes off, you run. If you're a good runner and you've trained well and you've got someone pacing you whom you respect, and once the gun goes off you forget about all that, then you run well. You're in an environment where something can happen. And a good script is that way too. You can't create great moments. You can only create the pockets and space for them to happen.

The Versatile Writer-Director

Brad Silberling is one of those rare writer-directors who is able to shift between projects of varying scope. *Ten Items or Less* (2006) centers on a famous Hollywood actor who hasn't worked in a while who runs into Scarlet, a frustrated clerk at an express checkout line, and develops an easygoing, mentoring relationship. *Moonlight Mile* (2002) concerns a family and a fiancé's struggle to come to grips with the loss of the bride-to-be as the fiancé finds himself under his not-quite-in-laws' roof, forced to be the son they never had and, by proxy, the daughter they lost. On an entirely different note, Silberling has the multiplex hit *Lemony Snicket's A Series of Unfortunate Events* (2004) and 2009's *Land of the Lost* along with numerous TV episodes on his list of directing credits. In addition, he was nominated for Best Original Screenplay by the Phoenix Film Critics Society for *Moonlight Mile*.

Can you tell me what led you to screenwriting?

Very shrewd words of my father who was neither a writer or in film production but was working as a television executive. As a kid, I decided when I was eleven I was going to be a film director shooting short, silent films. My father said, "Honey, there are a lot of other boys' sons who want to be directors too. You're going to have to start writing because you're going to need to truly create your own work." And this was back in the seventies. The competition was stiff and if you weren't pro-active, you were in trouble. So I backed into making those silent shorts and my own scenarios but not cognizant of the fact that I was writing. I didn't take any courses in film as an undergrad. Then came my natural love of the process.

As a result, did you ever have a total indie experience, total control over your vision or anything close?

I have had. Actually in one film, Morgan Freeman and I owned the movie. I wrote, directed and produced the movie with a Spanish actress entitled *10 Items or Less*. Purely for the love and experience of the movies about everybody aligning themselves with their art and their passion. It can't get a whole lot more indie than that. You know, everybody assumes the worst of the studio experience, but I had a similar experience with a movie I wrote, directed and produced called *Moonlight Mile*. I was completely left alone. I cast Jake Gyllenhaal in the lead role and the studio said, I don't know about this kid but we'll go along with it. It was Jake and Dustin Hoffman and Susan Sarandon and Holly Hunter. But then the head of the studio left the job and a new regime came in and what is beyond your control is how a movie gets marketed. This new regime at Disney began living their dream of making large tent-pole movies out of theme rides, pirate movies—you know, than an actual character-driven drama. But you have to pay the piper according to what their agenda is.

What was the evolution of *Moonlight Mile* in terms of inspiration and storyline? For instance, a dramatist once told me you're not truly ready to write until one of your basic assumptions is threatened.

Well, yeah, sure. I had a girlfriend in Los Angeles who was murdered. It took about four years and I wanted to find a way to—really what I was so struck by was all the unspoken and unwritten rules. A connection with the survivors. My girlfriend who was an only child had a set of parents who were extraordinary people. We didn't know each other that well but all of a sudden because of the event we were thrust into this new family paradigm. Very complicated and moving and difficult. You would certainly say that that's having a challenge that inspires you to put it down on paper. So I went off and created. It's a total piece of fiction but it made tangible what was emotionally true. I turned something concrete what was before metaphorical. And that's even true of *10 Items or Less*. That came out of the experience working with Dustin Hoffman in *Moonlight Mile*. At the time, he hadn't done a picture for three years. He was in such a plateau of success that he was scared that he might fail. Suddenly he was starving himself, wasn't really doing his work. I was really struck by that so I wrote a film about, again, what's your worst fear? Your worst fear is that you've let your art down. So that was the root of a fairly simple character relationship that all takes place in one day. So I always come from a place where there's always got to be an emotional connection.

And that's the same way Anthony Minghella works.

He's a friend. We talk about this a lot. It always surprises you that even when adapting material it's the same thing. Because whether it's a novel or your own life or some incident you see on the street, you're always adapting because your emotional centers go off. And you have to be willing to cling to that story for a year or five years. You can't work just according to a formula. I was watching *The Last Detail* the other night, a perfectly wonderful film that was revolutionary in its time. But a screenwriters handbook would just choke on it. Unfortunately kids are always looking for the quickest road to success. In film school, they all want to figure what the shortest line is. Maybe you get lucky and do that. But then what? What kind of investment are you going to make in yourself and your work?

Which brings us back to Dustin Hoffman and Holly Hunter who may have, through their own integrity, in some way influenced the process.

Surprisingly, Dustin Hoffman clings to the foundation of the screenplay. He and I engaged very early on in pure character conversations. The character he played was a composite of my girlfriend's father and elements of my father. And we got into conversations about his. So his was an indirect contribution. I would take these conversations and add a detail that I thought was startling. I would take a gesture of his that was repetitious and sneak it into the screenplay and he would laugh. In Holly's case, her character was based on an actual person and I was able to hook her up with this attorney I knew who was a D.A. And then what was great was that Holly would come back to me and say, there's this thing that she does or this turn of a phrase. So we would incorporate that and kind of re-craft it. And that's the beauty of the freedom of the process.

Now can we talk a little about the influence of the place and the location?

It was shot in and around Marblehead, Massachusetts, right off the water. My mother's family is from just outside of Boston. We spent time back there every year and it's sort of in my blood. The original story didn't take place there but I loved having it there to access it. It all goes hand in hand. There was a certain effortful quality that affected the lead character, the young man. And also a kind of effortful quality that exists in this particular community. He's being thrust into a typecast role. He feels like a thousand watt bulb in the darkness where he can't really hide. He's dying to be invisible and sit on this secret but this community is perfect because Marblehead has very few even planes. It forces him to worm his way into a frame and also made him feel nakedly exposed. It's a rabbit warren. That's the thing about it. It's a very tight little community. The streets keep spilling onto each other. It's not a place for secrets. It was a perfect place to stick this kid who had to sit on a secret for most of the movie, play this part and be a stranger. So we took great advantage of all of that and take the images to support the characters.

Shifting back for a moment, did any of your early TV writing have any effect on the way you write?

It did on a number of levels. It forces you purely in terms of survival. The pressure of handing in some new pages when you're under the gun. You learn to trust your intuitive skills and think on your feet. You get very good at boiling things down. You don't have time to over-think. The process is so fast, to get to the root of the story, the root of the performance. And just the overall economy of it. And the format—forty-two, forty-seven, forty-five minutes. It is ruthless. So you learn not to forget the essential story of the scene. You just have got to get to it. You can't handpick your orchestra; you've got to work with what they hand you.

Taking all this into account—and putting aside the pressure of certain

shows and formats—left to your own devices, are there certain circumstances or dilemmas that you always feel drawn to?

Interesting, as others have said before and as a mentor told me, you'll be telling the same story your whole career. The characters may change their wardrobes but you've got to be working on the same story. I think I'm fascinated by stories of people learning to trust the truth in relationships. There's a certain throughline in a lot of the films I've written where you've got characters who are difficult enough to find antipathy in life. And if they can be strengthened and not broken by honesty and truth that has got to come out, will that crumble a relationship? Interesting, you're never conscious of it in many different and wildly different genres. But I know when I write I'm interested in these kind of stories. They don't all have to be on a small scale like *10 Items*, which was really a two-hander. We did it in fifteen days for $2 million. And then I've done much larger scale pieces. But there's still usually some essential character quality, some kind of perseverance coming through an ordeal that I'm interested in.

And what's really going on underneath.

Yes. How can you honor that subtext and give it a voice? Is that voice going to be too powerful for people sometimes or disconcerting and it's always—I'm fascinated by that. That in a lot of these stories the truth is finally exposed. Is it going to destroy everybody or is it going to strengthen them? And that's often the fulcrum in these stories that I'm interested in. Those are really rich dramas and I'm always interested in how they play out. As family secrets come out to see how they ripple through.

Shifting focus again, what happened in your mainstream experience with Lemony Snicket and especially the hyper comic Jim Carrey, who seems to be desperate for approval?

I haven't met or worked with a stand-up comic who doesn't have that potential deficit. I mean, they all work in different ways but have to get that attention, that sort of love even if it's negative love, I guess. So you know that going in as a writer and as a director. They have to know that they're killing as a comedian and they're really doing well. But that's going to be a different performer from somebody who doesn't need that [in interpreting the script and in being directed]. And what's going to happen to everyone else in a long shoot like this, over a hundred and twenty-one days.

In adapting the three books, I assume there were parts that were left out, parts that were added as you shaped the shooting script.

Oh yeah. I had read the first three books but the two studios involved had planned to work from the first and the third book. But to me the third book was vital in terms of the lead character's emotional growth. So for contrast so they weren't just living one experience the whole movie but seemed to have a bundle of hope and then the hope is dashed and all those good turns. There were constant choices that had to be made in terms of what was included or not. There's a very repeated rhythm in each book. In our case, you couldn't repeat a rhythm three times. You had to create incidents that would create transitions. You had to hold back certain conflicts that couldn't play out at the end of the third act of the movie. So we definitely had to work on some narrative architecture. Then again, the novelist was wonderful. He was constantly in the process. I dragged him in all the time. Even though I was shifting from one book to another, he was very constructive and helpful.

One last question. Has your approach evolved over time or do you take each project as it comes?

Well, I tell you. I just went up to be a mentor or creative advisor or whatever they call it at Sundance. And I was dealing with a lot of first time writers and directors who are all looking to find some sort of nugget of truth. And what I do know is true, and I think that it pertains to every facet of writing, directing and even choosing projects to work on. And it's this movement toward the intuitive. You learn to rely on yourself more. You learn to let yourself know you have the tools to survive. You don't have to become over-obsessed with planning and backup plans but if you are, movies are only interesting in terms of the life that comes out of them. You have to be in tune with what's happening and that can't happen if your nose is stuck inside your script. It has to come from the discoveries you're making and little accidents because you discover something on the way to work and you put into your movie all these things. I notice that in the creative process and with all the directors I admire or am friendly with. This essential trust in storytelling. I mean, in *10 Items or Less* I wrote that script very quickly. And, other than as a director in choosing my locations, until the moment of doing it, I was going to trust it. And that's where the thrill is in terms of the evolution of my work. First and foremost you have to hire wonderful actors and you may have a plan. But the film is never what you set out to make. It's all about the actors and having a good enough story to hang the work on.

The Hollywood Writing Partners

Bruce A. Evans and Ray Gideon engage in their writing process around a long wooden table in a spacious, secluded, semi–Mediterranean home off Sunset Boulevard. Their work first came to prominence with *Starman* (1984). Among their other screenwriting ventures that came to fruition are *Stand by Me* (1986), *Made in Heaven* (1987), *Kuffs* (1992), *Cutthroat Island* (1999), and *Mr. Brooks* (2007). *Stand by Me* earned them an Oscar nomination for Best Screenplay on material from another medium and the Writers Guild Award. Bruce Evans also won a Special Jury Prize as director for *Kuffs* and often directs as well as collaborates with his writing partner, Ray. Ray Gideon, in turn, has appeared in feature films and has many acting credits on television as well.

What if we started with books and seminars?

RAY: I haven't read any of the books. All I know is that none of the authors have ever had a film produced. Maybe they're not interested in having anything produced, I don't know.

BRUCE: Robert McKee is doing very, very well. His seminars are making a ton of money and lots of people show up.

RAY: What happens, what the result is, is scriptwriting courses, whether they're alive or in a book, is that they're often attended by a lot of aspiring studio executives. They come in as assistants or interns and try to follow the system so rigidly they'll go, "Well, the character hasn't done this here. On page 13 you have to have your first plot point."

BRUCE: There's a theory that's led to the homogenization of movies. It's not the writers, it's the executives. They are the ones. The executives, the agents, they've all gone to take the course to understand what the structure is supposed to be. If you're working with a manager or agent and you have a script that's ready to sell, they have been to the course and the studio executive has also been to the course. You have people trying to fit everything into a box.

RAY: A story, a screenplay, whatever, will have a natural rhythm. In other words, it's like telling a joke. La la la, la la la, and there's a punch line — one, two, three. And yes, plot points now have to be closer to the beginning of a movie, say 12 or 13 pages in, because we're moving so fast. Warren Beatty said this to us once, he said, "What's changed the world is this remote control. You can only keep my attention so long." Commercials tell you a story in 30 seconds.

BRUCE: If you look at the old movies, they moved very slowly. Very little information compared to the movies today.

RAY: A lot of them, you go look at them and you say, let's go re-look at that piece and in terms of today's world they have only about 30 minutes of story.

BRUCE: What stands up is *Notorious*, which is wonderful to see. And *Casablanca*. They have more going on and their characters are so strong that they push you forward.

RAY: And with *Casablanca* they never knew how it was going to all turn out. Paul Greengrass, who did *The Bourne Ultimatum*, was saying that he likes to not know entirely how a scene is going to be on the set because things can happen.

So, somewhere apart from the seminars and many of the old movies, we have the successful work of the two of you. What led you to this craft and your particular way of working?

BRUCE: What happened, the journey that led us to screenwriting was that we didn't become movie stars. We were both actors. If we had become movie stars, I would have never written. Why would you write if you could become a movie star?

RAY: I'm from an Indian reservation in Eastern Canada. And like everybody, you sit in a darkened movie house and you watch a movie and you come here and you want to be Paul Newman. And you want to be whomever. And when you get here...

BRUCE: You look around and you go, "Jeez, there are a lot of Paul Newmans."

RAY: And a lot of guys from the reservation. To survive, I taught French at Berlitz and I managed a little movie theater and did every little play in every little house. And got involved in an improv group with Rob Reiner, Albert Brooks, Richard Dreyfus, Teri Garr, etc. We all swore on blood that we would be there for two years. But two weeks into it, Rob said he had an announcement to make that he got this TV series, *All in the Family*, but didn't think it would go well. And Richard was going to Montreal to shoot a movie and Albert was going to Vegas. Within two weeks the group dissolved and evolved into a group hanging around the Evergreen Stage on Fountain here. And lo and behold, Bruce and his girlfriend at the time showed up and a friend said he wanted to do a short film. He was looking for a story and I sketched out a story for him called *The Frog Lady* featuring Bruce's girlfriend.

How did you know how to write the story?

RAY: Actually I was at a party and a guy said he had this story but it wasn't a story, just an idea about a guy who comes out of a bar, sees a frog and kisses it and it becomes a beautiful princess. I told him what to do. He didn't like it so I told it to the guy at the playhouse. He said to write it up because it was exactly what he was looking for. I wrote it up, had to pay for half the shoot and starred in it as a showcase. It won an Oscar nomination and a bunch of awards. A month after that, Bruce showed again after hanging around the set and said he needed a master's thesis for his thesis at UCLA: "Do you want to sit down and write something?" I had never written anything beside the short.

BRUCE: And the commercials I was doing were putting me through film school. I never said anything to anyone at school about being an actor because they would want me to act in their things. And I didn't think I was a very good actor.

RAY: So we sat down and wrote a short thing, a kind of tongue-in-cheek murder mystery. Bruce's parents put up half the money and I put up the other half, because I was doing all those commercials, upon condition that I starred in it. And it almost became a series at Fox.

But still and all, you must have had some guidelines to go by, some touchstones you picked up along the way.

BRUCE: My teacher at UCLA, William Froug, had a book of interviews with screenwriters—just like this one, the one you're doing with us—which he handed out. And I had read that. However, for both of us the best writing training was the acting training. I had classes and Ray had had classes and I did a lot of improv work. There it's basically how you got into a scene as an actor, what you wanted in that scene and how you would progress the scene forward as the actor. What were your goals, your moment to moment goals, your overarching goal?—all of those things, that became our way. We were always writing for actors to play it. We weren't writing in a vacuum. We couldn't do that. We also asked whether this scene would entertain us if we saw it. This most valuable interview in Froug's book was the part when Nunnally Johnson basically said that when he started going to the movies there was a hat rack under your seat. Men came in and put their hats under the rack. He said, "My job as a screenwriter was to keep that man from reaching for his hat and to stay and see what happens." That was to us always the motivating thing. Can you keep the audience interested and keep them from reaching for their hats? That was the one tip that stayed with us.

RAY: Basically, the best course in writing is to get an acting teacher and get involved in improv and do plays. If you're out there and the audience says you're dying....

You mean if the energy isn't triangulating. They aren't feeding you or validating your work so that you have something to keep you going. By extension, when you're writing you have to sense that same positive energy somehow, that something that keeps you progressing.

RAY: Yes. Nunnally Johnson also said that in a screenplay, the word should advance the sentence, the sentence should advance the paragraph, the paragraph should advance the scene, the scene should advance the movie. There used to be a critic here for the *L.A. Times* that said...

BRUCE: "There is no substitute for the story that keeps you caring about the lives of characters, whether they live or die or get what's coming to them."

RAY: Basically, when you come right down to it, if you don't have a story to tell, you can't write. You need the story. You basically need that energy. There are a ton of movies being made that don't have that basic energy. They have no character. None of these movies would you want to see a second or third time.

Are you including the slacker movies with main characters who have no drive or wit, and things that just happen to them? How do they fit into your ideas about caring about characters' lives, a basic story to tell and energy? Or are the slacker movies the exception?

BRUCE: Which captures the lie about all the theories of how to do it. There is no real answer to how to do it. This is how we do it, what we look for. You do a story and it hits the zeitgeist of the moment and you are successful. Which may hugely out-gross *Chinatown. Chinatown* may have been too taxing for them. *Shampoo* couldn't be made today because of its moral ambiguity. It would be difficult for a studio to green-light it. Ideally, you're involved in the life of some character. Truffaut once said, "The difference between American and European movies is in a European movie you're watching a plane take off. It takes off beautifully into the sky and you watch it and watch it and it disappears. In an American movie it takes off and you watch it and it explodes." Now you have, why did the plane explode? and now you're off and running on that. The American movies are certainly doing well around the world but it's just a different sensibility. Hopefully there will always be room for both of them. The fear is that the corporatization of the movie business will rule out movies like *Little Miss Sunshine* because it will be difficult to get the money to do them in the search for some formula that will guarantee the greatest financial success.

RAY: However, as Paul Greengrass said, the big hits will trickle down and allow the smaller movies to be made.

BRUCE: And we really do need them. And Ray and I really do like to entertain people. When people ask us about a film like *Mr. Brooks*, "What's the hidden meaning?" the hidden meaning is that this is the kind of movie that I would like to go see. It's scary, it's funny, it's totally twisted and original.

And in originating it, in doing something you'd like in your particular way, how did it start?

RAY: We had done, all essentially so far, PG family films. Since, as Bruce pointed out, we were now adults, we decided to do a totally adult film. So it's like, what do you write about? What if? What if? What if? Oh, addiction is interesting. We're all addicted to something. To movies, some people are addicted to alcohol, clothes, shopping. We thought the ultimate addiction would be murder. And that kicked it off.

BRUCE: People have kind of slammed us because they say that killing people is not an addiction. But reading about the sexual thrill some of these guys got, it becomes very addictive. You look for that high. It feeds something, it supplies something. Like an alcoholic needs to take that drink, that guy who needs to take that drug, whatever it gives you.

So can we say there's the borrowed frog-story idea and many what ifs? that followed? Have there been other kinds of springboards?

RAY: The first screenplay we ever wrote, after we'd done the short, we took the cinematographer out for dinner, passed a construction site for the future Independence Bank and the cinematographer said, "Hey, guys, let's rob the bank." Bruce and I looked at each other and knew that that was our screenplay *All About Adam*.

BRUCE: It was one of the first really good lessons in screenplay writing. If you have a screenplay called *All About Adam*, you should have a character named Adam in the screenplay. Instead, what we did was metaphorical. It was all about man. Man doing his job from the outside instead of the inside, pushing a few buttons, passing the alarm system and walking in. Then, taking the money, pushing a few buttons, resetting the alarm and getting away with everything. But it takes time for the building to go up and what lives do they lead while they're doing this? A guy falls in love with this girl and on and on. But not one of them is named Adam.

Did you have an agent at this time who encouraged you?

BRUCE: No. I was at a party, there was a guy there who had co-directed *Performance*. I cornered him, told him I had written a script that he had to read, I'd seen *Performance* and loved *Performance*. "Please, please read the script."

No agent. Selling a spec script by making a direct contact, just like _The Player_.

BRUCE: Yeah. And he said to send it to his agent and I said if we send it to your agent you'll never get it. Please, we want you to read it. We knew enough even then not to send it to the agent. So he said to show up at his house, he gave the address, tomorrow morning at 8 A.M. because he was leaving for Europe the next day. He'll see if he likes it and we'll go from there. So Ray and I were at his place at 8 in the morning and he opened up and there were two beautiful Asian women right behind him and we thought, we're in the wrong end of this business. We handed him the script and in a couple of days we got a call and he said, "I love this script and I'm going to give it to Donald Sutherland." Two weeks after that, Donald Sutherland called and said he loved it. He bought it for $100,000, which was more money than we had ever had.

RAY: And now the price for that spec script would have been much much higher.

BRUCE: Luckily it got made but not as well as we would have wanted. Donald called and said, "I think we screwed up your movie but I want to take you to lunch." We stayed in touch, and later his son Kiefer got the part in _Stand by Me_, not just because we knew him but because he came in and got the part. He was an excellent actor.

RAY: Everybody else who auditioned was doing a bad imitation of James Dean.

I'm still trying to zero in on your process. Putting aside the frog story and the chance encounter with a construction site, how do the two of you generally work? How does a script usually evolve?

BRUCE: Ray shows up between 9:30 and 10. We read the paper and what we've done the night before. We make some changes and go to lunch or go work out. Come back and go through business with the agents if there's something to talk about. And at the end of the day, we really get into it and write until midnight.

RAY: Sometimes we'll get up and act it out. What if? What if? What if? But if it's not going anywhere....

BRUCE: You scream at your writing partner. Why can't he think of the answer? Or we'll switch to a another piece.

RAY: And one of the best lessons to learn is that sometimes you have to throw out your best scene.

BRUCE: Then you're back to What if? What if? and you go from there.

RAY: We usually know how it's going to end. I'm at the computer. And the reason I'm at the computer is that when we first started, I was the only one who had enough money to buy a typewriter. It was electric. We were going to switch off but the way Bruce was pounding on it, I said, "Bruce, you're going to ruin my typewriter." Anyway, it's like you start across the country at night with your headlights on. You can only see as far as your headlights but eventually you make it all the way across the country. The most difficult thing is coming up with the first scene. It's like that movie you mentioned, *The Hours*. When Nicole Kidman comes down and said, "I have my first line," then right away any writer who's ever written knows what that means. The first line is the most difficult thing.

BRUCE: They're all difficult. So it's a What if? and you move forward.

All the way through the first draft?

RAY: No. When you read our first draft we've rewritten every scene 5 or 6 times. We never finish a scene and say we'll come back to it. No. If it's not right we get it right or we throw it out.

BRUCE: Some guys can write real fast in days. Maybe 110 pages a day and say, "That works for me." Then go back over it.

RAY: Alvin Sergeant writes a scene and thinks it'll fit in somewhere. We can't do that.

BRUCE: Alvin will write a scene. Gary Ross will write an extensive outline. And he works and works on the outline. Apparently he works on a 200 page outline. I think that the methods, if you go to the guys who write, everybody has a different method. And if you do go to a book, it's what's applicable to you. You somehow work that into your method or into your thinking. The Nunnally Johnson thing; that stuck with us. And there are a bunch of other writers in Froug's book, and that stuck with us. And they all work different ways. But it's very difficult to write if you don't have a story to tell. Even if it's written beautifully.

RAY: Lorenzo Semple Jr. was giving a class at NYU film school and said that this student was going to write a screenplay about a clothing designer and the big crisis in the whole thing was that he couldn't find a pin for the hat. And Lorenzo Semple said, "Marines in a blinding snowstorm could not drag people off the street in to see your movie. What are you talking about?"

BRUCE: It may be fantastic, it may be great. But give yourself a chance with the subject that you choose, to get it on. Once you get it on, hopefully people will come. The idea is how you process it. The great line in *Sunday in the Park with George* is where he says, "Everything's been done." And his mother says, "But not by you." So that's the difference. Find the story that's been told umpteen times and still tell it your way. And it will be different enough.

RAY: Give yourself those energies, give yourself a story. Two nuns walk into a building into an elevator to see the dentist. The door closes, they go up and go to the dental appointment. That's not a story. Two nuns get into an elevator and press the button for the 4th floor and just before the doors close a psychotic killer gets in. And now the doors close and the thing he hates most in the world is religion and nuns. Except one nun happens to be not going to the dentist, she happens to be a black belt and has a gun. Now you have those energies. Who comes out of this alive?

BRUCE: We have to hope that the material and the voice we've developed has enough of that kind of difference.

RAY: Enough entertainment value because everybody will give you 10 pages. They'll read 10 to 15 pages of your script. If you haven't hooked their interest by then, forget it. One producer said to us, "I usually only read 10 pages, but because you're friends, I'll give you 17 pages."

Okay. As an attempt at closure, can you relate a story about what can happen to a script: one project that had a happy ending and one that was perhaps less satisfying?

BRUCE: We wrote *Mr. Brooks*. Kevin Costner read it and said, "I read a lot of scripts and have read 4 or 5 perfect scripts. This is one of them. We're not going to change a thing. But we're not going to do it within the system. Because you'll lose the same possible addiction in the daughter in the end. And the businessman serial killer going free. They will totally eviscerate the script. They'll turn it into pabulum and we can't do that." Through Kevin Costner we did it the way we wanted to do it.

RAY: In the case of *Made in Heaven,* the difference between what we wrote and what appeared on the screen was 180 degrees. Scenes were cut out. Alan Rudolph, the director, didn't want to do the special effects that were called for but decided to do them in the camera the old fashioned way. Within the first 10 pages in our script, a guy loses his life, loses his girlfriend and goes to heaven. In heaven he meets the perfect life. There's only a complication. She's about to be born and come back here to be a new soul. He'll meet her again sometime in the century.

BRUCE: They'll get together sometime in the course of eternity.

RAY: But he says, "No, I want her now."

BRUCE: And he decides he wants to leave heaven and go after her with no guarantee that he'll ever find her again. And if he doesn't find her, he'll forever be unhappy in love.

RAY: By the time Rudoph got through with it, there was no magic and no chemistry. It was flat and there were no special effects, no magical wonderful heaven. That's not the way he works, not the way he sees things.

BRUCE: We all start down paths that we think we can do. As Greengrass was saying, "People ask, how do you do the action?" And he said, "That's what I like. The percussive quality of the rat-a-tat-tat. I like it. I can see it. But some people can see something else much better than I can."

RAY: With us, we love love stories and what separates people. Like, he's Jewish, she's Irish. Because nothing separates people anymore, in *Starman* we thought, ah, what if he's an immigrant from the stars? Then there's, you go to heaven and you meet your perfect love but she's born here. Ah, I have to go find her. Anyway, we love movies. I'm 12 years old when I sit there and it's a fantasy ride.

BRUCE: We see as many movies as possible. We just love going. And we always keep in mind how difficult it is to make a movie. And it's just as difficult to make a movie that doesn't work.

RAY: It's a miracle if a movie gets on.

BRUCE: And, in the end, it delivers what it promises to deliver. When people can go and say, "It gave me what I wanted when I bought my ticket."

The Emmy-Winning Chronicler

Peter Lefcourt's writing studio is tucked away in a Beverly Hills high-rise just south of Sunset Boulevard. The stack of unproduced scripts lining the shelves of an entire wall aside, his writing credits include another of his send-ups of Hollywood, *The Deal* (2008), and well over 60 teleplays, a few screenplays and a number of best-selling novels. In addition he has produced over 25 TV episodes and served as creative consultant on over 11 more. His primetime Emmy and two Writers Guild awards for his scripts for *Cagney & Lacey* and other nominations round out his prolific credentials, along with the fact that he is on the board of directors of the Writers Guild.

First question: how did you get into the entertainment business?

I was living in Vermont and writing things that weren't selling. I wanted to write novels and I consider myself a fallen intellectual. My sister's husband's sister worked in the television business and she said, "Why don't you write some television?" She set up parties for a TV studio and knew everybody. One year when I came into New York, she set up a meeting with Frank Price, who used to run Universal Studios. He said, "Well, if you have any television movies...." This was the time when movies for television were starting to break out. So I went back to Vermont and I actually had a script that I had been working on. It was a gothic murder mystery about these two women who pick up a hitchhiker and chain him to a barn. I toned all the sexual implications down, put it into an envelope and sent it to Frank Price at Universal in California. About six weeks later the phone rings and it was Frank Price and he said they wanted to buy my script. Would I come out there for rewrites? I learned lesson number one. There is no such thing as a script that isn't ready to be rewritten. It's what I call the presumption of guilt. When you submit or hand in a script, the first thing the secretary says is she's going to set up a meeting for notes and rewriting. And I always said, "How do you know you're going to have any notes? Maybe it's exactly what you're looking for." Anyway, I flew out to L.A. and took a meeting with William Frye, who had produced all the Boris Karloff horror movies. He was charming and said they were going to make the movie and I can use his office to interview agents. So I had a whole bunch of agents trooping in to see me because I had a deal. I got an agent, Frye and I worked on the script at night and he essentially took me to school on how to write a screenplay. I had talent to write dialogue and the stories were interesting but the form was entirely invented.

Do you remember anything he told you that was significant?

The basics were very simple. Show, don't tell. Get in later and get out faster. Don't divulge something until you have to. If you have a mystery in the script, you don't just spill it out. Also, much less exposition, don't over-explain things. So, I was given a check for $2,500. I had never seen that amount of money at one time in my life and my agent said, "Don't worry, kid, they'll be plenty more where that came from. Come out to L.A. and we'll make a lot of money." I went back to Vermont and spent the money quickly and learned another lesson. Never count on anything. I get a call from my agent telling me the network has killed my script because they thought it was too violent. But he told me to come out anyway and write movies. So I put everything I owned in my Volkswagen and arrived at the time Nixon had swept to office in a landslide over McGovern and started to write television movies. And I had a hard time. My agent soon forgot about me because I was no longer the hot young thing. Eventually I sold something. I was two weeks from working at Denny's when I sold a movie to Universal called *Let's Switch*. I sold it as a high concept. It's very simple about two women in their 30s who decide to change lives, one of them married with children, the other one single with a classy job. It was a little bit like "the grass is always greener." They lapped it up and immediately got someone to rewrite it. One of the other things you learn in this town is that nobody ever tells you anything. It's called the sound of silence. Bad news travels slowly. When you don't hear anything you know it's bad news. The other adage is, "A fast no is the second best answer." I was living in Venice where there were a lot of out of work actors and writers and no one could afford an answering service, so we would answer each other's phones. If you were going out, you'd leave your door open and you'd pick up the phone and pretend you were the answering service. Anyway, it was rewritten by some pretty good people and I wound up with a story credit. So I was able to forestall Denny's for another six months or so.

And then you got jobs in episodic television.

Kate McShane, which was on for six episodes about a female lawyer. I started little by little and they paid—you make good money as a television writer. Enough for each episode to live on for four or five months. Then I got my first staff job on a sweet show called *Eight Is Enough*. This is where you go to an office every day and you work on stories. I had seen one or two and I wrote one as a freelancer. There were freelancers and staff writers and nowadays its almost all staff writers. When a pilot episode was picked up for a series, they invited writers to watch the pilot and then come in and pitch them stories. As television evolved, it became harder and harder to do that. The stories became more modular, there were similarities from episode to episode, going from one to another. It involved characters that freelancers didn't really know about.

But luckily there was *Cagney & Lacey* and another pair of your contrasting women: one footloose lady cop and her partner trying to juggle life on the beat with her duties as a wife and mother.

You know, what's interesting, I didn't create *Cagney & Lacey*. I came onto the show after it was created. But that was the subtext. Two women, one of whom had a happy marriage and children, the other one single, and they each sort of complimented each other. But I was approached to do an episode and—.

Eventually earned an Emmy.

Actually I got an Emmy as a writer-producer for an entire season. Producing in television is really writing. Almost all producers in television are writers. Writers have gotten to the position where they can control their own material. At the time, I was the head writer. The episode that was chosen was called *Heat* when Tyne Daley [Lacey] was kidnapped and put into a boxcar by Michael Madsen. The two Writers Guild awards, for which I have plaques, were for an episode called *Jane Doe 37* where Sharon Gless [Cagney] investigates the death of a bag lady. That happened to be my original idea. Nobody touched the script because I was the show runner. The story always interested me because single women are often only a couple of months of rent from being on the street if you don't have any connections. Here Sharon Gless was a single woman with very little family. She's got a good job in the police department but subconsciously she was always worried, "What's going to happen to me when I go?" So she really identified. It's very simple. They find a body, the body has no name. Besides finding out who killed her, the Cagney character is obsessed with finding out her name. She had to have a name. She shouldn't be buried without a name. That was the subtext.

Isn't the title "show runner" a recent development?

It's essentially a producing job. You have a staff of writers and you sit with them and you bounce ideas back and forth. The show runner is ultimately responsible but you don't write all the scripts. You rewrite the ones you want to rewrite. It's often a writer-creator but sometimes not, who is the person who runs the show and is the final authority, not just on the script but casting and cutting. Television is much different than features. The writers run television. Once you're into production on features, the director drives the bus.

At some point there was a shift in tone and your work became much more ironic. When did that start or when did you begin to notice it?

When I brought in some of my own pilots. One was a wacky, one-camera film-comedy for ABC about a mythical American embassy on a mythical island in the middle of the Indian Ocean which was a little bit like *Dr. Strangelove*. It was the halfway point between the maximum nuclear payload between Moscow and New York. So this little Peter Sellers kind of island with very nice people had spies from Russia and the United States crawling around. And how the people kind of played the spies off, very much like in *The Mouse That Roared*.

And how was this satire received?

As it turned out, that was the problem. It was much too sophisticated. But they made it and it had really good actors in it. I think that was the voice that was trying to get out. I did another show called *Rivkin: Bounty Hunter*. It was based on a true story about a guy who lived in the Bronx named Stanley Rivkin who was a freelance bounty hunter. He would go after people in the city and stuff them in the trunk of his car, get them to the bail-bondsman and get his money. The character was kind of a Jewish urban cowboy.

More or less, the sense of irony continued or seemed to follow you. Like the time you were in the south of France working with Joan Collins on a mini-series where she played a spy, captured by the Gestapo, and wanted a change of wardrobe in her cell even though you advised her that the Gestapo wasn't going to go for that. Then there were other jobs and other ventures until something happened.

I just started fighting a lot of people. The television business is micro-managed a lot of times. People in suits who tell you how to write. I would bristle. There was a strike and at that point I decided to write novels. For me, the best that screenwriting will ever be is architecture. You create the architecture for a good movie. Movies and television to some extent will always be a director's medium. A writer realizes that on some level. You go to a college campus and ask them to name five great screenwriters, they'll name five directors. So I wrote *The Deal* as a swan song. It's actually the prequel to *The Manhattan Beach Project*. It's about getting a movie made for all the wrong reasons. It became a cult book out here on the West Coast. A black comedy about the movie business. I thought studios were going to be so incensed that I wrote this satire about what shallow, stupid people they are, that they would never hire me again. But suddenly I became very recherché as a writer, I don't know why. Suddenly I was offered a lot of work again. And I also wrote another book called *The Dreyfus Affair* about two baseball players who fall in love and cause this enormous scandal for public relations of organized baseball. How do they explain this? Baseball is the most homophobic of all sports. And that book sold very well.

Why is it called *The Dreyfus Affair*?

I was very interested in the real Dreyfus Affair in France. I always wondered, what does it take to rip a country apart the way the Dreyfus Affair ripped France apart? A whole nation polarized by this event. People weren't talking to each other. It was fascinating to me how this guilty man could frame an innocent man, everybody took sides and he was sent to Devil's Island. Almost 100 years later, what could happen in America that would do this? And I said, What would happen if two ballplayers fell in love and were thrown out of baseball? This was before civil unions. That was my premise. What institution was as ossified and conservative as the French army was? Baseball. Baseball is Norman Rockwell America. Most of the book is how baseball tries to deal with this public relations problem, trying to pass it off as a substance abuse problem and cover the whole thing up. So finding a way to do that in a screenplay was tricky because it wouldn't have the charm of the book: the internal monologue of the guy who has been in the closet his whole life, married to a beautiful woman with two kids who finds himself attracted to his second baseman and trying to deal with his feelings and puzzle this out. He thinks like a baseball player. I had him go to a psychiatrist and talk about this. He winds up with a psychiatrist from hell. It's been optioned and almost got made with Ben Affleck as the blond, blue-eyed guy and a black second basement. But Ben Affleck got cold feet. His agent said he shouldn't play a gay guy because it would be a career suicide. But it wasn't anything a heterosexual would be embarrassed to see. It's funny. It's a comedy, how the other ballplayers react. Anyway, he dropped out and the financing collapsed. It did cause a lot of attention and I started getting more work off it.

In film.

One of the Princess Di movies. CBS hired me because they knew I traveled to Europe a lot to go over to London and research a movie about Fergie and Andrew and the scandal she was causing. Diana was then having some problems, caught in cell phone conversations. CBS called and said to put Diana in the movie and we'll call it *The Women of Windsor*. We'll make it three hours instead of two, that's their idea of creativity, and I said, "Why not?" They put it on very quickly, they had an airdate. If they have an airdate and a star, they don't care very much about the script. It did very well in the ratings, not embarrassing but pretty silly. I also did a satire on politics for HBO. I wrote more books, one based on a media scandal in Schenectady, New York, another political satire. Meanwhile I'm doing a lot of good work in Los Angeles, so one career is feeding off the other. A series for Showtime called *Beggars and Choosers*, a satire on the television business. Also a book about the sentimental education of a young man who had been involved with 11 women all named Karen. A little bit of an exaggeration. I had been involved with three Karens at age 10 in the fifth grade. Then another book about Charlie Berns [a down-and-out film producer], one of five hustlers all going to the Cannes Film Festivals with different agendas. *The Deal*, the first of the Charlie Berns stories, of course, has been made into a movie.

With the inevitable changes.

The rule of thumb is, a movie is just based on the novel. If they're going to buy my novel, it's fairly clear to me that I have no legal right to approve of what they do. I've done adaptations of my novels that have been optioned but not produced. It's a challenge. The problems that you solve in the novel you can't get away with in screenwriting. If you say that the Polish cavalry comes over the hill, somebody is going to have to find the Polish cavalry. The directors are going to have a vision, the actors are going to have a vision and you have to collaborate. Then again, a lot of writers become directors and producers if they want to protect their script. But that requires a different muscle, a visual intelligence to see things in the frame and a lot of them aren't very good at it. And it takes a great deal of hubris to say, "You're going to spend $25 million and you can't change a word." It's interesting, when you're a screenwriter, no one wants you around. Screenwriters are sort of the unknown soldiers. But we don't complain because we get paid a great deal of money and we can always leave and do something else.

But more specifically, back to the prequel, Charlie Berns and *The Deal*.

Bill Macy came to me and said, "We love your book, we want to do it but my partner and I want to write the script." He wanted to build up a love story to attract Meg Ryan because Meg Ryan attracts a lot of money. I had already written a script which was optioned by Showtime. Macy and his partner didn't even want to look at it. I said I'd rather write the script but if that's your condition—I knew that Macy could get it made. The book had been out there for almost 10 years and nobody was making it. This was a chance to get it made. I would make some money but it wasn't about the money. They kept the basic story about a down-at-the-heels producer who options the world's least commercial book about Benjamin Disraeli and turns it into a karate movie. What Charlie Berns does to get it done is very funny. And he winds up winning an Academy Award. So it goes from a guy trying to commit suicide to winning an Academy Award. Macy kept that and that's basically what the movie is about.

So again, like *The Dreyfus Affair*, it can go either way.

Like Bill Goldman's famous line, "Nobody knows anything." It's so true. When you think you're putting together the optimum deal—these stars, this story, that director—it can't miss. And then you get something that comes out of left field like *My Big Fat Greek Wedding*, suddenly everybody has to go to see it. There really is no rule. I love this quote. "The movie business is a crap shoot masquerading as a business masquerading as an art form."

But within this masquerade, as a writer, if you had to sum up what characterizes your work and makes it special?

A central comic idea. Not funny necessarily, but ironic. I kind of know where I'm going but I don't know exactly how I'm going to get there. And in the writing of it, I make discoveries. I surprise myself. I also keep in mind that nowadays the marketing people are driving the truck, but I don't mean to be pessimistic. I think people still need to have stories. They will never lose this.

The Master Storyteller

Donald E. Westlake has won Edgar Awards (Edgar Allan Poe) in three different categories: Best Novel, Best Short Story and Best Motion Picture Screenplay, *The Grifters* (1991), and another Edgar for Best TV Feature *A Slight Case of Murder* (2000). In 1993, the Mystery Writers of America named Westlake a Grand Master, the highest honor bestowed by the society. His script for *The Grifters*, adapted from the novel by Jim Thompson, was also nominated for an Academy Award and a WGA award. All told, 16 films have been adapted from his novels and he has written the story and screenplay for four other films and the story and teleplay for three television productions. In addition, under his own name and the pseudonym Richard Stark, he has over a hundred novels to his credit centering on crime, with an occasional foray into science fiction.

Something, somewhere must have started it all.

Just a love of story. I began as someone who was in love with story. When you're so young that the sun hasn't set yet when they make you go to bed, the way I got through my childhood was to tell myself stories. It starts with story. I'll tell a story in any format you want. I started with short stories.

And how did those stories evolve into crime capers?

For me, one of the basic elements of story—in one way or another, the story is very often about the underdog, a person who has to try very hard to get something. There's no way to be more of an underdog than to be something society doesn't want you to do. So I kind of gravitated into that direction. Evan Hunter and I had a conversation. He wanted to write about cops, so he was on civilization's side. But I would say that cops have got cars, they've got laboratories, telephones, they've got everything. They don't need my help. The guys on the other side need my help.

What influence did movies have on your work?

Richard Stark, my pen name, "stark" came from the idea that the writing should be stark and lean. "Richard" came from Richard Widmark in the crime movie *Kiss of Death*.

Dortmunder, one of your continuing characters, though on the wrong side of the law, is almost comic, so unlike the maniacal Richard Widmark character from that film.

Actually, in that one I was looking for a story about a guy who's rather short tempered. If he had to steal the same things several times over and over, it would really annoy him. The more I thought about it, the more comic it was. Because the worst thing you can do with a tough guy was make him inadvertently funny. He loses all credibility. I liked the idea but I had to find somebody to take that story for me. A few months later I was in a bar and one of the signs was "Dortmunder Action Beer." I said, that's what I want, an action hero with something wrong with him. I saw the guy, he's dogged, he refuses to give up his expectations of success—I saw everything about him. I never expected him to be a series. I was just doing something that interested me. A couple of years later, at that time I had a weekend house in New Jersey near the Delaware Water Gap, there was a bank off Route 23 that I would pass twice a week. They tore down the old bank and put up a new bank and for a year the bank was operating out of a mobile home next door. I thought, You know, an enterprising fellow could back up a truck and take the bank away. And I think I've got the group to do it.

Dortmunder and his gang, which leads us to *The Hot Rock* and then your life in the movies.

What happened was, I was a successful crime novelist living in New York and didn't expect to do anything else. A few of my books had been bought and made by the movies. The last one at the time was *Point Blank* with Lee Marvin. Then I got a call from a studio exec named Eliot Kasner saying it was time for another *Rififi*, they wanted me to write it and to discuss my ideas with an associate, Jerry Bick, who is coming to New York next week. My ideas? William Goldman was doing the screenplay of *The Hot Rock* at that time which would star Robert Redford. But I didn't have any connection with Hollywood at all. Kasner's first movie was *Harper*, with Paul Newman, which was Bill Goldman's first screenplay. So I called Bill and told him this and he said, "If Eliot called you, that means you're about to be hot because he knows everything in the movie business. He'll tell you that he loves your work, but print has never crossed his eyes. If you want a career in movies, Eliot will get a movie actually made. He'll get it made with the wrong cast, the wrong director and the wrong budget. And then you'll have a credit. Then you'll have a career in the movies. So it's up to you." Then this guy Jerry Bick came to town when New York was really at its low ebb. And at lunch Jerry said, "Unlike the uncle who sees the child three or four times a year, New Yorkers don't see how bad this place is." In response, and since every story begins, What if? I said, "So, what if two New York City cops are tired of how grungy this city is, decide to pull one robbery disguised as policemen? And using all the equipment they can get their hands on." Jerry said, "That sounds good." And this was *Cops and Robbers* which came out of that lunch.

And this idea just popped into your head in response to Jerry Bick's complaints.

Yeah. And Bill was right. Eliot got the movie done with the wrong cast, wrong budget and wrong director. But he got it done and I got a credit.

And all this without consulting a screenwriting manual or going to a seminar.

The two things they mostly blather on about which are completely irrelevant are the arc of the story and that it's all in three acts. It's not in three acts. There was one thing that I knew about movies was that they're relentless. Television is in acts with commercial breaks. I've also written for television and that's more like writing a novel because you put the zinger at the end of the chapter. There's no point in putting a zinger in the middle of a movie. It just keeps going.

As for the screenplay format?

I had seen a draft Bill Goldman had done. So I called him again and told him I was going to do this thing and asked if he had a few more screenplays so I could see what they looked like. I started to do it and very quickly realized that if I wrote at the same pace as thinking and writing a novel, the screenplay would be 5,000 pages long. I've to get rid of this and I've got to get rid of that. And just go here and do that. And his saying this gets rid of those 8 pages. It's compression. That was the most important thing to learn. It's only going to be 120 pages.

And the element of seeing through the camera?

I've always been a very visual writer. I always describe the look and sound of things. An old friend of man from college once said, "The world of Donald Westlake goes ching, chang, chung!"

As for your own special screenwriting procedure?

In anything, whether it's a novel or a screenplay, one of the most important things is the front door. Which means, where does it start? That's the first thing. With *The Grifters,* I turned *The Grifters* down. But a week after I turned it down I got a phone call from England. "This is Stephen Frears [the British director]. Why don't you want to do my film?" I said, "It's too gloomy." We talked for 45 minutes. He said, "If you think of it as the son's story, then it's the story of defeat and death. As the mother's story it's the price of survival." But I said the problem is, we have to meet the son first. The story begins when the bartender hits him in the stomach. The author says that he doesn't know it, but he's bleeding internally and he's going to be dead in three days. So we have to meet him first. We have to meet his girlfriend second for her not to notice that there's anything wrong. Then we have to meet the mother third to see there's something wrong and save his life. She's connected with the mob and she calls the mob doc who tells her there's nothing that can be done. And she says, "You'll save my son's life or I'll have you killed." And he says, "I'll get right on it." So I said to Stephen Frears that I didn't know how to start. How am I going to tell the audience that this is the mother's story if she's the third one to come in? And at that point he said, what eventually they all say, "Well, you're the writer." Six days later I called and said, "What if we do a triptych? Start off with the three characters in three different places going through three different doors into their lives? So that for the audience it's a level playing field to begin with. And then I can let the audience know that the mother is the one we're supposed to watch. And he said, "Fine, do that." And I did. The mother drives into the parking lot at the racetrack and goes in and up the stairs. The screen splits and the girlfriend goes into the jewelry store to peddle some jewelry. The screen splits again and the son walks into the bar. The mother is making the bets, she's dealing with the jewelry while he's dealing with the bartender. And we go on from there. The action is the son being hit in the stomach. But we had to get away from a story about a guy who gets hit in the stomach. It's a story about his mother.

If you had to rephrase it as an overall motif, what would you say?

What this is a story about is three ferrets in a box. And the top of the box is open. And any of them could get out but they would rather stay in the box and bite each other. That's what the story is about. So I said to Stephen Frears, anytime they're indoors anywhere, I would like them to be able to see the outdoors so we know they could leave. When the scene is interior, the escape is visible to us but not to them.

Is the front door always a prime consideration?

Yes. I'm staring on a screenplay now taken from one of my earlier novels and there is almost the identical problem. This time there are three other characters that have to do things before the main character is even on the same continent. So we see him in Alaska in a job that is extremely boring. He says that something has got to happen. Then we go to Africa and set it up so then this guy says to this guy, "I'm going to need you on that all along. Hire somebody to do your other duties." Then he makes a phone call to the guy in Alaska. So if we start with the guy in Alaska, even though he isn't doing anything, that's the thing. Who you see, what's happening in that very first instant. He feels stuck and says that something must happen. In a movie, that means that something will happen. Someone once said that nobody ever coughs purposelessly in a movie. If there's a cough in a movie, it's there for a reason.

The front door then initiates something that's going to propel the story forward.

Yeah. That opening, that first scene says there's a story here and there's a reason for you to be interested. It has to be done at the very beginning. When I was doing *The Stepfather*, I didn't know how to start that one. But in comedy or it's scary or whatever it is, I always like to push as far as I can. I decided we start with a guy carries a suitcase into a bathroom and the guy has blood on his hands. And he showers, he shaves, he puts contact lenses in to change his eye color and puts on glasses and different clothing. All of the bloody clothing he puts in a suitcase. He goes out and sees a couple of toys, picks them up and puts them in a toy box. As he goes down the stairs you see streaks of blood on the walls. When he gets to the bottom, in the room behind him you see bodies and complete chaos as if the dust is still settling. There are a couple of more toys on the floor and he puts them away neatly. He goes out and picks up a newspaper that a kid has thrown on the lawn and starts whistling "Camptown Racetrack." He gets on the Puget Sound ferry and drops the suitcase over the side and goes into his new life. There's been no dialogue, nothing has happened. He showered and shaved and got dressed, that's all that happened.

But you knew that would carry in the movie, unlike writing a novel.

A novel is all me. A movie is very little me. The actor embodies the character. I don't have to spend pages or even paragraphs telling you who this person is. The minute he appears on screen you say, "Okay, I know who that is." By how he looks, how he speaks, how he holds his body whether you recognize the actor or not. There's a scene in *The Hot Rock*, the first time you see the lawyer they're standing on a street corner and he comes hustling up wearing his black suit with all these manila envelopes in his pocket. And you realize that that's his office. And he takes a card out of a pocket and says, "My card." Maybe Bill Goldman wrote it, maybe Zero Mostel the actor did it, maybe Peter Yates the director did it. I spent almost an hour talking to someone in pre-production on *The Grifters* about what the cars say about the three main characters. What does the mother care about? Money and security. Her car should be a great big brush-gold tank. The girlfriend, a world-class bimbo, her car was a swimming pool, a bright blue convertible. The son, who is a con artist who doesn't want to be noticed, his car is the most anonymous vehicle you've ever seen in your life. It was the color of olives and water. Something I would brush by in writing a novel becomes very important in a movie because it's only what you see and what you hear.

How involved are you in this pre-production phase?

In a good production the director will involve the writer to some extent. In one project, I wanted the killer to bring home a bronze eagle to put over the mantel and the director wanted him to bring home a puppy to give to the step-daughter. We argued for a while and then negotiated. I said, "I'll give you the puppy, but promise me one thing. At no point in the movie will anybody threaten the puppy with a knife." He said, "It's a deal." But if they want to go off and do what they want to do, they will. When you're writing a screenplay for a studio, you're an employee. And you can be replaced. And overturned.

Back to *The Hot Rock*. How did you feel about Bill Goldman doing the screenplay of your book instead of you?

Anybody who does a screenplay from his own book has a fool for a client. You've already told the story in that form in that field. And now you're going to try to rethink it? Take a cold eye on it? You have to have a distance from it. You have to say, "That goes out." The first thing that Bill did, there was one scene in *The Hot Rock* that, in my book, I thought was a definite movie sequence. The first thing Bill did was cut it out. The lawyer [who has stashed away the "hot rock"], in order to escape from Dortmunder and his gang, has checked himself into an insane asylum out on Long Island. In the book, it had long ago been a fenced-in factory building. So the old railroad tracks were still there. So the gang gets a full-size Tom Thumb locomotive and drives through the fence onto the yard, grabs the lawyer and backs out again. Bill said, "If I have that in there, then I have to have the whole thing about the circus in there and I have to have the guy who drives the train and three minutes of dead time for a 10-second gag." "Ah," I said. It was the best course in screenwriting I could have had.

And ideas keep coming to you because there's always something wrong somewhere.

That's right. It could come from something I might find in the paper. Like insurance scams based on false deaths with some kind of foreign element to them, a claim someone had drowned overseas, casual record keeping in some places and it's hard for insurance companies to investigate. You don't need an actual body to get a death certificate. You just need three people to say they saw him and he was dead. You can start with a couple in desperate money trouble and the only thing they haven't tapped is their life insurance policy. But you can't borrow against the policy, you can only die. Which way the story will go, you never know. Ultimately at the end, you find out what you were writing about. Much more than an insurance scam, it was about love and trust. Do you really trust each other? Will he go back to the states and set things up so that he can come back as her brother? She's going to be the one collecting the money. If she doesn't come through, he's stuck there. So eventually you discover it turns into a story about true love.

In other words, underneath it all and apart from all the great what-ifs and provocative front doors, the essentials are...?

Emotion and peril.

The Screenwriter and the High Road

For a writer of mainstream Hollywood movies, John Fusco is an anomaly. When not working on location or engaging in studio business and conferences in Los Angeles, he much prefers to live at the Red Road Farm he has created high up in Vermont's Northwest Kingdom close to the Canadian border. So high up and close that on the proverbial clear day you can see the ridgeline of Canada just over the next rise and the hawks riding the thermal currents below. In the near distance, a bit further down, are the acres of pasture for his rare Spanish Mustangs, Choctaw Indian ponies and retired movie horses like Hidalgo. In 1988, John was adopted and made a relative of the Oglala-Lakota Nation and given the name Wakinyan Ca'mte which means Thunderheart, named for the title of the screenplay he was working on at the time. Stephen Redbow named his farm in honor of John's sincerity and dedication. In Native American terms to walk "the Good Red Road" is a deep commitment and responsibility. In other walks of life it's often referred to as taking the high road. Starting with *Crossroads* (1986), his film scripts have continued on to range from the two *Young Guns* movies (1988, 1990), to *Thunderheart* (1992) and *Hidalgo* (2004), to *The Seven Samurai* and *The Forbidden Kingdom* (2008), with other produced screenplays in between and new projects to follow. Apart from his deep association with the heyday of the American West and Native American history and causes, he also has a background in the martial arts and holds the advanced rank of Red Sash in Shaolin Kung Fu. Among his awards are two back-to-back national Nissan-Focus Awards, two Western Heritage Bronze Wrangler Awards for *Young Guns* (1989) and *Spirit: Stallion of the Cimarron* (2003) (the latter his only animated feature which also garnered him an Academy Award nomination), and the Western Writers of America Spur Award for *Hidalgo* (2005).

When we first met and you were playing Deputy Sheriff File for me in *The Rainmaker*, you had a kind of rock-blues band at the time and were always dressed in Western garb even though you lived in a conservative section of Connecticut. You also wanted to borrow an original script that my actor friend gave me for *Where Has Tommy Flowers Gone?* to study the format. All of that surely is as good a jumping off place as any.

It is. At the time, I was writing a novel that kept turning into a screenplay and it was called *Blues Water*. It was about a half–Seminole Indian musician playing the southern bar-and-grill circuit. Trying to come to terms with his ancestral past and racism down south in Florida and Indian communities. The music I was playing at the time kind of informed it. Then File became a part of that I sort of drew on. And you encouraged me to be who I was and use it. I had been out of school for so long. I dropped out of high school at 16 and went off playing music. I had this epiphany at 21 when I was on the road with the Dixie Road Ducks as the front man playing my original music. They were all in their 30s and 40s and bona fide Southern musicians. I started to reflect on how I got there. Why? I was able to summon my original love for writing and film, trying to get in touch with the happiest I had ever been. And I found that feeling in the times I was writing these short scripts and filming them in Super 8 and casting kids from the neighborhood. My father was very blue-collar Italian American and my mother was a real dreamer. She was very supportive and she used to say, "Well, you should go to Mickey Rooney's acting school." So I held onto that dream. I would go into class and make the announcement that I was going to be leaving soon to go into Mickey Rooney's acting school. I had this real love for acting and film and really wanted to write screenplays. So, on the

road I had this epiphany and decided I was going to go back to school somehow. In the band, I was acting out but my true love was suppressed. In lyrics
and performance I found a world but it was not for me. I was going to back-
track to that kid, pick it up from there and believe. Pursue it even if it killed
me, give it a shot. The band tried to hold me hostage but I literally escaped,
shimmied down the gutter at an old inn we were staying at to my girlfriend
at the time's convertible while the band was watching the door.

And somehow you wound up in my theater workshop and production.

I went straight from the road life. Your course was the liaison and gave
me the confidence. It was a profound experience because my father came to
that show. I remember the acting exercises we did. In one of them, we stood
in a round circle and we all went around and each did an improv. It was getting closer and closer to me and when it got to me I pulled out a harmonica and started wailing on it. And you said when we go around again for me
to lose the harmonica because I couldn't go through life depending on a harmonica to get me through. And it all eventually led to NYU.

**David Mamet is always putting down film school or any course of study.
I'm hoping you'll tell me your experiences at NYU were all worthwhile.**

Absolutely. I was a finalist in the Focus Awards, a national competition for college and university students. I only heard about it the last minute.
It started out as a 10-minute assignment for a 10-page short and I started
writing it and writing it and *Blues Water* wound up be a feature. Most of the
class didn't turn in their 10-page short and most of them don't ever turn one
in. I turned in a feature and Professor Lamar Sander really liked it and I
entered the script. Out of 800 scripts, that script was selected as one of the
four finalists. So I was flown to Los Angeles. This was my first semester at
NYU. The first prize was a new Nissan automobile. We were taken around
meeting studio execs. At the award ceremony, Rob Reiner was the host. I
won first place. I thought I sold the script. I was surrounded by producers
and thought, "Wow, this is it." But I got an agent who was with William
Morris.

Still in your first year in NYU's film program?

Yes. So I signed with William Morris and went back, tending bar and
sold the car so I could keep going through. I thought *Blues Water* was going
to sell. It got great feedback, but the studios thought it was a little too arcane
in order to market it. But I had an agent and he said, "What's next, what's
next?" The next semester, there was going to be a special screenwriting seminar where only 12 students would be selected taught by Waldo Salt, Ring

Lardner Jr. and Ian McClellan Hunter. Three of the blacklisted screenwriting masters, all with Oscars. They were going to teach this class sitting at the head of a table and work on 12 scripts in development. We were supposed to turn in the first 12 pages and a kind of rough outline. So that was *Crossroads* for me. Waldo took a real liking to that project.

Do you remember anything he told you that affected the structure or influenced your writing in any way?

They were all completely anti-paradigm and step system. It was, you know, write from your heart; it was about character and conflict. With Waldo it was all about honesty of character, really having conviction, What do you want to say? Getting to know your characters and letting them tell the story. Never first act, second act, never really even talked about it.

So, in a way it was just like acting class: in character, working your way in and around and through each obstacle. A feeling of the first time and not knowing exactly where it's going to take you.

That's right. We talked about having rough signposts. You can kind of light your way and get there or you might change direction. My ending changed several times through that workshop. I made discoveries. They made me turn around and look back and decide if that's where I really wanted to go. "Look what's happened back here"—that kind of thing.

And what about your visual sense of it all, seeing through the camera, or was that intuitive?

I've always written cinematically. Even when I started out writing short stories, I saw the shots. I always saw it as a movie. But Waldo was all about, "What's happening between this young kid and this old blues man?" By the time I finished the script, the competition rolled around again. I submitted *Crossroads* and won first place again. A second car and this time I got to keep it.

Even though it was the same judge who wrote the well-known handbook about plot points at certain intervals.

But I knew it's really a cinematic sense, pacing—movies were really my literature. Good movies, not, "Oh, boy, my first act is going on way too long, I need to hit that plot point. Uh-oh, I don't have the big hook up front." I went to see *Van Helsing* and it kind of starts with the third act. It blows you out of the seat and then what? It's the new theme ride. It's over the Matterhorn. It's exhausting. It's not engaging. What this is doing to young screenwriters now is they look at this stuff and they're kind of conditioned. A young film student from Italy came over once and said after *Hidalgo* came out, "I very much like this movie but too slow, too slow. I liked the race, the race with the horses." And I said, "If we're really going to care about this character, wouldn't it be stronger to know that he felt involved in the Wounded Knee Massacre? And that this sets up his whole mission and what he needs to resolve in his personal life?" And he said, "I know, I know, the Indians, but I want the race to start. Sometimes it stops and talks too much. I like it fast, fast."

Were you always able to protect your story from the "new theme ride?" When they made *Crossroads*, did it all go the way you had planned?

It did not. The experience for me was difficult. *Crossroads* doesn't represent the whole accurately because that was a baptism by fire. I just felt lucky to be there. My head was spinning, Columbia was buying the script, it won the second Focus Award. All of these directors whom I admired wanted to direct it. Sean Penn wanted to play the lead role. So they flew me out to L.A. and Walter Hill was going to direct it [Hollywood screenwriter and director of *The Long Riders* (1980) and *48 Hours* (1982)]. I was a fan of a lot of his stuff. I wasn't too far from playing File and the world where I got the story, from traveling, playing the blues and meeting these kind of characters and love for this culture. But Walter said, "Kid, I don't think that ending at the old rail yard is doing it enough. I'd like it to take place at the devil's church. And I don't think it should be an old black man. I think we should get a rock star like Keith Richards. And we're casting Ralph Macchio from *The Karate Kid,* and because he's so nice in that movie, I want him to be a little edgier in this movie." I just felt like this guy has got to know. I'm this film-school kid. I've got to trust in him, got to believe him. And little by little it got away from me.

Because of the director.

Yes. Walter came in and said, "I love the terrain, I love the material. But how much can this kid really know what he's doing? I'm taking over." I'm still ticked off with what they did to that script. Students still come and check it out of the library at NYU. A professor told me that I wrote a shot of bourbon and Walter served up a glass of milk. It lost its edge and soul. And that all led to my leaving my agent and telling him that this isn't working for me. I just wanted to get a place in the woods in Vermont, hole away and write. He said my career was just starting; "It's career suicide and it's going to be tough getting development deals if you're not in town." I said I didn't want to write on development, I wanted to write on spec. He wanted to know what I had in mind and I said, "a Western." And he said, "So you're leaving L.A., moving to Vermont and writing in a genre that's been dead for 20 years." So we did it anyway, my wife and I, went up there and I holed up and wrote *Young Guns*. It sold to Morgan Creek Productions and opened number one. The Western hadn't made any money since *Butch Cassidy* at that point. That enabled me to stay in Vermont. The agent said, "Okay, do what you're doing and write a sequel."

If Westerns were so out of favor, how were you able to succeed?

A lot of the wags out there in Hollywood said they tried to do the young west, the brat pack on horseback. They had no clue about Billy the Kid. Paul Newman in *The Left Handed Gun*, he was up there, much older than 21. Johnny Mack Brown dressed in black. I was fascinated by how young Billy the Kid and his Regulators were. How young the Wild West was. You were lucky if you lived past 21. I hit that angle because of my outlaw rock background when I was that age. It came from a pure place. I created that mood and tried to make the reader, the studio and the audience aware of that: "The barn doors burst open, here come the six riders; if it was a hundred years from now they'd be on Harleys." They started to salivate over the demographics; it all lined up and every young guy in Hollywood wanted to do it. Tom Cruise wound up being in the movie uncredited. He showed up on set and wanted to get shot. He got shot off a roof. I still remember sitting in the little Morgan Creek trailer on the lot with Joe Roth who gave the green light to that risky film, which did well for them and got them going, and Joe went on to run the studio.

This time were you able to protect your work?

This is where things started to change. Because I cared about the material and grew up real fast from the *Crossroads* experience, I talked to my agent about it and said I wanted to attach myself as a producer. They don't get it without me coming along and retaining some kind of control of the project. Of course the studios tried to get rid of that. But I was involved in meetings and that enabled me to be on the set. A friend of mine said for me to make sure I told you that this is atypical. Straight-up screenwriters don't usually go on the set. Usually they want to get rid of the writer, as you know. As an executive producer, what it does is give you an opportunity to get into the room with the director and the casting and music and everything. Let the director and the creative team see that you are a part of the DNA of this material. It would be in their best interest to have you around. That's the important thing. They always say, "Oh, we've got this script. Now we're going to hire technical advisers." The writer should be the best technical adviser. She should know more about that subject than any technical adviser they can bring in. A case in point is *Thunderheart*. I'll go in and speak Lakota to the medicine man. I'll go to the tribal president who adopted me into his family. Then tell them, "If you're going to shoot here, you'll have to do this in the spiritual way. I've practiced this way. I've lived this world, I've gone into it so deep." Then they figure, "We'd be stupid just because this guy is the screenwriter to cut him out of the process. We're going to need him." And then the actors stay close to you. I mean, I've had a lot of experiences when the actors have finished a shot and the director says, "Okay, that was a good one." The actors look past the director and look at me because I know the material and the background. It's very important for writers to be aware of that. The idea is to be invited to the early parties to be able to let them see that it would be in their best interest to keep me involved.

Are you actually able to say, "This isn't going to work" or "We have a problem here?"

Sure. Along with that you try to establish a strong relationship with the director. You come in and the director realizes you really know this stuff and are going to make it easy for him. So he's on my side. Because to be a director is a lonely job to be out there and the studio is sending notes because they don't like the dailies. Michael Apted, who is known as a cantankerous British director, he and I had this relationship where I covered his back. You try to make the director see you want to be his ally. I have to say that about in every film, I've had that relationship. When there's only a month left of shooting, they'll say, "You're what? You're leaving? No no, you can't."

Did this all hold true on *Hidalgo*?

One of the funny things that happened there with Joe Johnston, who was kind of a traditional director like, "Okay, I've got the script, now who's going to write it?" Or, "Who's going to write it next? I'll put my scent on it and it's now mine as the director." Casey, the producer said to me, "Joe's kind of wondering about dialogue polish. You've got to get into a room with him." And so I did. And Joe started to realize that I know horses, know this world, know about this esoteric character few people know about. From that meeting on, we established this relationship. He would ask, "John, they don't want to give me the money for this shot? Can you call Casey and can we kind of team up?" I went out to the deserts with them, I was on the set for the whole thing. At the end of the movie, Casey said, "John, you're going to see something when you come to the first screening that's unprecedented. Watch those end titles real closely because it blew my line but really speaks toward how you pulled this off with Joe." I go and watch and it says, "A Joe Johnston, John Fusco film." Joe said, "Hey, I'm not going to take all the blame myself." It meant a lot to me and I think it's relevant to all this because it shows that it can be done. If you try to serve the project and say, "How can I really help?" So they can see that you just want to do the best thing for this movie.

And where did the concept for *Hidalgo* come from?

The paint horse that Jack Palance rode in *Young Guns* came home with us. I fell in love with him and started researching the history of the paint horse, which got me back to the history of Native American horses. In that lore was this incredible little story that no one knew. In 1890, Hopkins, this half–Lakota cowboy, entered a 3,000-mile race across the Arabian Desert on a paint horse and won. And the horse's name was Hidalgo. So I would try and find stuff on this guy Hopkins and I found very little. But I told my wife, Richela, "That's a movie, it's in my heart and one I really want to do." And Richela said, "You've got the guy and the horse, you've got the beginning, and you've got 3,000 miles of sand. And there's so little known." And I said that could be a plus. If I can research the period, create the drama, research endurance racing, look at the types of characters that would be in there, look at this Lakota background...."

But why Arabia?

Because Hopkins had been in the Buffalo Bill Wild West Show and his horse had been billed as the greatest endurance race horse in the world. There were Arabian horsemen involved in the show and he was challenged by a sheik. The Arabs take their horses very seriously. They believe they have the best bloodlines that go back to Mohammed himself. The thematic—a mustang, which comes from the Spanish and means half-breed, half-wild, and a half-breed guy. I started imagining his life, his drama. Eighteen-ninety. That coincides with the massacre at Wounded Knee that many people view as the end of the free West. This was all under it. Researching more on Hopkins, putting together little pieces, I found out that he had been associated with Wounded Knee. He was a horseback messenger who was famous for being able to cover territory in record time. What if he was the one who delivered the message on horseback to the U.S. Army that we have a problem on our hands, put these Indians down? What if he denied his culture because he was the son of a U.S. Cavalry officer and a chief's daughter? So it was taking those factual elements and creating fiction.

So with all that underpinning, it was no longer just an endurance race.

That's right. I came across Lady Ann Blunt from England who had come over with her father to Arabia in search of the purest Arabian bloodlines.

They took it like a religion. So I created her as a character. There was this whole class conflict looking down at this Indian mustang. This is a real underdog story.

Consistently then, there is an integrity to it all and something you truly care about.

It all comes from this well of childhood passions. Passions and interests that started at a really young age. And I go back to that well because it's where my heart is. Native American themes. The Old West. The blues. And as a kid I was very passionate about Chinese martial arts. Kung Fu and the philosophy. My father, who served in the Korean War, had all these exotic stories and knew secret things that were taught to the soldiers. He said, "I could teach you, but you would become a very dangerous man." And so I was always fascinated by it and eastern philosophy which has a real parallel with Native American philosophy. About nature and the universe and the Tao. I would take the *I Ching* with me because I loved those passages. When I was a kid, I made a couple of Super 8 films with a martial arts theme about this wandering monk. I played a Chinese in them. I studied martial arts and, little did I know it, but that was also in the well, in the writer's well. I showed my son old Kung Fu movies when he was five or six and he was just riveted. I found a Shaolin Kung Fu master in Burlington, Vermont— I had dreamed of finding that exotic spiritual practice—and I've been training there. Like Native American spiritual practice, Shaolin is based on animals. At one point my son was afraid of the dark and I started telling him stories. He had a talisman that he used with his martial arts heroes, so-and-so the monk who would protect him. So I read him *The Monkey King*, which is China's most beloved folk hero. He was sort of this man-monkey master of stick fighting who lived up on a mountain and he was like Coyote in Native American lore. He was a trickster and he was finally captured and imprisoned for 500 years in Five-elements Mountain because he was immortal. Then was finally freed to go on the famous journey to the west. It all grew into a made up story in which a young, troubled American kid is bullied, because my son was afraid of bullies then too. He has all these fears. So this troubled American kid in my story watches Kung Fu movies to get courage. Obsessed with it, he goes into Chinatown and buys these bootleg DVDs and there is this old blind Chinese man who runs this pawn shop. One day the kid sees something he recognizes from a dream that keeps happening, an antique bow staff, a fighting staff. The old man feels something about this kid's attraction. In the Monkey King legend the story drops the part about his all-powerful staff. My little play on it was, what happened to that staff? Here it winds up in a little Chinatown pawn shop where it's been sitting for hundreds of years. This kid is then transported back to ancient China to free the Monkey King. This kid who lives in a shallow world of Kung Fu movies who gets beat up by these local bullies, now has to go through an authentic journey. He has to learn the true principals of Kung Fu and what it really means. And be prepared to fight all these elements as he goes through Five-elements Mountain to free the Monkey King and get him his staff. As he travels, he encounters characters from Chinese mythology and classic martial arts novels and is pursued by villains from Chinese literature, incorporating all these nightmares and mentor relationships. Basically, it's a Kung Fu *Wizard of Oz*. You know, is it a dream?

I think it goes without saying that it's a movie.

Yes. Jackie Chan plays two characters. He's the old guy in the pawn shop and he's the drunken eighth immortal whom the kid meets wandering. So I basically told the bedtime story to Casey Silver, the producer of *Hidalgo* who for 12 years was the president of Universal. I told him the story makes my son feel a lot better. And Casey said, "Keep going, keep going." And then he said, "John, John, this is next. Let's do it. Let's develop it and take it to Universal or develop it from my fund."

It also goes without saying that every screenwriter should have a producer like that.

Who he believes in and who believes in his work. To protect the writer, let the writer hide in Vermont while he goes out and fights the battles. I also get notes from Casey but he has a great story sense. He knows my work really well. He always goes for the high road. "What's the theme, what are we saying here? I want to know the kid more, I don't get a sense of this." I'll do another draft for him. Then he might say, "I think we need to lose another five pages here and really tighten it up." It's like having a real partner. I never feel like I'm getting studio notes. It's the two of us facing the studio. Casey doesn't give up trying to get the right elements to get the movie made. It was called *The Monkey King* and now it's called *The Forbidden Kingdom*. Casey asked me who I saw in this movie as the drunken immortal and as the Monkey King. I said, "I see Jackie Chan and Jet Li together for the first time." Jet is a Buddhist monk, very serious and very classical. Jackie Chan is the Buster Keaton of martial arts cinema and people have been trying to get them together for years. The characters are all well-rounded, it's funny, physical and there's a lot of emotion. So, as it turned out, they both wanted to do it. We wound up with a dream team of that kind of cinema.

All the attractive elements attached at just the right time.

That's right. Everybody wanted in. It's a high concept in itself: Jet Li and Jackie Chan.

But obviously it doesn't always happen that smoothly. And you probably have other projects still waiting in the wings.

Like *The Highwaymen*, the true story of the two retired Texas Rangers who finally tracked down and killed Bonnie and Clyde. It's the flip side of the Warren Beatty–Fay Dunaway film, stripping off the veneer of the romance of Bonnie and Clyde and media and celebrity criminals. It shows the untold story of these two old guys, Manny and Frank, who ride the high country and were called out of retirement to do one last job. It's a road story between the two guys who make the transition from horse and Winchester to '34 Ford V8 and machine gun and come to terms with what they have to do. I always had an interest in the true story of Frank Hamer, who was mocked in the Arthur Penn film, to give him his due. In the same way I was interested in what was behind Billy the Kid. I got to meet Frank Hamer Jr. down in Texas, drove the Bonnie and Clyde Trail where the killings took place, and wrote the screenplay.

And the well never runs dry.

As long as I find an access code and how it's related to something I love and to my childhood, the rain barrel is always filling up. I have to have that initial true passion and that linkage.

Is there a final word, something we may have left out?

Yes. For the first 15 years of my career, I started writing at five A.M., five days a week and usually wrote for 10 hours. When I won those national screenwriting awards I was writing night and day while observing a lackluster work ethic all around me. I go easier now, but that's what it takes.

Afterword

Someone once wrote that any pursuit can be viewed in one of two ways: as a finite game or an infinite game. If the choice is finite, there is a clear beginning, middle and end within prescribed boundaries and a time limit. More often than not, it's also defined in terms of a contest. The greater the prize, the stiffer the competition and the greater the odds. Whoever is calling the shots and keeping score will announce the winner or winners at the final gun while the rest of the pack will just as clearly realize they have lost. Just as in *The Player, Adaptation* or *Wall Street*, contestants often toss around expressions like, "You've got to have an edge, an angle, an ace in the hole," "Every battle is won before it's fought," "If you're not a comer, you're either nowhere or on the way out." For the losers, every outing becomes tougher, the odds longer as the scorekeepers and powers that be set up the process of elimination. Under these circumstances the quips and clichés are apt to go something like this: "Well, it's back to the drawing board," "Don't count me out; I just need a little break, that's all, maybe get some better coaching. I mean, there's always a way." Within this framework, you're always trying to get your foot in the door or make a comeback or trying to stay on top no matter what it takes.

As for the infinite game, as the term suggests, there is no time limit, it's never over. No one is calling the shots or keeping score because the locus of control is internal, not external. In this way there are no opponents to outmaneuver and no enervating pressures or a life constantly bouncing between extremes. Instead, the player creates his own standards and, ideally, within a cooperative framework. At the outset, with every venture that strikes a chord, there is a feeling of engagement in a task that's challenging but attainable and provides immediate feedback every step of the way. The experience itself is the goal, the doing of it the reward. You can always change direction or make mistakes and learn from them and move on. Even rest for a while until the urge strikes again or rework a discarded notion that takes on a new meaning seen in a new light. There is, of course, the opportunity to enter the fray just to see what it's like and enter again and again if you've a mind to, making sure never to hang your ego on a single result. If and when the chance comes to share the work, feedback is measured in terms of your intent and the opinions of those you admire or care about. If the work deepens and evolves and comes to something and goes on to touch more and more people, that is surely rewarding. If it doesn't, there is always the next time, and the next, and the next because the options are always open. Needless to say, for the screenwriter who understands and loves the process, it's all an infinite game.

Appendix A: Glossary

Auteur   The presumed or actual author of a film, usually identified as the director.

Camera angle   The position of the camera in relation to the subject: looking down (high angle); horizontal, on the same level (straight-on angle); looking up (a low angle).

Canted framing   A slanted view causing the frame to seem out of kilter and not level.

Classical narrative   An unfolding storyline based on the assumption of clear causal factors (the desires, decisions, choices and traits of characters opposed by counterforces and affected by natural or social dynamics or circumstances) resulting in a striking chain of events and eventual closure and significant changes in the status quo.

Close-up   A camera shot emphasizing an actor's facial expression or the details of a gesture.

Continuity editing   A system of cutting designed to made all the bits and pieces appear to be continuous and to maintain clear narrative action.

Crane shot   A shot accomplished by having the camera above the ground, moving through the air in any direction to capture a panorama or a bird's eye view.

Crosscutting   Editing that endows the film story with a great range of unrestricted knowledge (cause and effect or simultaneity) by alternating two or more lines of action occurring in different places.

Deep focus   A use of a certain camera lens and lighting that keeps both close and distant subjects in sharp focus.

Elliptical editing   Presenting an action through cutaways or dissolves so that it consumes less time on screen than it would in a conventional story form.

Establishing shot A shot that takes in all the important figures, objects and setting.

Extreme close-up A framing in which the scale of the object shown is very large or part of a face or body.

Extreme long-shot A framing in which the scale of the object shown is very small—e.g., in this way a building, landscape or crowd of people will fill the entire screen.

Fade-in A dark screen gradually brightens as a shot appears.

Fade-out A shot gradually disappears as the screen darkens.

Following shot Any camera shot that keeps a viewer's attention fastened by staying with a moving figure or subject and keeping it onscreen.

Framing The use of the edges of the film frame to select and compose what will be visible onscreen.

Hand-held camera The use of the cameraman's body as a camera support either holding it by hand or using a harness.

Jump cut A noticeable interruption—e.g., figures change instantly against a constant background or the background changes instantly while the figures remain constant.

Long shot The scale of the object or figure(s) appear to be small or far away as the background dominates.

Long take A shot that continues for an unusually long period of time.

Medium shot A framing in which the scale of the object shown is of moderate size; a human figure would be seen from the waist up and would fill most of the screen.

Montage A juxtaposition of images to create ideas and relationships not present within any shot, setting or period of time.

Motif A significant element, usually thematic, that is repeated.

Natural lighting A reliance on natural or realistic sources (the shadows and illumination cast by a streetlight on a figure in a doorway or through the blinds in a room, the effect of the twilight afterglow on a landscape, etc.) to create realistic textures as opposed to the slick or flawless look of a film shot on a major studio lot.

Offscreen sound and space Sounds that come from a source that is assumed to be present but beyond what is visible, and action that is assumed or can be readily imagined that is also just beyond the frame but part and parcel of the ongoing moment.

Pan A horizontal camera movement turning to the right or left.

Point of view (POV shot) A shot taken with the camera placed approximately where a character's eyes would be, showing what the character would see.

Rhythm Adjusting the length of shots through editing: the rate of sounds, shots and movements within each shot; the pulse and accents or elements that are stressed, and tempo and pace.

Sequence A moderately large segment of film involving one complete stretch of action often equivalent to a scene.

Shot or take One uninterrupted run of the camera with a single static or mobile framing.

Storyboard Comic-strip-like drawings of individual shots or phases of shots with descriptions written below each drawing as part of the planning phase.

Three-point lighting The common use of three directions of light on a scene from behind the subjects (backlighting), from one bright source (the key light), and from less bright sources balancing the key light (fill light).

Tilt A camera movement scanning the space, swiveling upward or downward on a stationary support.

Tracking or dolly shot Mobile framing literally on a track, traveling forward, backward or laterally as the mounted camera tracks the action.

Wide-angle shot Using a lens of short focal length to affect a scene's perspective, distorting the space laterally and exaggerating the distance between foreground and background planes.

Zoom A shot movement shifting to a telephoto range enlarging the targeted image and flattening its planes, reducing clues for depth and volume (creating the illusion that a figure running toward the camera is taking a long time to cover a relatively short distance) while a shift toward a wide-angle range does the opposite.

Appendix B: Conventional Three-Act Format

ACT ONE (approximately 30 minutes)

Main plot
Turning point or disturbance (approximately 10 minutes in)
Introduction of subplot
Main plot crisis

ACT TWO (approximately 40 minutes)

Continuation of main plot and complications
Continuation of subplot and complications
Mid-act crisis
Cliffhanger

ACT THREE (approximately 20 minutes)

Main plot driving toward conclusion
Subplot heading toward resolution
Major crisis and decision or action
Resolution scene

In the conventional movie, at the beginning of Act One, a protagonist is going along with his normal routine in pursuit of whatever. A strong disturbance changes his course of action, turns his life around and sets up a major dilemma or challenge. The subplot acts as a counterpoint. It can provide a frame for, or resonate with the situation the protagonist finds himself in, or affect his relationships and his new pursuit. This secondary line of action can also serve to drop clues and allude to secrets or traits about the protagonist that will develop later. More often than not, the subplot reveals what is going on simultaneously in direct opposition to the protagonist's new, irrepressible course of action that will strikingly compromise and complicate matters. Things then swing between positive and negative or highs and lows leading to an event or decision that intensifies the protagonist's situation and, in effect, creates an even greater disturbance—e.g., a young apprentice stockbroker gets taken in by an unscrupulous corporate raider to the dismay of his friends and family; during the Great Depression of the 1930s, a down-and-out but proper maid finds herself accepting a job under false pretenses as a social secretary in a madcap world that is quite immoral but provides her with temporary food and shelter; the leader of the neighborhood lads agrees to pull a foolproof robbery with his mates to solve their mutual financial woes, unwittingly pitting himself and his friends in direct opposition with nefarious drug dealers and crooked policemen.

The second act advances the story and the protagonist's problems, resulting in escalating obstacles and turning points. The second-act climax results in a cliffhanger because relationships and circumstances have changed drastically, setting up another crisis and decision with far more dire consequences. Secrets are revealed, things go from bad to worse, the protagonist has reached a point of no return. The apprentice stockbroker is now totally at odds with his father and his family and in jeopardy of being caught engaging in insider trading; the masquerading social secretary finds herself juggling her ditsy employer's assignations with a nightclub owner, a callow producer of West End Musicals and a lovesick piano player; the lads have pulled off the robbery but some of the gang members have been caught by the villains, threatening harm if the lads' leader doesn't turn over some highly inflammatory missing ledgers and photographs, goods the leader is totally unaware of.

The third act propels itself toward closure. The conventional wisdom here is to resolve the conundrum in due course so that the audience won't leave feeling the story should have ended 20 minutes before the final credits. The excitement builds, the pace becomes faster. Conventional wisdom also assumes that the audience comes to see the final 20 minutes in order to get what they wanted, but not in the way they expected. They especially have no patience with false endings (just when we thought she had died in the bath, she pops up again) which have by now become tiresome. After the satisfactory climax, all the loose ends in this standard recipe are expediently wrapped up. In other words, in this third segment, unexpected events have led the protagonist to the brink. Everything is disintegrating around him. He must do something to resolve everything and, typically, get what he needs instead of what he initially was after. The young stockbroker blows the whistle on his unscrupulous mentor and goes to jail but saves his dad's company. The faux personal secretary reveals her true self and exposes the other two lovers for what they are and urges her ditsy employer to give up fame and fortune for the love of the piano player as all three wind up on the street, broke but sincerely happy. The leader turns the table on the mobsters and the crooked policemen by calling their bluff, agreeing to an exchange for the release of his mates, and then turning the loot and ledgers and photographs to the proper authorities in return for amnesty for himself and his wayward but essentially goodhearted pals.

As we've seen, and as the following excerpt from James L. Brooks' draft of *Broadcast News* illustrates, the standard scripting template is designed to generate a standardized blueprint. By employing this blueprint, the screenwriter readily indicates the style, shot-flow, tempo and progression, etc., shot that makes a given project.

FADE IN:

EXT. WASHINGTON D.C. STREET—MORNING

JANE and AARON walking to work—agitated.

> AARON
> They didn't hire Peter Stiller from the Times
> and he had a great audition tape.

> JANE
> You want to start going over who they could
> have gotten? They can't take on people like
> this for network news. For God's sake. What's
> going on?

INT. NEW BUILDING LOBBY—DAY

TOM arrives for first day of work.

INT. ERNIE MERRIMAN'S OFFICE

ERNIE MERRIMAN is the network's Washington Bureau Chief. He is in his early 60's, has worked for the network about 40 years—part of the golden age—a family man, an honorable man, a good guy. Right now he is welcoming TOM to the network. As he hands TOM his credentials:

> ERNIE
> Any particular area you feel strongest in?

> TOM
> To be honest, I was best at anchor.

ERNIE gives him a long look—is he kidding?

> ERNIE
> Why don't you take a few days observing

the system? Then we'll put you on
general assignment.

EDITING ROOM—NIGHT

Two small TV monitors—a smallish room. JANE goes over her timing
notes which correspond to the time code SUPERED on the monitors.
BOBBIE—an extraordinarily silent man—is doing JANE'S
bidding. On the monitor we SEE the mercenary piece which JANE is
editing against a tightening deadline. The PHONE RINGS periodically—
JANE conducting abrupt conversations while continuing to edit. The pressure is palpable and builds and builds. Through it all, JANE remains calm,
her focus is amazing.

                    JANE
              (consulting notes)
    Go back to 316, Bobbie. The sound bite
    in the cab—it starts, 'I don't know how
    I'll feel...'

                    BOBBIE
    We could...

                    JANE
              (interrupting)
    Please, Bobbie, we're pushing.

As BOBBIE expertly reverses the tape, TOM'S face appears in the glass
doorway and then he enters the already crowded room—JANE'S eyes
click to him briefly. She makes not a move to welcome him. He pauses,
but is committed and tries to find a place for himself against the wall.

                    TOM
    They said it would be okay if...

                    JANE
    We're working here! You can stand over
    in the uh, uh, uh...

SHE momentarily can't think of the word 'corner.' Then back to BOBBIE.

                    JANE
    Play back the last line.

                    BOBBIE
    He said something about...

> JANE

Let me hear it!

BOBBIE, taking the sharp commands with ever increasing, yet still repressed resentment.

The Assistant Director, BLAIR LITTON, enters the editing room. Ever since she got her job she has been the first to crack under pressure.

> BLAIR

We'll need it in ten minutes. We're putting it
directly into...

JANE holds up a finger of warning to BLAIR as she picks up a ringing phone and talks to BOBBIE at the same time.

> JANE
> (into phone)

Craig, just a second–
> (to BOBBIE)

Let me hear it!

> MERCENARY
> (voice over)

It's been a long time since I've seen
my folks and all but ... I don't expect
any big-deal homecoming.

> JANE

Stop there.
> (into phone she's
> been holding)

I want to shoot a picture from a book I
have in the office.

> BLAIR

You don't have time. Not a chance.

> JANE
> (into phone)

I'll be right down. It's very tight.

> BLAIR

I've got to tell Ernie ... because there
isn't enough time.

> JANE

Yes, there is.

BLAIR charges out as JANE gathers up her notes.

> BOBBIE
> (smiling secretly, speaking
> for the first time)
> I don't think she's going to make it.

Appendix C: Hollywood Mythic Formula

Archetypes

(Reflections of aspects of the human psyche based on the theories of Carl G. Jung)

The Mentor—a Merlin-like character, helping or protective, often wise and older, providing a conscience for the untested hero who answers the call.

False or Dark Mentors—a person or forces who lure the hero away from his goal and into danger.

The Threshold Guardian—obstacles or characters who make it difficult to cross the first threshold.

The Herald—the one who brings news and warnings of the future, good or bad.

The Shadow—the hidden nature of the hero or villain; darker for the hero, more vulnerable for villains.

The Trickster—provides comic relief and undermines the status quo.

Shapeshifters—archetypes male and female who go through unexpected changes from ally to foe, visa versa or anywhere in between.

Others—the king or father who leads or oppresses; the queen or mother who nurtures or controls; the warrior who enforces what is right or wrong; the magician who makes the invisible visible to balance the natural order or manipulate it; the artist or clown who reveals undetected beauty or folly; the lover who provides positive or debilitating sensuality; the rebel who challenges the order of things for positive or negative ends. In addition, there can be demons, scapegoats, masters, servants and slaves, seducers, villains and sworn enemies, a temptress, boon companions, etc.

The Odyssey

STEP ONE: SEPARATION

The Ordinary World
The Call to Adventure—by chance, provocation, loss, unexpected happening, illness or whatever promises to put the hero in danger, facing the unknown, forced to give up his safe haven.

Meeting with the Mentor
The Approach—whatever forces the hero to cross the first threshold, met by difficult obstacles and, often, mysterious sirens of desire.

STEP TWO: INITIATION, DESCENT AND THE ROAD OF TRIALS

Movement into a Dark and Incomprehensible Landscape
The Ordeal—overcoming of fear, the need to prove one's self worthy as more archetypes come into play as needed and to fulfill their functions.

Meeting a Succession of Tests and Almost Superhuman Tasks—
e.g., slaying the dragon (physically or metaphorically), escaping from the enemy; possibly led astray by a temptress, brought back by a mentor or wise woman, facing and overcoming the wrath of a father figure or all-powerful force.

The Final Test—battles, defeats, moments of illumination and ultimate triumph.

STEP THREE: THE ROAD BACK

Bringing Home the Elixir or Trophy—making his way back, stronger and wiser, ready to face the last obstacle which is *home*, the hero returns bringing wisdom, peace of mind, or whatever has been lost or missing to put his former world right. He is now the master of two worlds having achieved both self-realization and a much wider view of life beyond his initial, immature self-absorption and preoccupation with the safe and predictable. He now truly has something to give.

Appendix D: Resources

The Writers Guild of America

Membership: Admission is based on the sale or licensing of previously unpublished and unproduced literary or dramatic material totaling 24 units of credit. Sales of a motion picture screenplay or teleplay 90 minutes or longer to a company or other entity that is signatory to the WGA's minimum basic agreement earn 24 credits each. The 24 units must be accumulated within the preceding three years of application. The schedule of units of credits can be obtained by contacting the WGA West or East. The WGA also represents cable and interactive writers.

Benefits: A collective bargaining agency establishing negotiated minimum payments for various writing services. The improvement of conditions under which those services are performed. A WGA health fund. A staff of attorneys to review contracts and the policing and collection of residuals and, when requested, arbitration for screen credit based on a percentage of creative contribution (with a bias in favor of crediting the original writer). An original movie and television script depository, a script registration service, a pension plan, and a film society that offers first run screenings of most studio releases.

Addresses:

WGA West
7000 West Third Street
Los Angeles, CA 90048–4329
(323) 951–4000

WGA East
555 West 57th St.
New York, NY 10019
(212) 767–7800

For more information: *www.wga.org.* Offering advice, interviews, lists of agents and agencies, research links and databases. You can also call or write the office in your area.

Additional Writers Guilds

Writers Guild of Canada
366 Adelaide St. W, Ste. 401
Toronto, Ontario
Canada, M5V IR9
(416) 979–7907

Australian Writers Guild
8/50 Reservoir St.
Surry Hills, NSW 2010
(0) 2 9281 1554

Writers Guild of Great Britain
15 Britannia St.
London, England WC1 C9JN
(0) 20 7833 0777

New Zealand Writers Guild
P.O. Box 47 886
Ponsonby, Auckland
(0) 9 360 1408

Magazines

Creative Screenwriting
6404 Hollywood Blvd., Suite 415
Los Angeles, CA 90028
www.creativescreenwriting.com

New York Screenwriter
655 Fulton St., #276
Brooklyn, NY 11217
www.nyscreenwriter.com/2000.htm

The Hollywood Reporter
5055 Wilshire Blvd, 6th Floor
Los Angeles, CA 90036
www.hollywoodreporter.com

Script
26707 W. Agoura Road, Suite 205
Calabasas, CA 91302
www.scriptmag.com

Hollywood Scriptwriter
PO Box 10277
Burbank, CA 91510
www.hollywoodscriptwriter.com

Variety
5700 Wilshire Blvd.
Los Angeles, CA 90036
www.variety.com

Fade In
289 S. Robertson Blvd. Ste. 467
Beverly Hills, CA 90211
www.fadeinonline.com

Written By
(published by The Writers Guild)
7000 W. 3rd Street
Los Angeles, CA 90048
www.wga.org

Additional References and Services

DRAFTS AND SHOOTING SCRIPTS OF PRODUCED SCREENPLAYS

www. ScriptGuy.com
www. script-o-rama.com
www. screenwriter.com

SCREENPLAY FORMAT GUIDE

www. Screenplayguide.com
www. Oscars.org/nicholl/format_a.txt

GUIDE TO SCRIPT AGENTS

F+W Publications
4700 East Galbraith Road
Cincinnati, Ohio 45236
www.guidetoliteraryagents.com
(also distributed in Canada, the U.K. and Europe and Australia)
www.screenwriting-source.com/literary-agents.asp

(includes other industry contacts)
www.absolutewrite.com/ebooks/ebookAgents.pdf
www.writerswrite.com/screenwriting
(includes links to producers and industry information)

STORES AND SUPPLIES

Writers Store
2040 Westwood Blvd.
Los Angeles, CA 90025
(800) 272–8927
www.WritersStore.com
(also carries *FrameForge 3D Studio 2* storyboarding software)

The Screenwriter's Store
10–11 Moor Street
London W1V 5LJ
+44 020 7287 9009
www.screenwriting.com

Selected Bibliography

Books

Bordwell, David, and Kristin Thompson. *Film Art*. New York: McGraw-Hill, 2004.

Engel, Joel. *Screenwriters on Screenwriting*. New York: Hyperion, 1995.

Field, Syd. *Screenplay*. New York: Dell, 1984.

Froug, William. *Zen and the Art of Screenwriting*. Beverly Hills: Silman-James Press, 1996.

Gaspard, John. *Fast, Cheap & Written That Way*. Studio City: Michael Wiese Productions, 2007.

Goldman, William. *Adventures in the Screen Trade*. New York: Warner Books, 1983.

_____. *Which Lie Did I Tell?* New York: Pantheon Books, 2000.

Lefcourt, Peter, and Laura Shapiro, eds. *The First Time I Got Paid for It*. New York: Perseus Books, 2000.

Lehman, Ernest. *North by Northwest*. London: Faber and Faber, 1999.

McCreadie, Marsha. *The Women Who Write the Movies*. New York: Birch Land Press, 1994.

McKee, Robert. *Story*. New York: Regan Books, 1997.

Ondaatje, Michael. *The English Patient*. New York: Vintage Books, 1993.

Polish, Mark, and Michael Polish. *The Declaration of Independent Filmmaking*. Orlando, FL: Harcourt, 2005.

Schulberg, Budd. *On the Waterfront*. Carbondale: Southern Illinois University Press, 1980.

Seger, Linda. *Making a Good Script Great*. New York: Dodd, Mead, 1987.

Silver-Lasky, Pat. *Screenwriting for the 21st Century*. London: B.T. Batsford, 2004.

Suppa, Ron. *Real Screenwriting*. Boston: Thomson Course Technology, 2005.

Thompson, Emma. *The Sense and Sensibility Screenplay & Diaries*. New York: Newmarket Press, 1995.

Truby, John. *The Anatomy of Story*. New York: Faber and Faber, 2007.

Articles

Dargis, Manohla. "Gold Rush Mentality at a Hustlin' Sundance." *New York Times*, 16 January 2007. E13.

Gelbart, Larry. "A Beginning, a Muddle and an End." Revision of *Monster* by

247

John Gregory Dunne. *The New York Times Book Review*, 2 March 1997. http://www.nytimes.com/books/97/03/02/reviews/gelbart.html.

Gold, Sylviane. "A Dark-Humor Master Gets a Camera." *New York Times*, 13 January 2008 AR 11, 19.

Holden, Stephen. "In Art's Old Sanctuary, A High Priest of Film." *New York Times*, 31 July 2007. B1+.

_____. "A Chronicler of Alienated Europeans in a Flimsy New World." *New York Times*, 1 August 2007. B1+.

Lahr, John. "Disappearing Act: Cate Blanchett Branches Out." *The New Yorker*, 12 February 2007: 38–43.

_____. "The Impersonator: Peter Morgan Fills in the Gaps of History." *The New Yorker*, 30 April 2007: 34–39.

Lane, Anthony. "Drifters: Hal Hartley's *Fay Grim*." *The New Yorker*, 21 May 2007: 90–91.

_____. "Lone Sailors." *The New Yorker*, 27 August 2007: 78–80.

Mitchell, Elvis. "Turning the Big Screen Into the Small Screen." 22 November 2002. *http://movies2.nytimes.com/mem/movies/review.html*.

Powers, John. "Open City." *Los Angeles*, July 2007: 20–22.

Scorsese, Martin. "The Man Who Set Film Free." *New York Times*, 12 August 2007. AR9+.

Scott, A.O. "The Seven-Year Itch, Days After the Wedding." *The New York Times*, 5 October 2007: E10.

Scott, A.O., et al. "Hollywood Plays it for Laughs" ("Falling-Down Funny" etc.) *The New York Times Magazine*, 12 November 2006: 21–116.

Stanley, Alessandra. "A Person Could Develop Occult." *New York Times*, 14 October 2007. AR1+.

Tapley, Kristopher. "His Screenplays Get Made, Except the Ones That Don't." *New York Times*, 19 November 2006. AR 15+.

Thompson, Anne. "Closet screenwriter Arndt comes into light." *The Hollywood Reporter*, 17 November 2006. 1–3. *http://www.hollywoodreporter.com/hr/content_display/features/columns/risky_business/e*

Wimberly, Rachel. "Morgan Creek Productions." *Script*, July-August. 78–83.

Personal Interviews

Bill, Tony. 17 October 2007.

Evans, Bruce. 24 July 2007.

Fusco, John. 7 September 2007.

Gideon, Ray. 24 July 2007.

Lawson, Steve. 20 June 2007.

Lefcourt, Peter. 31 July 2007.

Neufeld, Mace. 27 August 2007.

Scott, Campbell. 23 October 2007.

Silberling, Brad. 25 October 2007.

Stille, Lucy. 18 December 2007.

Westlake, Donald. 28 April 2007.

Other

"A Conversation with Peter Morgan." Charlie Rose. www.charlierose.com/guests/ 23 July 2007.

A Personal Journey with Martin Scorsese Through American Movies. Dir. by Martin Scorsese. DVD. Mirimax, 2000.

Black & White to Color: The Making of The English Patient. Canadian Broadcast Corporation, 1996.

Filmschool: Interviews. University of California, Irvine, 13 February 2007. kuci.org/filmschool.

"Letter Perfect: Tod Williams and John Irving Discuss Writing *A Door in the Floor.*" *Writers Guild of America East*: 1–2. 8 October 2004 http://www.wgaeast.org/features/2004/08/10/door_in_the_floor/.

Little Miss Sunshine by Michael Arndt. Early draft. *www.script-o-rama.com/table.shtml.*

Little Miss Sunshine Special Features, Commentary by Screenwriter Michael Arndt. DVD. Fox Searchlight Pictures. 2006.

"Neil Simon & Larry Gelbart." *Writers Guild of America, East*: 1–18. 5 July 2007. *http://www.wgaeast.org/features/simon-gelbart.html.*

"101 Greatest Screenplays: The List." *Writers Guild of America East*: 1–5. 4 March 2006. *http://www.wgaeast.org/greatest_screenplays/2006/04/list/index.html.*

"Richard Russo Adapts *Empire Falls.*" *Writers Guild of America East*: 1–3. 6 October 2005. *http://www.wgaeast.org/features/2005/06/10/russo/.*

Index